From Strategy to Change

From Strategy to Change

Implementing the Plan in Higher Education

Daniel James Rowley, Herbert Sherman

 JOSSEY-BASS
A Wiley Company
San Francisco

Jossey-Bass books and products are available through most bookstores. To contact Jossey-Bass directly, call (888) 378-2537, fax to (800) 605-2665, or visit our website at www.josseybass.com. Substantial discounts on bulk quantities of Jossey-Bass books are available to corporations, professional associations, and other organizations. For details and discount information, contact the special sales department at Jossey-Bass.

 Manufactured in the United States of America on Lyons Falls Turin Book. This paper is acid-free and 100 percent totally chlorine-free.

Library of Congress Cataloging-in-Publication Data

Rowley, Daniel James, 1946–
      From strategy to change: implementing the plan in higher education/Daniel James Rowley, Herbert Sherman.—1st ed.
      p. cm.—(The Jossey-Bass higher and adult education series)
      Includes bibliographical references and indexes.
      ISBN 0–7879–5431–4 (alk. paper)
      1. Education, Higher—United States—Administration. 2. Strategic planning—United States. 3. Educational change—United States. I. Sherman, Herbert. II Title. III. Series.
      LB2341 .R6818 2001
      378.1'01'0973—dc21

00-011191

FIRST EDITION
HB Printing 10 9 8 7 6 5 4 3 2 1

The Jossey-Bass
Higher and Adult Education Series

Contents

Part One: A Framework for Assessing and Making Strategic Choices

Part Two: Implementing Strategic Choices

Figures, Tables, & Exhibits

Figures

Tables

Exhibit

Foreword

By the late 1990s the phrase, "it's not going to be business as usual," was a refrain popular with many business people. The economy was operating at full throttle, many industries were facing hypercompetition—every move by a competitor was met by a counter move, and those who could not keep up were driven from the industry. In the midst of all this competitiveness, colleges and universities seemed to be above the fray. Everyone needed an education, and demand was growing by leaps and bounds. Forty percent of high school graduates were entering college. A poll showed that over 80 percent of the general population believed that a college education was no longer a luxury but a necessity. Many observers, and academic administrators as well, believed that institutions of higher learning had little to fear. How wrong they were. In the last five years the educational environment has changed dramatically. Here, in the first decade of the millennium, "it's not going to be education as usual." Daniel James Rowley and Herbert Sherman have clearly spelled out in *From Strategy to Change* why this is true and what everyone associated with colleges and universities must learn if their institution is going to survive and prosper. The two central themes of this book are (1) the playing field is changing and (2) effective implementation of strategy is going to be the critical success factor.

The Playing Field Is Changing

About a decade ago a friend of mine was the vice president of finance at a Big Eight school. One day he happened to be in Miami on university business and I met him for lunch. During the meal he began telling me how a deal had just been cut in which the Big Eight Conference and the Southwest Conference were going to disband to create the Big Twelve Conference, which would be made up of the original Big Eight universities and four of the Southwest Conference members, including the University of Texas (UT) and Texas A&M. This was a surprise to me, an Oklahoma University graduate who prided himself on that school's ability periodically to dominate the conference in football. However, we always had a difficult time winning against UT. Why would we want them in our conference? Wasn't it enough that we were on their annual schedule and they would beat us regularly in the Cotton Bowl?

Then my friend explained to me why the Big Eight Conference was being reconfigured. The University of Texas and Texas A&M were big drawing cards. If they were combined with schools such as Oklahoma, Nebraska, Colorado, and Missouri, the conference would be an athletic powerhouse. The ability of the teams to attract star athletes would increase, television revenues would zoom, and the schools would earn much more money than before—much of which could be poured back into improved academic facilities. But the schools had to act now because the deck was being reshuffled and it might be fifty years before there were any significant changes like this again.

This story helps explain how athletics at the college level is changing. The best schools want to be in conferences with other outstanding teams because only through great competition can athletes rise to their full level of achievement. As this reshuffling takes place, the playing field is changing. Schools that do not get into these conferences have limited opportunity to attract the best athletes and win national championships.

Yet this story is more than one of college athletics in general or football in particular. Colleges and universities are changing in many other ways, thus altering the field in the process. A good example is online courses offered by well-known schools such as the University of Phoenix, which is currently the dominant university in this arena, as well as by lesser known institutions such as Baker College of Flint, Michigan, which has thousands of students enrolled in online courses and has close ties to the big auto manufacturers, who are happy to see their people completing their undergraduate and MBA degrees and are willing to pay their tuition.

Today, it has been estimated that approximately 70 percent of all colleges and universities in this country offer online courses. And one newly minted billionaire recently announced that he is willing to put up $100 million to create an online Ivy League University. Quite clearly, schools of higher education can no longer sit back and wait for students to come calling. In fact, private, prestigious schools are now offering early admission, scholarships, and a host of other incentives to high school seniors with high college board scores. The competition for the best students is heating up.

And to make things worse, corporations are now getting into the picture. Motorola is creating its own university, and so, too, is General Motors. Who needs to ask the University of Michigan to create a special type of MBA degree for engineering undergraduates at Cummins Engine or to persuade Stanford to tailor a master's program in information systems for Intel employees? Private companies can do it themselves—and they are prepared to do so. They know what they want and they can pay top dollar for whatever they need from faculty to brick and mortar to technology.

How can the local community college compete in an environment like this? How can a large state university stop private schools such as the University of Phoenix or Baker College from siphoning off their potential undergraduate, MBA, and, yes, even PhD students? How can research-based schools with high-quality doctoral programs in business such as Columbia University, New York University, Northwestern, Indiana, the University of Florida, and UT find sufficient doctoral students when schools such as Nova Southeastern University in Fort Lauderdale, Florida, and the University of Phoenix are offering doctoral programs for working professionals?

The answer to the questions I have posed is that university administrators, chair people, and faculty alike have to understand that the playing field is no longer what it was five years ago. It is not changing—it *has changed!* And administrators and their constituency groups must understand this and be prepared to respond to these new changes. This is one of the central themes of the book, which poses a series of critical questions and offers a host of alternative ways of dealing with the new academic world.

Implementation Is Critical

Eighteen months ago I had the opportunity to interview Michael Porter, undoubtedly the best-known name in strategic management in America, for an article in a major journal. One of the first questions I asked Michael related to how his thinking has changed over the last decade. His answer was that strategy implementation is a lot more important than he had given it credit for in the past. And this is true for many strategists. The formulation side is more enjoyable. After all, setting out a plan for what one wants to do can give the planner a euphoric feeling. However, the time to implement the strategy is where the rubber meets the road, and it is truly the hardest part of the strategic management process. Now the organization has to "walk the talk" and make things happen.

Many questions and issues need to be addressed in effectively implementing a plan. The first crucial part of strategy implementation is deciding what the institution will stand for. What do we want people to think when they hear the name of our college or university? Whatever the answer, it should be a result of a careful positioning strategy. And in positioning, I have found that two sides are critical: the physical and the psychological.

The physical side of positioning refers to qualities we can see. If a school wants to be known as a research-based institution, it has to have faculty that are getting research grants and writing articles in the top journals. It also needs doctoral programs that are turning out PhDs that can find employment at top-tier schools. If an institution cannot do this, its implementation is not in sync with its strategic plan. It has to go back and rethink what it wants to stand for and how to devote its resources to getting there.

The psychological side of positioning, in my view, is even more important because what people "think" about an institution is often more important than what the institution actually does: Perception *is* reality. So a university, for example, has to be careful not to confuse its constituency groups regarding what it stands for. The best personal example I have of this occurred many years ago when I first joined the faculty at Florida International University (FIU). FIU had opened only two years earlier, and the school was determined to become a major public urban university. I was in Miami only a few days and busily moving into my house when the phone rang. It was a professor from the Management Department at the University of Miami (UM), the large, private university located less than a mile from my home in Coral Gables. The professor told me that my basic management textbook was being used by the college and wanted to know whether I would be interested in teaching a class for UM. I drove over to the university, talked to the man, and agreed that I would ask my dean at FIU whether it was acceptable to teach a class for UM, and he would clear things at his school. The next day he called again and I told him that my dean had agreed that I could teach one class at UM. However, to my surprise, the professor told me that he had broached the offer with his dean and been rebuffed. This ended my relationship with UM, but I have often thought about it and realized that the dean at Miami was right. If he hired a professor from a state university with its low tuition rate to teach a class to a group of students who were paying premium price at a private school, one of two things might have happened. On the one hand, I might have been rated very poorly by the students, in which case the dean would have wondered why he had ever hired me in the first place. On the other hand, I might have been rated outstanding, in which case the students would have wondered why they were paying high tuition when they could go to school across town at a much lower price. By letting me teach at his school the dean would be blurring the image that UM was trying to project. So his decision was a good one, and it helped emphasize in my mind the importance of the psychological side of positioning.

A second critical part of strategy implementation is that of making choices. No academic institution can be everything to everybody. Michael Porter likes to point out that effective organizations do not straddle by trying to appeal to too many markets. They limit their field of activity to where they're most effective, and they let go of the rest. This book helps administrators deal with this subject by showing them how to decide what they stand for—and then stick to it.

A third critical part of strategy implementation is understanding how to deal with constituency groups. Academia has a large number of these groups, including faculty, students, alumni, the local community, employers, and administrative personnel, to name but a half dozen. And when one looks at the things that each group wants, it is not difficult to realize that a major balancing act is under way. For example, the administration at public research-based institutions would like to see faculty writing articles in top-tier journals and teaching at least two classes a semester in order to maintain enrollment targets. The faculty would like to see their teaching load dropped to one class with very few students. Students would like to get a degree that will help them command large salaries. Employers would like to see the university turn out top-flight students who are willing to work for minimum salaries. And so it goes, with each group arguing its own case and convinced that the other groups warrant less consideration than do they—regardless of the validity of the various positions. For example, a number of years ago a colleague of mine and I conducted research on the top twenty MBA programs in the country as ranked by *Business Week*. One of the issues we examined was the number of classes professors taught, the size of these classes, and the number of professors' publications. Our data were not statistically significant, but they did point toward the conclusion that professors who taught more students (for example, large lecture sections) tended to also have more publications per year, thus casting doubt on the argument that reduced teaching loads generate higher publication productivity. Quite simply, balancing the needs of different constituency groups often requires administrators to deal with fiction as well as fact.

Value of This Book

In this book the authors address critical issues facing current administrators. In particular, they emphasize the need to identify appropriate strategic choices. Some academic administrators think that the future is going to be a mere repeat of the past. As Peter Drucker likes to say about such statements—this is blatant nonsense! The future of academic institutions will be determined by highly astute, well-informed administrators who are capable of making the right choices. And this means knowing how the playing field has changed and what will be the best position to take on that field.

Many approaches are possible that can be used by administrators. In this book the authors provide models for understanding what these choices might be and how to decide which ones are best. The book could not arrive at a better time. A few years ago, two of my colleagues and I wrote an article on human resource management in the twenty-first century. We looked at the practices of world-class enterprises and at organizations that were farther back in the pack. Two findings emerged. First, the best companies tend to attract the best talent and, in turn, slowly but surely begin to pull away from the rest. Second, companies that emulate the "best practices" of world-class organizations can stay within competitive distance, but the rest become noncompetitive and cease to exist.

Today, the deck is being reshuffled in the world of academia. We are seeing the emergence of internationally focused universities with online programs that are appealing to students on all major continents. This book is designed to develop precise information for campus leaders and strategic planners regarding the strategic choices that exist in the new economy for institutions of higher education, and to describe several options for implementing the choices embodied in the campus strategic plan. *From Strategy to Change: Implementing the Plan in Higher Education* is *not* a book that belongs on every administrator's shelf; it is a book that belongs on every administrator's desk.

January 2001

Richard M. Hodgetts
Florida International University

Preface

Everyone has heard of strategic planning, and many campuses have engaged in a planning process they describe as strategic planning. However, not everyone has had a successful experience with the process, and many have become highly jaded about what strategic planning is and what it can do.

Although some campuses have engaged in successful strategic planning events and have made significant changes that have helped strengthen their programs and resources, many other campuses haven't been as lucky. To most of them, strategic planning has become a pariah, a terrible mistake, and something that should be avoided at all costs.

In attempting to be objective regarding these opposing outcomes, one might ask, Why the difference? Why might strategic planning work on one campus and not another? Is it the differences among campuses? Is there more than one model of how to plan out there? Is it an issue of who plans and how they plan? What's going on here?

As it turns out, there *are* differences, major differences, among strategic planning events from one campus to another. There is *not* a single model, there are several. The differences one finds from one campus to the next are gigantic, and attempting to use a cookie-cutter method of planning, let alone a method that is not sensitive to the unique circumstances and needs of colleges and universities, is bound to fail.

What is going on here is that strategic planning is complex. Not only is academic strategic planning different from the equivalent in the business world, but also those who engage in the process on college and university campuses need tools that help them more easily identify what types of strategies are appropriate for their particular campuses—tools that help them move from planning to implementation and that help them overcome many of the problems they may well encounter. Without these types of tools, it is highly likely that the strategic planning activities that a college or university engages in will fail.

Strategic planning *can* and *does* work. Furthermore, with the major paradigm and economy shifts that characterize the Postindustrial Age and emergence of the Information Age, strategic planning may be the only viable method of successfully reengineering higher education institutions to meet the needs of a highly technical, global, and competitive society.

This book takes the discussion of strategic planning beyond the basics to a problem-solving level. By examining a set of specific strategic choices, evaluating the appropriateness of various implementation strategies, and developing an understanding of how campus leaders and strategic planners can solve many of the problems they may encounter, those involved in the strategic planning event can be successful.

Our Goal in Writing This Book

In this book we build on and extend the work described in two previous books by Rowley, Lujan, and Dolence. Their first book (1997) described a successful model for strategic planning in colleges and universities that has worked well on several campuses in the United States and Canada. Their second book (1998) went on to describe the significant societal changes the Postindustrial Age and the Information Age have made and how these changes have challenged the academy as it moves into a new millennium. The central goal of this book is to go beyond the material in these two other books, develop more precise information for campus leaders and strategic planners regarding what strategic choices exist in the new economy for institutions of higher education, and describe several different options for implementing the choices embodied in the campus strategic plan.

By combining the material in all three books, campus leaders and strategic planners will have a complete schema of understanding how to plan, the context of that planning, the options relevant to the plan, and a choice of how to put the plan into place. The authors of the three books have all developed the materials specifically for college and university campus leaders and strategic planners as tools to help create effective, successful strategic plans.

Scope of This Book

It is not our intention to develop a scheme of strategic planning in this particular book. There are some very good models in the literature, and many of these have proven to be successful. Rather, our intention is to deal with the three problems that tend to plague any number of higher education strategic planning processes:

- What kinds of strategies are appropriate for colleges and universities?
- How can these choices be effectively implemented?
- What kinds of problems are campus leaders and strategic planners likely to face?

One can see very easily the need for answering these questions in reading over the strategic plans of many colleges and universities. (Most of these documents are public and may be accessed easily on the Internet and through library database searches.) What one first notices is how generic the plans are: The statements of missions are remarkably the same from one plan to the next; goals and objectives tend to be global in nature and lack specificity. The documents look more like wish lists than a plan of action, and they usually lack a stated plan of implementation. Such "strategic plans"—documents that have taken uncounted hours of work and the participation of a wide segment of the campus community, plans that really are not particularly strategic in nature—are destined for the back of the bookshelf, bottom file drawer, or the trash bin, despite their artistically printed final presentation. These are the plans that fail.

What is needed is a *plan to plan* that (1) clearly elucidates the need for planning, (2) identifies a planning method that will work on a college or university campus, (3) determines a clear, concise strategic choice or set of strategic choices, and (4) identifies how and when campus leaders can implement the plan. The last two of these imperatives are the major issues we develop in this book.

Who Should Read This Book?

From Strategy to Change: Implementing the Plan in Higher Education is a book that should be read by all leaders in higher education, both on the academic and administrative sides of the house. This book attempts to identify the strategic options that all such leaders will need to consider as they move into a strategic planning event or try to salvage an ongoing strategic planning process. Governing boards, presidents, chancellors, vice presidents, vice chancellors, deans, department chairs, and faculty governance leaders need to understand the issues raised by the academic strategic planning event and have a schema of choices that help them move toward a successful planning process. Classroom educators and campus researchers should also benefit from the messages in this book as they sit on the sidelines or are asked to participate in a strategic planning event themselves. Policymakers, governmental decision makers, and funding agencies should also read this book because of the close partnerships that exist between them and the college and university campuses for which they are responsible. And finally, anyone who is interested in the strategic planning process as it works in public organizations, such as colleges and universities, can benefit from reading this book.

Organization of the Book

In this book we attempt to provide substantive information regarding two fundamental issues in creating and implementing a successful strategic plan in institutions of higher education:

- Precisely what are the strategic choices that a college or university can make to help develop and sustain a competitive strategic advantage?
- How can campus leaders and strategic planners effectively implement their strategic choice?

Figure A provides an organizational scheme for the book and demonstrates how we address these two issues. As you can see from Figure A the book is organized into two parts.

Figure A. Organization of the Book.

Part One

> **Forces for Change**
> • External • Internal
> **Chapter One**

Types of Colleges and Universities (Industry Structure)

The Classics	The New Breeds
1. Research colleges and universities	1. Co-op colleges and universities
2. Comprehensive colleges and universities	2. Composite universities
3. Small colleges and universities	3. Perpetual learning colleges and universities
4. Community colleges	4. Virtual universities
5. Specialty colleges and universities	5. Virtual college and university indexes
	6. Self-directed teams within colleges and universities
	7. Assessment and competency-based colleges and universities
	8. Corporate universities
	9. Company universities
	10. Alternative colleges and universities
	11. Emerging
Chapter Two	**Chapter Three**

Competitive Position of Colleges and Universities

Competitive Advantage	Strategic Approaches
1. Low cost leadership	1. Prospector
2. Differentiation	2. Defender
3. Breadth of competition	3. Analyzer
	4. Reactor

Chapter Four

Positioning the College/University (Strategy Formulation)

1. Analyze institution	3. Analyze market position
2. Analyze competition	4. Market Repositioning

Chapter Five

Part Two

The Strategic Change Process (Strategy Implementation)

1. Forces of change and resistance	2. Preparing for change	3. Structural change	4. Tweaking/cementing change (strategy evaluation)
Chapters Six, Ten	Chapter Nine	Chapters Seven, Eight	Chapters Eleven, Twelve

Part One describes sixteen strategic choices that one can identify in higher education today and the issues that surround them. These represent the macrolevel choices for a college or university such as, should we seek to become a research-1 institution, or focus our resources into becoming a specialty college or university? The book goes on to place these sixteen choices within a model that is defined by the resource base and philosophical direction of a campus. With a basic model in place, this section of the book then identifies many of the issues that affect the choice a campus might make by examining the effect of competition on the strategic planning process. Finally, we provide a tool that campus leaders and strategic planners can use to determine where they fit within the model and demonstrate how planners might use it in designing a strategic plan that moves the campus to where it ought to be.

Part Two looks at the specific choices campus leaders and strategic planners have as they look forward to implementing their strategic plans. We identify eleven strategies for implementation and discuss their appropriate uses based on the specific situation of the campus. These range from highly participatory implementation schemes to top-down forced change. This wide range of choices should be welcome information for campus leaders who are excited to have completed a good plan but have no idea how to sell it to the campus. We also identify several specific issues that can and often do interfere with the planning and implementation processes. Many of these issues have to do with the human element. We describe several strategies for dealing with problems that arise as various campus individuals or groups attempt to derail or kidnap the strategic planning initiative, including a chapter that takes the practice of organizational development and applies it to the setting of higher education. It is our intent to provide the reader with a series of practical tools that will help make strategic planning on college and university campuses a success.

The condition of the academy today, the challenges of the Information Age, the global economy, the explosion of technology, and the development of a worldwide communications system all demand that each college and university campus develops an effective way of looking at itself and its conditions in determining the best path to security and prosperity. All the evidence continues to support strategic planning as the best way of helping campuses achieve these ends. We hope that this book will help campus leaders and planners achieve their goals.

Daniel James Rowley
Greeley, Colorado

January 2001

Herbert Sherman
Southampton, New York

January 2001

The Authors

DANIEL J. ROWLEY is the department chair of the Management Department at the Kenneth W. Montfort College of Business at the University of Northern Colorado in Greeley, Colorado. He holds a master's degree in public administration from the University of Denver and a doctoral degree in organizational and strategic management from the University of Colorado at Boulder. Dr. Rowley has served as university strategic planner, chief of the president's staff, secretary to the board of trustees, and assistant secretary to the board of trustees for planning, all at the University of Northern Colorado. He has coauthored several Jossey-Bass books on strategic planning in higher education institutions.

HERBERT SHERMAN is the director of the Professional Studies Division at Southampton College of Long Island University in Southampton, New York. He is also the head of Southampton's Small Business Institute and Social Research Center. He holds a master's degree in management science from Polytechnic University in Brooklyn, New York, and a doctoral degree in management from the Union Institute in Cincinnati, Ohio. He has authored and coauthored many articles and conference papers on strategic management. This is his first book with Jossey-Bass.

From Strategy to Change

A Framework for Assessing and Making Strategic Choices

Chapter One

Forces of Change and the Importance of Strategic Planning

Laughter drifted through the hallways as several faculty members gathered informally to share the latest gossip about the turmoil in administration. "It's just plain unbelievable that we're going to have to go through another search process so soon for another president. This will be the fourth new president since I've been here." Harold Maude, a physicist with ten years of service with the university (yet the junior member of his department) was reacting to the news that the board of trustees had just formed a search committee to locate and hire a new president.

"You're right," said Jeremy Johnson, a senior member of the biology department. "And I was just getting use to Hilliard's enigmatic behavior and his great parties—what a shame!" he said facetiously. "Hilliard might have had the personality of a pompous ass but, boy, he knew how to spend university money. Are any of us going to forget how he blew twenty grand on redecorating his office?"

This evoked hearty laughter from the group, especially from Sam Ellison, the head of the faculty senate and a thirty-year veteran of the university. "Is that all?" asked Sam rhetorically. "I thought that the twenty grand was merely the price tag for that imported Persian rug. Last estimates were that he spent over one-hundred thousand dollars on office decorations including several 'objets d'art'." This led to further laughter, since it was widely known that President Hilliard prided himself as a painter and hung many of his own works in his office. Public opinion of Hilliard's artistic talent, like his managerial skills, was less than flattering.

President Hilliard was gone, and no one seemed to miss him. The board had fired him in a very public manner for failing to turn things around. The board cited him for not developing and implementing an effective strategic plan, which had been the mandate when they hired him. Though Hilliard had developed something he called a strategic plan, it was extremely unpopular and had engendered little support across campus. Now, with his abrupt departure, others on the campus were working quickly to reverse everything that Hilliard's plan had begun.

As the board began its search for a new president, they knew that the task ahead for the new leader of the 12,500-student campus was going to be even more difficult than what Hilliard had inherited. Student numbers continued to decline. Endowments continued to shrink. Several top professors had left. There was anarchy among the staff, and remaining top administrators were all busy looking for other jobs on other college campuses. The campus was getting close to a crisis situation. So it's not surprising that the board was in a quandary as to what had gone wrong and what they needed to do to move the campus forward. Dare the board mandate again that the new president use strategic planning to solve campus problems and develop stability? If so, what were the chances that the new president would be able to implement it, given the bad press of the most recent strategic planning attempt on the campus? Who would support it? Would it work? Something had to be done, and it had to be done soon. So the board began its search, hoping for a miracle.

This example of an actual college situation is not, unfortunately, an isolated example. Many colleges and universities have faced and are facing circumstances similar to that of the university we briefly describe here. More disconcerting, several colleges and universities that have turned to strategic planning have seen the process fail. Other colleges are wary of attempts to engage in the strategic planning process, regardless of the widely heralded promises of strategic planning or even its documented successes in business and several not-for-profit organizations.

The Nature of Strategic Planning

Over the past several years, nearly every campus has engaged in some sort of strategic planning for a variety of reasons:

The governing board has mandated strategic planning to solve campus problems or improve campus performance.

Campus leaders have pushed for strategic planning because they have felt that the campus was not headed in the appropriate direction or was not taking advantage of proper opportunities.

"Everyone else is doing it."

Strategic planning is no longer simply the purview of business, and many campuses hope to duplicate the success that many businesses and not-for-profit organizations have had in developing and implementing their strategic plan.

As a result, most colleges and universities in the United States and around the world have become involved with a strategic planning process.

However, as most colleges and universities have also learned, getting involved with a strategic planning process is no assurance that the campus will be able to develop a good plan or implement it successfully. Further, campuses quickly learn that the strategic planning process within the academy is hardly a simple process. Many campuses get mired in process, lose their confidence in strategic planning, find that they really don't want to change, discover that the costs involved are greater than they are willing (or possibly able) to pay, and learn that implementation is unbelievably difficult.

The best initial intentions too often result in failure. Typically, the planning document ends up on a shelf or, more often, in a wastebasket. In the postmortems, faculty, administrators, staff, and members of the governing board all blame the general process of strategic planning. Often one hears, "If the campus could just stop all this ridiculous nonsense about strategic planning and let things go back to the way they were, everything would be fine once again."

Some critics become passionate. One of the authors of this book was attending a strategic planning meeting during which a faculty member rose to his feet, holding a book high, and stated, "Look here, even Henry Mintzberg says that strategic planning doesn't work!" He was holding up a copy of Mintzberg's *The Rise and Fall of Strategic Planning* (1994a), which the mistaken faculty member had gotten hold of but had not read. The faculty member, who had been involved in several campus planning events, was upset this time by some of the provisions of the current, developing strategic plan. Along with a coalition of others (including faculty and several unhappy administrators), he was trying to make a case for ending the planning process on this particular campus once and for all. This type of systematic resistance to strategic planning is not uncommon. The resisters claim victory when campus leaders abandon the process and the threat of change goes away.

Then reality settles in. The problems have not gone away. Major opportunities continue to be missed. The endowments have not gone up. Student numbers continue to dwindle. Revolt in the faculty continues to be more the norm than the exception. Conflict among campus constituencies, particularly between the faculty and the administration, has not lessened and in fact may have become even greater. Perhaps the president or chancellor has been fired, as in our brief case example. Understandably, as the campus tries to make sense of what has happened and what went wrong, the last thing anyone wants to hear is that the campus needs to go through yet another round of strategic planning.

Of course, revisiting the strategic planning process is precisely what does need to happen. Ironically, many of the failures attributed to strategic planning have had little to do with the strategic planning process and much more to do with misconceptions and false expectations about strategic planning. No doubt, prior bad experiences make the mere notion of another round of strategic planning abhorrent to some campus constituents, and for administrative and faculty leadership to suggest that the campus buckle under and try again is going to involve a monumental sales job. What people throughout the campus need to understand, however, is that the failures they experienced did not invalidate strategic planning as a viable process; the failures were the result of planners' inability to identify clearly the appropriate strategies to take the campus where it needed to go, or the inability of the campus (on all levels) to implement those strategies properly, or both.

Hope for more successful results with strategic planning processes comes from a full understanding of what strategic planning is in colleges and universities and how it can actually work.

Today, there remains no better method of determining what changes the campus needs to make and how to put those changes into place than strategic planning (Nutt and Backoff, 1992). For strategic planning to be successful, however, college and university administrators, faculty leaders, and strategic planners need to understand that the complex process described by Rowley, Lujan, and Dolence (1997), Dolence, Rowley, and Lujan (1997), and others (Shirley, 1988; Morrison, Renfro, and Boucher, 1984; and Bryson, 1989, 1995) cannot be shortcut or short-changed. Further, they need to realize that global goals and strategies are basically useless when it comes time to understand specifically what the strategic plan for the campus is designed to accomplish, let alone when it comes time to actually begin the change process.

People who reject strategic planning outright or, at the other extreme, those who put too much hope in the strategic planning process, sometimes do not fully appreciate the nature of the phenomena they have begun to deal with. They are unsure of what their real choices are, and often they are also oblivious to what it will take to put a strategic plan into action. One of the original theorists in the academic field of management, Fredrick Taylor, provided some wisdom in this area when he pointed out that processes that are not fully understood cannot be effectively programmed (1911). What is interesting is that Taylor did his work long before the idea of strategic planning was ever associated with organizations, let alone colleges and universities. Further, as Mintzberg pointed out (1994a, 1994b) in the book we alluded to above, strategic planners need to be realistic about what the plan can actually do. It cannot do everything, but it should not be allowed to do nothing. There must be a balance based on real needs and real solutions. Taylor and Mintzberg remind us that organizational leaders and strategic planners, including college and university leaders and strategic planners, need to be knowledgeable about what they expect the strategic plan to do and then put it into practice. Without the necessary homework, it is unlikely that the process will succeed.

As noted in the Preface, we hope to provide in this book substantive information regarding two fundamental issues in creating and implementing a successful strategic plan in institutions of higher education. Precisely what are the strategic choices that a college or university can make to help develop and sustain a competitive strategic advantage? and How can campus leaders and strategic planners effectively implement their strategic choices?

In this chapter, we set the scene for making strategic choices that will allow the college or university to take maximum advantage of its opportunities and overcome its threats. The cause of all these challenges and opportunities is change, change that is driven by outside forces and is powerful and inevitable as it pervades the academy. As they begin to recognize the impacts of change, many individual colleges and universities start to discover a variety of choices in terms of how they will address and respond to the challenges of change.

Many colleges also discover that the practice of higher education is at a watershed. Numerous issues with which the academy traditionally has been unconcerned are now not only a reality of everyday life, but they impact the very survival of the individual academic institutions: change, competition, accountability, marriage of laboratory and field research with applied research, development of strategic alliances, *learners* instead of *students,* lifelong learning as a new definition for continuing education, effective responses to stakeholders, and many other issues. These forces for change exist, and it is now time for each campus to determine how it wishes to respond to them. The strategic planning process, again, continues to offer the best hope for effectively managing desirable changes.

Issues of Change in Academia

The important role that higher education plays in society is crucial, particularly as we move into the Information Age. The academy creates needed change. As Pascarella and Terenzini (1991) remind us, college and university campuses offer "a setting in which the impetus and opportunities for change are substantial, perhaps unsurpassed by those of any other social institution" (p. 59). Yet when these campuses need to change to serve the emerging economy in a different manner, that form of change has proven to be much more difficult.

One of the major issues facing colleges and universities is the necessity to break away from the traditional academic mold and find new educational models with strengths that match with new market opportunities. Colleges need to have a better fit with their environment. Atwell (1998) describes the academy as being plagued by a single model of educational excellence, the major research university. He proposes that this is a model that perhaps only fifty colleges and universities in the United States have been able to achieve effectively. He further suggests that many institutions are inappropriately trying to emulate these national treasures when the new environment clearly dictates the need for multiple models. Elsewhere, Carnevale (1991) describes the new environment as being driven by a new, consumer-like learner, one that demands high levels of quality, convenience, timely responses, and customized products and services. Further, Thurow (1992) reminds us that in such a dynamic environment, competition increases as consumers migrate to institutions that best supply their needs at a price they are willing to pay. This is the development of a market model of education (see Kiker, 1971, for further discussion).

These are significant environmental forces that are reshaping academia. Although Rowley, Lujan, and Dolence (1997) suggested that most colleges and universities are slow to change, there are several alterations occurring in academia that are both interesting and encouraging; change is taking place.

Over the past few years, an impressive number of institutions of higher education have wrestled with the challenges of this new environment and have moved away from their traditional orientations to a variety of new directions. As we describe in Chapters Two and Three, there are today some sixteen choices for delivering higher education. Many colleges and universities around the world are instituting new programs, establishing new delivery systems, creating strategic alliances with other colleges and universities (as well as with business concerns), and developing new and innovative ways of meeting the educational needs of the Information Age society. Along with these changes, however, several large issues are emerging, particularly from the perspective of the strategic planner and strategic manager.

- *What* are appropriate strategic choices for a particular college or university?

- Once determined, *how* can these choices be implemented?
- *What* types of structural changes are needed to facilitate the new programs and new delivery systems?
- *Should* colleges and universities form strategic alliances, with whom, and for what purpose(s)?
- *What* needs to happen to match academic innovation to twenty-first century educational needs?

Emerging Faces Within the Academy

As Atwell (1998) suggested, there is a need for a variety of models of educational excellence. This does not mean that the traditional models of the research university, liberal arts college, comprehensive university, and the myriad large and small colleges and universities in the United States and around the world are all going to go away or transform into something completely different. On the contrary, some of the institutions that have achieved wide recognition as centers of excellence and have large resource bases will not change dramatically in terms of either program or mission. Although nearly all academic institutions will change certain learning methodologies and pedagogies and reexamine the role of the professor, many will also find that they need to restructure themselves to be more efficient and responsive. Campuses that have tried to emulate Research One (Carnegie classification) colleges and universities may well find that they need to change dramatically in direction and form. In the end, only colleges and universities that are already centers of excellence will face changes that are minor compared to their sister institutions that have been unable to establish a similar competitive advantage.

Stated more bluntly, many institutions of higher education may see dramatic shifts in both their mission and their program offerings over the next several years (Blustain, Goldstein, and Lozier, 1999; Duderstadt, 1999; Farrington, 1999). As more and more colleges and universities begin to restructure themselves, a specific pattern of choices is emerging. Success depends on a college or university

- Developing a particular pattern of academic programming that meets the specific needs of a college or university's service community

- Making proper strategic choices and implementing them in a timely fashion
- Acquiring needed resources and using them properly
- Doing the most good for the most people
- Finding a strategic niche in its market domain and developing and maintaining a strategic advantage to help assure long-term health and survival

Inevitability of Change in Higher Education

Why do we have to change things? Why can't we just go on doing things the way we've always done them? What's to be gained by throwing out all the familiar traditions and successful ways of operating just to try something new? These questions, and others like them, are not unusual around the halls of college and university campuses. Many faculty, staff, and even administrators are skeptical about the needs for change and about how those changes will affect them and the work they do. Many learners who come to these institutions seem to have a better handle on the realities of the new economy and subsequent changes in the new millennium than many permanent members of a college or university campus who have difficulty understanding that change is needed in higher education.

This reluctance to change is fully understandable, given the history of the academy. Colleges and universities have been the fountainheads of knowledge creation since the Middle Ages. They have had the franchise, so to speak, and have experienced minimal competition. In this monopolistic setting, the Ivory Tower has become revered almost as a holy place where knowledge is created and disseminated to all who care to visit. Why should this change?

The reality is often not grasped by denizens of the Ivory Tower that the academy has not kept pace with the explosive needs of the Information Age in terms of either knowledge creation or dissemination. It is hard for many within the academy's traditionally insulated intellectual walls to realize that what it does and has done traditionally throughout the ages is no longer as highly revered or regarded as in the past. The reality, however, is that the entire course of civilization has changed dramatically over the last half century, and what society needs and demands of those who create and disseminate knowledge has changed right along with it (Duderstadt, 1999). The danger is that unless individual colleges and universities adapt to these changes, the forces that have created these changes are powerful enough to destroy any academic institution that fails to fulfill their needs and demands.

Monumental Changes in the External Environment

The simplest way of addressing the changes in the external environment is to look at the transition society has gone through in moving from the Industrial Age to the Information Age. The components of this overall change have literally shattered old tenets of belief and created new ones (Dolence and Norris, 1995). The staggering advances that have come from the development of new technologies and new economies has transformed everything.

The fall of Communism in Eastern Europe, the advent of the Internet, the growth of cheap and fast transportation, and the increased ability to communicate instantly anywhere in the world have meant that new systems of getting things done had to be discovered. New ways of organizing how things are accomplished had to be developed, and new ways of working with each other in a worldwide community had to be created.

The role of the academy in all this is complex. To better understand this role, it is important to remember that most of these changes occurred outside the academy. This is significant because so many societal and economic changes have come from the academy (Rowley, Lujan, and Dolence, 1998). This time, however, the changes were different, and instead of leading the change process, the academy finds itself following the change process. There are exceptions—many academic researchers and professors have been part of the new paradigm from the beginning, at least from an analytic distance. Innovations in teaching and learning have popped up around the world to meet the demands of today's learners. So many other campuses, however, have tried to use the traditional approaches to education, regardless of their appropriateness. Inevitably, college administrators and faculty become surprised when student enrollments go down, endowments drop off, and their best faculty take flight, thus lessening the colleges' ability to provide programs of excellence. Once the quality of their programs drops, and colleges lose their distinct competencies, it is not hard to predict the decline and possible fall of these institutions.

Changes in the Economy

How people work and the work that they do in the new age is clearly different from how they worked and the work they did in the previous age (Katz, 1999). Globalization and computer usage have transformed the economy of all industrialized nations throughout the world (Western Interstate Commission for Higher Education [WICHE], 1992). Indeed, a whole new industry has been created, the information industry, that doesn't just serve the industrial base, it has replaced it altogether in many ways.

Creating, refining, controlling, disseminating, and analyzing information is big business today beyond the boundaries of the campus. It has created huge new companies, such as Microsoft, that have quickly grown to dominate much of the national and world economies. These are companies that work with information (and make large profits in doing so), or as we know it in another context, knowledge—the traditional role of the university. If the local college or university is now challenged by an entire business industry in knowledge creation and dissemination, how does it mesh or compete with this new industry? How does it maintain its tradition of testing information and creating better understanding? What is the proper role of the academy and its individual institutions in the Information Age?

This is the primary challenge to today's colleges and universities. Each campus needs to redefine or reaffirm itself within the new age in an economy where control of the development and dissemination of information (knowledge) is no longer a monopoly. Certainly there is still need for the many activities of the academy that are not currently addressed by outside information companies, both in terms of research and in teaching, yet there are growing competitive forces today that challenge even the most sacred of academic traditions and activities (Blustain, Goldstein, Lozier, 1999; Katz, 1999). Dealing with competition, especially from nonacademic organizations, is new to most colleges and universities and presents new challenges and problems.

Changes in the Learning Needs of the Populace

The other major change is the transition from student to learner (Trachtenberg, 1997; the Education Resources Institute [TERI], 1966). No longer adequately referred to as the *student,* the *learner* brings a new set of needs and circumstances to the issue of how best to disseminate knowledge. *Students* might be considered those who seek knowledge but are passive in deciding what knowledge they need or how teachers will provide it to them. Students are passive when they receive that education and conform to the dictates and traditions of the college or university that provides that education. Students are not creators of knowledge but are the receivers of the results of research.

Learners are different. Like students, learners seek knowledge, but the resemblance ends there.

• Learners take the initiative in deciding what areas of knowledge they need to learn.
• Learners look for methods of being taught that match their time constraints, available resources, and work-related requirements and restraints.
• Learners understand that much of today's knowledge base is changing and are anxious to be part of the knowledge creation process as well as in the refining and analytical processes that go along with it.
• Learners understand that they have choices and use those choices to get what they want when they need them.

From this description, two conclusions become obvious. First, the nature of today's learner requires a different form of educational response from colleges and universities if the educational process is to be effective and if we assume that the primary purpose of education is to provide knowledge to help individuals, groups, and entire societies improve their lives and the lives of others (TERI, 1966). Second, the learner can take full advantage of a competitive world of education and is fully capable of doing so (Farrington, 1999).

Learners are also consumers, and as consumers, believe that they have a say in the products they purchase. This notion introduces higher education to traditional business competition, a setting with which it is unfamiliar and uncomfortable. Beyond the issues of the transformation of the student to the learner and the learner being a consumer rather than a receptacle, in the modern academy, a variety of kinds of learners have different needs and wants. These include

- The *traditional learner*—the individual who goes directly from high school into a traditional college or university and seeks a degree in a particular discipline.
- The *nontraditional learner*—the person that may have started out as a traditional student but dropped out and comes back much later in life to complete a college or university program; this can also be the person who didn't go to college following high school but decides in later life to get a degree from a particular college or university.
- The *traditional graduate learner*—the individual who seeks master's or doctoral level degrees soon after completing the preceding degree. Many of these people become involved with the research side of higher education, particularly in the Carnegie Research One and Two, as well as Doctoral One and Two, colleges and universities.
- The *professional graduate learner*—the person who seeks a graduate degree to enhance professional status. These people seldom become involved with major college or university research agendas.
- The *casual learner*—the individual who periodically signs up to take a class either for personal interest or for professional enhancement.
- The *lifelong learner*—the person who is always seeking new knowledge and new knowledge bases. This person exemplifies trends developing within the Information Age.

Among the various types of learners, two types can be particularly challenging to even the best of the traditional colleges and universities: the lifelong learner and the nontraditional learner (WICHE, 1992). In today's economy, not only is knowledge developed at breakneck speed, but also those who work with that knowledge have to continue learning to keep up with their work. Therefore, people of all ages have educational needs, and many turn to colleges and universities to help provide for those needs. Further, these learners have different needs and are more informed about their rights and about the benefits that higher education should bring them than traditional learners. There is simply no good reason for even attempting to teach these learners in the same way as traditional students, particularly as the numbers of lifelong and nontraditional learners increase.

The lifelong learner is a particularly interesting challenge. Having perhaps already received a college or university degree, these members of the Information Economy have the same needs for leading-edge knowledge that the nontraditional learners have. Instead of getting involved in a directed educational degree program, however, these learners need updates in certain fields and single courses (or maybe just parts of courses) for others. What this means is that the basic college or university degree program can no longer be viewed as a complete knowledge package. Like knowledge itself, learners seek updating. Why wouldn't these learners expect degree-granting institutions to provide those updates?

These examples of the new learner present significant challenges to traditional education. Traditional education doesn't do a good job in meeting these needs. While some might argue that the traditional student will continue to exist, and there is truth in this, overall the academy cannot package itself as useful only to traditional students. As more high school students are becoming aware of their choices, the basic appeal of the traditional campus may begin to fade. Further, in refusing to change to meet the needs of today's learners, certain colleges and universities risk irrelevance, and this irrelevance could be fatal.

The Importance of Developing and Maintaining a Competitive Advantage

If the notion of having to change traditional values and methods is difficult for some campus constituents to accept, the notion of having to become competitive must seem cataclysmic. Remember that the traditional academy has regarded itself, as well as having been regarded by others, as almost a mystical place. It was a place apart from the outside world where knowledge was created and disseminated. The appeal of this world is strong, and it is understandable that this pristine aura of academic life has its protectors and supporters. In such a world, there is no room for competition among institutions—only creativity, scholarly analysis, and excellent teaching.

Once again, however, these views clash with the demands of those who provide the means that allow colleges and universities to exist (Katz, 1999). Learners and other consumers of higher education's products and services want to be assured of receiving higher levels of quality, timeliness, and responsiveness. Should one campus refuse to meet these needs, learners and consumers simply go to the next campus, whether it is the college or university next door or the one in cyberspace. Not liking competition is not the same thing as not having to deal with it. Competition exists and campuses really have no choice but to confront it head-on (Farrington, 1999).

Competitive Advantages Are Not Just for Businesses

In business, strategic planning and strategic management have long been known as effective tools for creating a competitive edge, taking advantage of particular market conditions and distinctive competencies, and forging a niche that a company can dominate. The reputation of competition and phrases such as "dog-eat-dog world" are unappealing to academics, so their resistance to having to become competitive is understandable.

As businesses have learned, however, creating and building a competitive edge is often a critical issue—business operations can be as easily lost as they can survive. Businesses can succeed or fail based on whether they become a major player in their particular competitive environments. Further, competition does not necessarily imply a predatory stance. Certainly, much of the literature on strategic management today describes and defends business practices that do not propose obtaining competitive advantage by annihilating a company's competitors. Win-win situations are possible (such as strategic alliances, joint ventures, and network arrangements) and in many cases are preferred. This truism of businesses can also apply in the academy.

The Meaning of Competition in the Academy

Competition in the academy has two faces. One is the face of competition for resources (Katz, 1999; Levine, 1997). There just are not enough resources to go around in either public colleges and universities or in private colleges and universities. In public institutions, colleges and universities not only often directly compete against each other for funding but also with other state agencies as well. This sort of double jeopardy means that top administrators, budget officers, and lobbyists must spend a great deal of time in the state capitals arguing their cases, cajoling the legislators who they believe are friendly to their cause, and swapping influence back and forth to get the best results possible. In an era when the general bent of the conservative coalitions has been to reduce spending, reduce taxes, and reduce services, however, the case for increased funding for public colleges and universities has become a harder one to sell.

For private colleges and universities, there is competition for gifts and endowments, and here, too, the fight is not just between schools but also between academia and other organizations that must compete for philanthropic dollars. As is true for public institutions of higher education, many private institutions have also seen public monies be severely reduced or dry up altogether. This has forced them to engage in seeking individual and corporate sponsors, just as private (and to a lesser degree public) not-for-profit institutions do. This increased competition intensifies the difficulties in raising adequate gifts or funding endowments for the private college or university, thus further stiffening the competitive environment.

There is also competition for students and faculty and to some degree for administrators and staff. In the case of students, colleges and universities want students who (1) are academically qualified to become college students, (2) show an ability to complete a program, (3) will add to the prestige of the institution, and (4) help meet specific quotas (such as minorities and women in certain programs). High school students who come out of high-quality programs, have high SAT scores, and come from the upper end of their graduating classes are the ones to whom colleges and universities are most attracted. However, because there are only a limited number of students in the top 1, 2, 5, or even 10 percent range of their graduation classes, competition for these students is created. Each college or university wants to be the one that the top students will select. To get these superior students, as well as more minority and protected-class students, colleges and universities have had to add significantly to their scholarship pools to entice desired students to accept their offers. This is a significant additional cost that affects resources.

The other side of the issue of student candidacy is that of needing to fill space. The airplane analogy is very apropos here: The major fixed expenses (in the case of colleges, their physical plant, faculty salaries, etc.) must be met before the plane leaves the ground. Although a campus might want to fill its classrooms with only top students, the reality is that the college or university will continue to reduce admissions standards until they have admitted enough students to fill their available seats and have met, if not exceeded, overhead expenses. Here, too, in order to get students into the classroom and generate enough cash flow, more campuses are forced to increase nonacademic scholarships and other incentives (equivalent to offering discounted tickets on an airplane).

The second major face of competition is the drive for excellence (Rowley, Lujan, and Dolence, 1998). Throughout the world there are certain colleges and universities whose very name implies tradition, quality, and excellence. To many of the rest of the institutions of higher education these few "name schools" have become role models and quality benchmarks.

According to Clark (1995), however, the name schools are not necessarily better than their less-renowned sister institutions. Their prestige often suggests educational qualities that are actually no better than one can find at lesser-name institutions. As Atwell (1998) advised, noted at the beginning of this chapter, it's not so much that every college or university cannot be a Harvard or a Cambridge or a Heidelberg, it turns out that they really don't want to be. Every college or university has the ability to develop particular programs that can rival the name schools, as well as the opportunity to develop excellence in areas that the name schools have been unable to attain. For example, Southampton College (part of Long Island University), with a student population of only fifteen hundred students, has developed an excellent reputation for its undergraduate program in Marine Sciences. The Culinary Institute of America, just ten miles north of an Ivy League school, Vassar College, has developed a world-renowned reputation for producing exceptional chefs.

This face of competition—the competition for excellence—is the ability of a given college or university to say that one or two (perhaps more) of its programs are outstanding. Excellence will draw students, faculty, grants, gifts, and endowments to the institution that will help that college or university sustain its competitive advantage and long-term success. By understanding that not even the name schools can be everything to everybody, colleges and universities can use the strategic planning process to develop their own resource base in ways that will build their institutions in a significant manner. This is a clear way of being proactive and helping to maintain a competitive advantage.

Issues of Values and Ethics in Academic Competition

Perhaps much of the resistance to the notion of being in a competitive environment or acting in a competitive way for many academics is a lingering feeling that, somehow, competition means that one side wins while the other side loses. Such an outcome might appear unethical, particularly when we are talking about the rich gifts and capabilities of the academy. It also may suggest that the intellectual and collegial values of higher education are no longer valued in today's world.

Fortunately, depending upon how one approaches the issue of competition, there does not need to be a downside to becoming more competitive. It is possible for colleges and universities to work side by side and still compete. For example, two campuses might combine their efforts to reduce costs by increasing their economies of scale in purchasing, printing, public relations, or lobbying efforts. At the same time, both institutions continue to recruit the same students and faculty. To carry the example further, the two campuses might even decide to trade certain programs and act as feeders to each other. (One campus gets rid of its MBA program and shifts resources to bring its undergraduate program to excellence, while the other campus pares way back on its undergraduate business program and shifts resources to bring its MBA program to an excellent level, thus giving both campuses a greater opportunity to create excellence in their surviving programs while providing immediate and seamless access between programs on the different campuses.) "Win-win" situations are possible, and there is nothing that challenges either the ethics or value system of a campus by adopting such a strategy.

Why Strategic Planning Can Work in Colleges and Universities

The basic strengths of strategic planning are its abilities to help better align the organization with its environment (that set of internal and external forces that can positively or negatively affect the activities of an organization). This rubric is true in business and it is also true in the academy. Unfortunately, with the massive shifts in the world economy over the past several years, many elements of the environment have become less defined, less predictable.

The environment is also pervasive and invasive. Either an organization interacts in a desirable and effective manner with the environment or the environment proves its strength by destroying the organization. An analysis of the demise of several of the dot.com companies shows that good intentions do not always prevail in the face of marketing preferences or financial realities.

This environmental imperative does not diminish in force or intensity simply because the organization happens to be a college or university. As too many present-day presidents and chancellors fully appreciate, maintaining campus stability, building a relevant program mix, developing excellence, and acquiring needed resources are all challenges that continue to intensify and become harder to solve as their campuses try to discover how best to be successful. Many presidents and chancellors have already turned to strategic planning to help better define ways of moving toward success, and many have been disappointed. We argue that it isn't strategic planning that is at fault, but the approach to planning that campus leaders and strategic planners have adopted. More specifically, these less-than-stellar results are due at least in part to a lack of appreciation by these individuals that strategic planning in colleges and university is significantly different from strategic planning in business. As Mintzberg (1994a) has so eloquently reminded us, strategic planning works, but it isn't easy. By establishing a realistic approach to strategic planning, knowing precisely what the options are, and keeping in mind up-front what it will take to implement the strategic plan successfully, the prospects for success increase significantly.

Goals for Strategic Planning in the Academy that Will Work

The central reason for engaging in strategic planning, as we have stated, is better aligning the college or university with its environment. The market mechanisms now in operation bring with them all the positive results of successful and mutually beneficial interchanges, as well as the negative results of a mismatch. This does not suggest a change of values or ethics for colleges and universities but an understanding of the changes that have occurred in society vis-à-vis the development and utilization of knowledge. Colleges and universities will continue to serve the function of discovering and disseminating the knowledge that society needs. The methods colleges and universities use for knowledge distribution, the types of knowledge circulated, and who uses that knowledge, however, may vary more dramatically than in the past.

There are also other goals that are appropriate for a college or university's strategic planning process. Educating the lower socioeconomic level of the populace that has traditionally not taken advantage of a college education is not only a noble goal, but in the Information Age it is also a necessity. Higher education can play a significant role in preventing creation of an underclass that will become permanent as the less advantaged are left further and further behind. Developing new disciplines will be necessary as we develop not simply the Information Age economy but also the new economies that will follow. Continuing to develop new methods of knowledge delivery and pedagogy to improve the learner's ability to learn is another important goal. Seeking better ways of integrating the entire world community in peace through developing better methods of communication, encouraging cultural understanding, and developing mutual respect are additional worthwhile goals.

Strategic goals can also include the assurance that the college or university will survive for the long term because it has a foundation of at least one quality program as well as a healthy financial and capital base. Furthermore, colleges and universities can help improve the lives of their students, faculty, staff, and even administrators through a positive and fulfilling association with the campus. Finally, strategic planning can be a device a campus can use to help improve the community through inclusion, caring, and sharing. Every one of these goals is vital if a college or university is truly seeking to be successful in the long run. These goals are also long-term goals, as is true of the strategic planning process itself. Campus leaders and strategic planners might find it useful to test their perceptions of what strategic planning is and what it does against this list to see how close their expectations and goals really are to the goals of the strategic planning process.

The Inevitability of Problems

Unfortunately, there just is no way to avoid problems in the strategic planning process—in business and colleges and universities alike. The real issue is how will campus leaders and strategic planners choose to deal with these problems. What we emphasize throughout this book is that the real key to success isn't to avoid problems, but to face problems openly, honestly, fairly, and with the knowledge and appreciation that strategic planning is a human process. There is no way to avoid problems but there are many ways to confront and work through them.

We believe that this is part of what Mintzberg (1994a) is telling us. When planners go into a strategic planning process believing that the strategic plan will solve all their problems, they have just created their first problem. Because strategic planning takes place in a volatile environment and is a human process (and the more we can make it truly a humane process, the better), and because no one can ever successfully predict the future, problems will occur.

So is strategic planning so problematic that it really isn't worth trying? The answer is absolutely not. There is no portion of life that is not subject to problems, so why single out strategic planning as the one problematic activity that campuses should rigorously avoid? What is needed here is the understanding of what happens when strategic planning is rejected. Problems don't go away, they get worse. Life doesn't become less complicated, it becomes more so. And if campuses don't improve, they slide further and further into difficulty and thence oblivion. The key is to be realistic, patient, honest, and open. Allow the strategic planning process to deal with numerous campus issues but don't expect it to solve all the college or university's problems.

The Importance of Staying the Course

For readers who have gone through a failed strategic planning process, we understand that it may be difficult to believe that the best recommendation for their troubled campuses is to try strategic planning again. There is no better method, however, of aligning colleges or universities with their environments; even failed campus strategic planning efforts can be turned around with the proper methodology.

In an era of tight budgets, dwindling resource bases, and frayed nerves, going back into a strategic planning process seems like asking a lot, but in reality, there is no other good alternative. The difference has to be that the second time around, everyone is better informed as to what the process is, what it can do, and how it should be implemented.

For readers who are contemplating becoming involved in strategic planning and have not yet done so, we hope you will not be discouraged from this task by others' failures and miscues. If you are considering strategic planning and are reading this book, you are trying to learn everything you can about the process before beginning. This is very wise, and in our experience, refreshing. Too many campuses have started out using the business model or have developed their own model (planning is easy isn't it? anyone can do it!), only to be disappointed. By understanding how campus leaders and strategic planners need to tailor the strategic planning process to fit the academy, by becoming more familiar with the specific environmental factors that affect colleges and universities, and by understanding what the specific choices and implementation alternatives are, informed beginning planners have a clear advantage over those who haven't done their homework.

Chapter Two

A Basic Choice Model for Traditional Academic Organizations

Within the context of strategic planning, campus leaders and strategic planners face a variety of challenges. As Rowley, Lujan, and Dolence (1997) have identified, one of the first major hurdles is to develop a scheme of planning that is unique to the academy and that reflects the complexities of a dual-governance system in which top-down planning (the general business model) doesn't work. However, once a group of college or university planners get past the basics of *how to plan,* they then face the issues of *what to plan* and *how to implement* the various strategic facets of the plan once the planners have identified them.

In this chapter and the next we address the issue of what to plan directly by looking at the various strategic choices colleges and universities have in their planning process. We do this from a macro perspective; that is, we identify major academic directions that a college or university might develop as the central pattern of academic activity within the institution or a major new segment of campus activity that is likely to affect most all campus constituents. On an individual level, a particular college or university might well decide that one of the models we describe here is a perfect fit for its campus. Another college or university might decide that adapting two or more of the models within a more multidivisional setting best supports its future. These decisions come out of the strategic planning process as campuses establish a firm understanding of the demands of their crucial external environments and the resource capabilities of their internal environments.

This done, they can begin to formulate their strategic direction by developing a better understanding of some of the more important issues inherent in the sixteen types of higher educational institutions we present here. The various strategic choices consist of the fourteen types of higher educational institutions that Rowley, Lujan, and Dolence (1998) have already suggested, along with two additional types. Understanding these sixteen types and some of the issues inherent in each should be useful to campus leaders and strategic planners, because if colleges and universities are to have a clear and concise plan for strategy implementation, they must first understand the types of strategies currently operating in the industry of higher education based on the different institutional characteristics.

The underlying bases for choosing one type over another in the strategic choice process is dependent upon two major realities of the college or university: the resource base of the institution and the institution's prevailing philosophical academic position. In this chapter and in Chapter Three we place each of sixteen types within a general model and also describe, in general terms, the expected structural characteristics of each. This is information that should also help strategic planners and campus leaders understand what type of college or university their institution most closely resembles as well as what other strategic options are available to them. Planners and campus leaders can then implement plans to support their particular strategic choice or choices (either by creating or reengineering) to achieve the maximum benefits of the institution's preferred strategic direction.

Purposes in Devising a Model

At the dawn of the new millennium, one can look around the general industry we call higher education and see a wide variety of forms that characterize its institutions. Many traditional colleges and universities in the United States look toward the Research One (R-1) college or university model as the one they see as most worthwhile to emulate. This is not to say that traditional colleges and universities are completely static or gravitating solely to the R-1 model. It is becoming evident that some changes are taking place, however, as discussed in the previous chapter, and as Atwell (1998) has stated so clearly, higher education needs alternative forms of colleges and universities. There simply is not the resource base to support all colleges and universities pursuing an R-1 strategy, nor does society want all higher education to be strictly R-1 dominated. Therefore, in order to flourish, many (if not most) colleges and universities must look at alternative forms of higher education.

This is an important reality in higher education today, and several other authors have added to our understanding of the issues involved. For example, Rowley, Lujan, and Dolence (1998) suggested that nearly all colleges and universities will dramatically change their structures, their technologies, and their curricula over the next several years as they seek to better align themselves with the complex educational issues that are emerging in the Information Age. Leslie and Fretwell (1996) not only mirror this view but state that academic institutions are not immune to the dramatic changes of the emerging Information Age environment and need to be proactive in developing institutional and industrywide changes. Elsewhere, Davies (1997) suggests that colleges and universities are coming more and more under scrutiny as different government entities have begun to question their investments in higher education and the effectiveness of the educational process in many sectors. Further, as Stitt-Gohdes (1999) reminds us, different people learn differently and therefore require various modes of instruction. It is evident that not only does developing a broader scope of learning opportunities make sense (when added to the simple competitive realities and forces involved as described in Chapter One), but also that several alternative types of higher educational models emerge in the Information Age economy. Therefore, we should not be surprised at the amount and diversity of change that is occurring already, even in traditional higher education. Change will be the norm for the foreseeable future.

As we move into the new millennium, a whole new set of environments is the reality for all organizations, business and non-business alike. These new environments require unique responses. For colleges and universities, much of this change may not be a free choice, as many external constituencies are becoming more militant in their involvement. For example, Davies (1997), in commenting on governmental funding, has suggested that this particular environmental force can simply impose negative penalties if colleges and universities fail to meet their expectations. This leads to the real concern, as expressed by London (1987) and even earlier by Lawrence and Lorsch (1967), that organizations that do not adapt to their environments will begin to atrophy, and many will simply not survive.

There seems to be no specific prescriptive manner in which college and university leaders and strategic planners can map out their current position and look at alternatives that make sense for them. Environmental pressures recommend or mandate change, but do not (as they *should* not) describe what those changes should look like or should accomplish. A basic model can be helpful to place individual campuses within families of similar institutions based on primary characteristics. Such a model can help campus leaders identify where their institutions are in relation to a particular family of institutions, and then illustrate what is required to become more typical of those institutions (in the event that initial placement puts a particular institution in a position out of line with its family type) or to move to another institutional type altogether.

As campus strategic planners devise their "plans to plan," they need to orient themselves among a variety of strategic choice issues. These include understanding what alternative forms institutions of higher education are implementing and the success or failures they are experiencing. Planners also need to analyze their campus's resource base and guiding philosophy and then tactically choose the most appropriate strategies that match those internal realities. Further, they also need to decide how to move forward by creating or reconstructing the structure of the institution to match the strategic direction.

Having determined these issues, planners can begin to match the discovered resources and philosophies of the campus to the primary constructs of the models we present in the next section. What they will then develop is a better knowledge of the drivers with which they have to work as they go on to construct their own strategic choice model.

The Strategic Constructs of the Basic Model

Figure 2.1 represents a schematic placement for different forms of higher educational institutions (described in the next section) within a two-dimensional model. The two major dimensions are those of the resource base of the institution and the guiding philosophy of the institution. The model also includes three distinct areas of risk.

Why these particular three dimensions? First and foremost, and very simply stated, resources provide the basics for all campus activity. Resources allow campuses to take action and grow and implement strategic plans, whereas the lack of resources prevents

Figure 2.1. Strategic Positioning of Information Age Colleges and Universities.

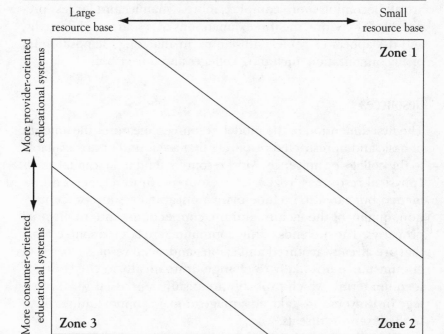

campuses from developing and perhaps even maintaining their institutions. Resources are probably the most important concern of any organization as it seeks to survive and grow (Pfeffer and Salancik, 1978).

Second, the prevailing institutional philosophy determines the direction the institution will pursue (Mintzberg, 1987). For many colleges and universities, this philosophy has been decided by others or by history and tradition. For example, if a state chooses one particular institution to become its premier, lead institution, that normally means that that particular college or university will become the state's leading R-1. That institution has little or no choice, nor do the other publicly funded campuses in the state.

Third, risk involves the relative ability to survive. As environments become more unstable and unpredictable, risk increases. As risk increases, the ability to survive becomes more threatened. As we move more deeply into the Information Age and the other challenges of the new millennium, one thing is certain: Environments are all becoming more complex, more dynamic, and far less predictable. Therefore, the three dimensions of resources, philosophy, and risk appear extremely substantive in analyzing the positioning of any organization, including colleges and universities.

Resources

The first dimension in the model, resources, measures the amount of basic and unrestricted resources that are found or are available to the college or university. Most resources tend to be capital assets (physical resources, real estate resources, funding, and endowments) but can also include many noncapital resources (reputation, quality of the faculty, alumni, connections, and intellectual property). The two ends of this continuum are large resource bases that are already acquired and stable, and small resource bases (a circumstance not likely to change dramatically in the short or medium term), which probably are insufficient assets for the college or university to take advantage of major opportunities or to fend off serious threats.

This dimension is important because the relative size of the resource base can either facilitate or diminish the ability of colleges or universities to make major changes or take advantage of major opportunities within their environments. It is also important because a large resource base gives an institution more freedom to pursue its mission while a small resource base forces an institution to consolidate its efforts and pursue limited strategic opportunities. Limited resources also means that institutions have a greater dependency on their stakeholders. Colleges and universities with limited resources tend to be highly influenced by crucial stakeholder groups and also find that they need to spend a great deal of time and effort to influence these stakeholders.

However, a large resource base reduces the relative risk experienced by a college or university in that there may be more available resources for new projects. Slack resources buffer organizations from environmental uncertainty and risk by providing a safety cushion of cash flow needed when the organization tries to implement changes dictated by increasingly competitive environments (Galbraith, 1977; Thompson, 1967). This means that colleges and universities with larger resource bases can initiate change (and deploy funds) faster than their poorer counterparts.

Institutional Philosophy

The second dimension is that of philosophy. There are essentially two approaches, both having to do with the institution's attitudes toward their students. Being *provider-oriented* refers to the disposition of the institution to follow a more traditional academic approach (internally driven) to knowledge generation and dissemination and provide resources to faculty to undertake research or teaching with a maximum of academic freedom. Certainly Atwell's (1998) top fifty U.S. treasures, all Research One institutions, would fall into this category. Along with rich resource bases, these top fifty and the next tier of research institutions, which are able to accumulate large resource bases as well, can more easily follow the traditional activities of higher education. They are provider-oriented in the sense that they create knowledge and then provide it to others. They also determine what their research agendas will be (not completely, of course, due to the influence of grant providers, governmental regulators, and even historic missions—but the research they do is original in nature and is guided by recognized campus experts within their fields). On such campuses, research is valued above teaching, and often the type of teaching that occurs, especially at the undergraduate level, is done by junior faculty or teaching assistants, not by the researchers who are creating the knowledge.

Being *consumer-oriented* refers to the disposition of the institution to follow a course that is more cognizant of market needs and demands in designing its research agenda and curriculum base. As Clark (1995) describes it, the university becomes a market. Most comprehensive colleges and universities in the United States and around the world are much more likely to choose or will be at least partially forced into this role. Many of these institutions will probably focus more on applied research, as opposed to pure (or exploratory) research, one of the hallmarks of the Research One institutions. Some will focus on teaching excellence as one of their primary appeals to an ever-increasing, selective, and demanding market of learners. Other institutions will seek to combine research and instruction via practical, hands-on learning experiences.

One of the primary drivers in the pattern of the provider-driven classification is the emergent role of the learner as a major participant in the educational process. As Dill and Sporn (1995) suggest, this phenomenon has shifted the traditional role of higher education as the provider to higher education as the server. They go on to describe this as a whole new knowledge industry (p. 149). Major segments of the academy will become, in Dill and Sporn's words, a type of "learning commons for society in general." These events are occurring because, as Kember and Gow (1994) tell us, students are becoming more and more vocal in the learning processes they are involved with. No longer passive, they are making demands for what their education should be like, and when ignored they go somewhere else. This has created a competitive environment that colleges and universities can no longer ignore.

As diverse as society is, it should not be surprising that several different forms of colleges and universities will become more evident as the Information Age emerges, and that many of these forms will become much more consumer-oriented than they are presently. The result will be a new landscape of institutions of higher education—some parts familiar, but other parts different from our traditional experience, and refreshingly so.

Risk

The model presented in Figure 2.1 also suggests a third dimension, that of risk. It further suggests three distinct zones of risk. Each of these zones is associated with both present and future risk conditions in the increasing turbulent environment of the academy. Zone 1 is the most risky due to the lack of substantial resources and the tendency to be inwardly as opposed to outwardly focused. Such a position tends to mock basic marketing standards for attracting and serving a knowledgeable constituency base, and therefore institutional types in this zone may find themselves at extreme risk, with the very real potential of collapse. Zone 2 represents conditions of moderate risk. It also represents a continuum of choices that blends higher levels of resources than what was available in Zone 1 with a broader philosophical orientation, moving from a position of high resource levels and more traditional philosophical orientations to lower resource levels and more consumer orientation. Finding an appropriate balance is the key to success here. Even so, perhaps the stronger driving force is still the resource base. The conclusion one might draw is that the best strategic choice for institutions without large resource bases is to become more consumer-driven. Again, the logic follows the basic marketing wisdom of giving consumers what they want if you want them to support your institution.

Finally, Zone 3 represents lower levels of risk. Though still risky (no institution, business, not-for-profit, or government is ever entirely insulated from environmental risk), based on state support and public demand for higher education, most comprehensive colleges and universities have little to worry about in terms of long-term survival. However, as the model suggests, the colleges and universities in this sector of the model *do* need to become more applied and consumer-oriented in their operations in order to avoid the burgeoning criticisms and threats of dissatisfied (and more and more vocal) constituencies. Since institutions in this sector (particularly comprehensive colleges and universities) have tended to emulate research institutions, individual campuses may not currently occupy the position suggested in the model. However, we suggest that, over time, this shift will occur more and more. Meanwhile, the colleges and universities that are more consumer-oriented should be successful, almost by definition, thus providing excellent benchmarking for other institutions who are still seeking a firm strategic direction.

Putting the Constructs Together

As the model indicates, all options are arrayed within a two-dimensional space. This is appropriate, given that individual campuses have different levels of resources and different attitudes toward research and teaching. What the model suggests is a theoretical, idealized positioning that we feel will be supported over time. If we are right, the positions on the model represent preferred, or idealized, conditions. For example, if an institution truly wants to become an R-1, it *must* acquire a large resource base (both capital and noncapital) and establish excellence in its chosen field(s) of research. Such an institution simply cannot survive with a low resource base.

We have already suggested there has been a drive to emulate the R-1 campuses—the historical tendency of most colleges and universities in response to the Soviet scientific advances of the 1950s and 1960s (Rowley, Lujan, and Dolence, 1997)—although the demands of the new millennium are vastly different. There is a much broader demand for a much wider variety of higher educational institutions. Therefore, not only does the model not suggest any one particular type of college or university as superior, it also suggests the possibility of mixing strategies as philosophy, resources, and environmental controls allow. Individual campuses will need to be able to scan their particular environmental sets, assess market shifts and demands, and be flexible enough to enact change in response to those shifts. According to Clark (1995), in such a world institutional differentiation is the key to success and should be rewarded.

The Sixteen Types of Higher Educational Institutions

Rowley, Lujan, and Dolence (1998) have described a variety of higher educational institutions as they looked at the changes brought about by the paradigm shift moving from the Industrial Age to the Information Age. In their discussion, they suggest that there are already fourteen specific identifiable institution types of higher education. Beyond those types, we believe we can identify two more. Table 2.1 identifies the sixteen types that are evident in this new educational environment, divided into two sets: the *classical forms,* and the *new breeds.* In developing this particular typology, the traditional academic model is present, but it is also augmented, remodeled, adapted, and in some cases discarded as new model types emerge.

In examining the full list found in Table 2.1, the sixteen types of academic institutions offer at least sixteen stand-alone strategic choices. However, combining models (for example, a comprehensive university engaging in a virtual university program) provides an even wider field of choices. Making a specific choice as to the appropriate direction a college or university should adopt is an issue embedded in the strategic planning process. In such a process, each campus examines its own institutional strengths and weaknesses and attempts to match them with the most promising opportunities, while raising consciousness about the potential threats, all found in the fast-paced learning environment of the Information Age. Beyond issues of strengths, weaknesses, opportunities, and threats, there are issues of mission, aspirations for excellence, governance, and resources, all of which play into the planning process.

Before going further into the issues of strategic choice and implementation, it is useful at this point for strategic planners to examine the sixteen types in more detail. In this chapter and the next, we provide this detail by describing each type, identifying their major structural characteristics, and explaining the reasoning for their placement in the model.

Figure 2.2 represents what the configuration would look like when we place the five types of colleges and universities referred to as the *classical forms* in the basic model. In this figure, one can

Table 2.1. Types of Higher Education Institutions.

The Classical Forms of Colleges and Universities

1. Research colleges and universities[a]
2. Comprehensive colleges and universities[a]
3. Small colleges and universities[a]
4. Community colleges[a]
5. Specialty colleges and universities[a]

The New Breed of Colleges and Universities

6. Co-op colleges and universities[a]
7. Composite universities[a]
8. Perpetual learning colleges and universities[a]
9. Virtual universities[a]
10. Virtual college and university indexes[a]
11. Self-directed teams within colleges and universities[a]
12. Assessment and competency-based colleges and universities[a]
13. Corporate universities[a]
14. Company universities[a]
15. Alternative colleges and universities[b]
16. Emerging[b]

[a]Identified by Rowley, Lujan, and Dolence, 1998.
[b]Identified by the authors.

see the schema of strategic decision elements that could be helpful in aiding the strategic decision maker better fit a particular institution into a particular strategic niche.

The Classical Forms of Colleges and Universities

As noted above, this chapter describes the first five types or families of colleges and universities—ones with which we are most familiar. The central purpose in doing so is to identify each of these families as specific strategic choices. Although the reader may

Figure 2.2. Strategic Positioning of the Traditional Families of Colleges and Universities.

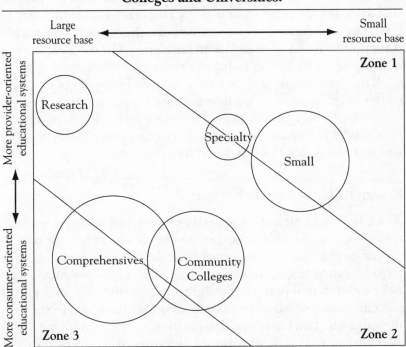

be familiar with the general descriptions of the classical forms we discuss here, it is important to view these forms as potential strategies, and to do so it is important to understand how they are alike and how they are different.

As the model has already suggested, and as the discussion in this and the next chapter will support, in order for an institution to *be* one of the types of institutions we describe in the model and to survive and prosper, strategic planners must benchmark their own colleges and universities against the philosophical, resource, and structural characteristics of that type of institution. This means, for example, that if one particular institution discovers that it does not have the characteristics it needs to be a research institution and it is not going to acquire them, it needs to choose a family of institutions that it is more suited for and develop its strategic plan in that area. It also means that if one particular institution wants to be a true research college or university, the model can provide direction in terms of what has to change within the institution's makeup so it can be successful as a research institution.

The next chapter will deal with the new breed of colleges and universities, some of which take familiar forms but apply them in new ways. To better understand those new forms, it's important to have a solid understanding of the description and structures of the classical forms that have spawned the newer ones.

Research Colleges and Universities

As we have said already, research colleges and universities have served as an extremely important model of what a college or university ought to be for well over four decades. Though we have already argued (along with other authors) that this one model cannot be the stencil pattern for all campuses, research institutions will continue to hold an extremely important position in the new millennium. The Carnegie classifications of Research One (R-1) and Research Two (R-2) form the majority of the institutions in this category. Also some Doctoral One (D-1) and Doctoral Two (D-2) may also fit here, provided the institutions support a primary mission of research and demonstrate a strong commitment to graduate education. Otherwise, D-1 and D-2 colleges and universities would fit in the category of comprehensive universities.

Basic Description

The research college or university is perhaps the most familiar type of higher educational institution in the world. It is characterized by its ability to provide leadership in basic and laboratory research, which is the most visible fountain of knowledge. It supports society's need for research and new knowledge, and after centuries of fulfilling that need, there is no expectation that its role will diminish in the next age. The research institution also supports graduate programming and the fostering of the next generation of college and university faculty, researchers, and campus leaders.

Although their primary mission tends to be in research and graduate education, research institutions continue to fulfill their role as educators. This becomes quite clear when one looks at the huge number of students at some research colleges and universities, such as the University of Michigan (36,995 students), Michigan State University (42,603), the Ohio State University (48,278), the University of Minnesota (45,410), University of Texas (48,857), Arizona State University (44,255), and the University of California at Los Angeles (UCLA) (35,558), just to name a few. Other research colleges and universities may not be as large, but they have developed excellent reputations as top quality research venues, such as the University of Massachusetts at Amherst and the California Polytechnic State University at Pomona in the United States, and Oxford and Cambridge in the United Kingdom, again to name but a few.

In such institutions, the primary mission tends to skew resources toward the fulfillment of research agendas, doctoral level education, and, to a lesser degree, master's level education. Very large undergraduate classes, teaching assistants, and very little individual attention often characterize undergraduate education.

Structural Characteristics
Due partially to size and partially to mission, research colleges and universities tend to be more bureaucratic in their structure. Academics and administrators tend to be the top of their professions; academics hold distinguished positions within their disciplines (the PhD from a Tier 1 institution is a given here), and administrators come to the research institutions with an admirable pedigree for their particular positions. Academic freedom is crucial to the success of their research agenda, so there is an odd pairing of high levels of administrative bureaucracy with highly unstructured faculty activities (outside the classroom, at least). The senior faculty members are treasured by the institution, and many of the resources available to the institution are earmarked for the work of these esteemed creators of knowledge. Tenure and promotion are often difficult to achieve, as to become one of the truly elite of a major research institution requires superior scholarship and, perhaps, proven grantsmanship. Power is concentrated toward the top

in this world, and the lower levels of the structure are tenuous places to be for faculty and administrators looking to establish their careers at these institutions.

Placement on the Model

Research colleges and universities depend upon large resource bases and in most cases are able to command them. Research and tenured faculty salaries are costly, and in order to be successful, research institutions must have large state revenues (for state institutions), higher than average tuition rates (a particularly important issue for private schools), large endowments, large grant and contract programs, and high-profile partnerships with governmental agencies and larger business organizations. This places them firmly on the left side of the model (Figure 2.2).

The dedication to research and the general mission to create knowledge push research institutions toward the top of the model as well. Although many grants and even many endowments will require specific types of research agendas, the work on those agendas is directed for the most part by academics. Therefore, in creating intellectual properties, there is little doubt as to who is in control of the research and what will happen to the results of that research. This makes the institutions primarily provider-oriented.

The model places such an academic type in Zone 2, a zone of moderate riskiness. This also appears to be appropriate because of the dependence upon large resource bases (which cannot always be fully guaranteed) and the potential for conflict between the research output and the expectations of grant and contract providers. Keeping everything in balance is the tricky obligation of research institution administrators, but this balancing act also places the institutions at a moderate level of risk.

Comprehensive Colleges and Universities

Seldom does one state have more than one Research One institution. It might have two or three smaller R-2 or D-1 public and private colleges and universities within its borders who are engaged in heavy research programs, but most other colleges and universities within a given state have other missions and serve other interests. We refer to most of these as comprehensive colleges and universities. Further, within this category are public as well as private colleges and universities.

Perhaps of all the families of institutions in the model, the comprehensive institution comprises the largest number. This is the group of institutions that has found that they need to really battle for resources if they try to become more like the traditional research institutions. This category includes some of the Carnegie D-1 and D-2 colleges and universities that have marginal graduate programs and marginal research activities. Still others originally were one-dimensional campuses, such as teachers' colleges, who were taken up in the post-Sputnik world, first, to become universities and second, to become R-1 look-alikes that never achieved their goals. In this group, one can also find colleges and universities that purposefully have devised missions and goals such as teaching or community service that they value over research.

It is unfortunate that in the emerging academic arena, this is the group of institutions that may have found themselves cut out of the lion's share of resources. Their missions are not as highly valued by governments, corporations, or donor groups as their research brethren's, and as a result their share of the resource base is proportionately smaller (lower salaries, smaller capital budgets, and less academic support funds). These institutions serve such a large percentage of the population, however, that their role in the economy is nonetheless vital. What is most important, these are the institutions that are geared to educate the growing number of learners emerging in our explosive economy. They are clearly needed and a vital resource in the Information Age.

Ironically, many of these institutions are just not sure about their appropriate role in the Information Age, given increasing market opportunities. This is why Rowley, Lujan, and Dolence (1997, 1998) and Keller before them (1983, 1994–1995) have argued so vehemently for strategic planning on these campuses. In a rapidly changing world with rapidly growing and diverse educational needs, it is clearly important for these campuses across our country (as well as around the world) to match their resources with the demands of their environments—both for their own good and for the good of the learners they hope to serve.

Basic Description

By and large, comprehensive colleges and universities are geared for more effective undergraduate education than are their research counterparts. They are degree granting at both the undergraduate and graduate levels, though graduate education tends to be more specialized and in some places even more applied than would be necessarily true of a research institution. They provide a solid liberal arts program along with specialization in a variety of disciplines that provide quality education to the average college-bound learner. They have a huge presence in this country and are major players in higher education as an industry. They include systems such as the California State System, the State Universities of New York, and many other state colleges and universities who form a huge second tier of academic institutions in this country and around the world.

As they move away from attempting to emulate the major research colleges and universities, many comprehensive institutions are becoming more specialized than they have been over the last four decades, as many of them have come to recognize two important realities: they do not have (and will not have) the large resource bases needed to become a major research institution, and they must develop and focus on centers of excellence to serve specific societal needs and the new age of learners they serve. They have had to become more marketing-oriented, and it should be an understatement to say that in order to thrive, these institutions need to be much more aware of the needs of their constituency groups, and they must be successful in meeting those needs if they hope to keep their support.

Structural Characteristics

Some comprehensive institutions can be very large. With size, bureaucracy takes hold. And in this world of reduced resources, there is a fair amount of attack on bureaucracy, at least the administrative side of bureaucracy. For example, many colleges and universities have conducted studies of administrative expenses and have recommended a series of administrative cutbacks designed to reduce administrative expenses and bureaucracy and shift those resources to academic salaries.

Faculty members tend to hold mostly doctoral qualifications from first and second tier doctoral-granting institutions, though it is not unusual to bring in doctoral candidates to teach as potential faculty members. It is also not unusual to find high-profile business leaders or community leaders serving as adjunct faculty (a practice also found in most research institutions). Administrators are also normally experienced elsewhere and have a proven track record, though it is not totally unusual for administrators to get their first administrative posts here. Staff tend to be highly professional, and in many states are part of a state system that could include unionized employees.

There are major movements in these institutions to give faculty more of a say in administrative affairs as one way of making sure that available resources go more toward academic programs than to administrative decision makers. The idea of shared governance is more of an issue in comprehensive institutions, and a fuller participation in campus administration is in evidence. Furthermore, on many campuses, even students have an important voice in the administrative affairs of the college or university, and in some cases, they even have a say in academic decisions as well (for example, faculty hires, academic standards).

Placement on the Model

This last point demonstrates some of the pressures that make the successful comprehensive campus more consumer-oriented than their research counterparts. As Johnson and Orr (1999) point out, the typical "Gen-Xers," who constitute most of the learners one finds in the comprehensive college or university, are different from traditional students. They respond better to educational techniques that include modeling, research, self-assessment, field experiences and journaling, guest presenters, mentoring, collaborative learning, and limited lecturing. Becoming more amenable to this new type of learner can be a severe challenge to many traditional programs, but the trends suggest that student interest in the quality of their education will grow, forcing even the most traditional college or university to alter its teaching style.

Consumer-orientation is not just an issue for students. State legislatures are becoming more intrusive in making certain demands on their colleges and universities. For example, as of this writing, thirty-four of the fifty states have passed laws requiring assessment and accountability in higher education—a move that challenges the traditionally held values of self-assessment and self-regulation. Further, the literature has been full of concerns for the quality of education by employers, parents, alumni, and others within the economy. These actions are forcing higher educational institutions, particularly the comprehensive ones, to become more responsive to the demands and needs of the society they serve. In terms of placement on the model, this pushes comprehensive institutions down toward the lower half (Figure 2.2).

Although their resource base is not as strong as that of their research compatriots, as a general rule significant state funding goes into the support of public comprehensive state colleges and universities, and private comprehensive institutions can usually depend upon their reputations to attract needed tuition revenues, outside grants, gifts, and contracts. Although there are clear signs that the states want their campuses to be more accountable, they nevertheless provide enough funding to allow faculty salaries to be competitive (for the most part) and classrooms to be maintained for quality education. Tuition rates have been allowed to rise (again for the most part), so that campuses have been able to develop a reasonable amount of flexibility in their attempts to provide high-quality education. This pushes comprehensive institutions to the left side of the model. As the model indicates, not only are comprehensive institutions a significant educational force in higher education (it's the largest group in comparison with all others), but they also have a broader range of resource and philosophical positions. Those with more provider-driven tendencies and lower resource bases are more risky (Zone 2), whereas those with larger resource bases and more consumer-oriented philosophies are less risky (Zone 3).

Small Colleges and Universities

Almost by definition, a small college or university has a small resource base. Of course, this is not always true. Some smaller colleges and universities have done a masterful job at attracting endowments, developing grants and contracts, and attracting high-quality, internationally known faculty.

This is not true, unfortunately, of very many small institutions of higher education (Hightower, 1995). What many such colleges and universities are finding is that in order to survive, they need to develop greater resource bases (which is particularly difficult given the high level of competition for resources), find some special niche or situation that will support them over the long term, or develop truly excellent reputations.

Basic Description

What we define as a small college or university is one that has fewer than five thousand students, and for the better part of this grouping, has many fewer than five thousand. These can be either public or private institutions. They place little or no emphasis in research (comparably speaking of course) and probably only have a single campus. They have a relatively small faculty whose primary discipline has been broadened to include related disciplines, in which the faculty may have had little training (for example, having a professor who was trained in marketing teach courses in management and finance). Small colleges and universities exist in large and small cities, rural settings, and suburbia. They are ubiquitous. They may or may not engage in sports, but if they do, it is usually in National Collegiate Athletic Association (NCAA) divisions and fairly far removed from Division 1. They usually provide a tremendous amount of interaction among administrators, staff, faculty, and students, though resources such as the campus library and the campus laboratories are woefully undersupplied and sometimes even antiquated.

The truly outstanding small colleges and universities may have a superior library, laboratories, and other campus resources. Again, this is not the norm. As a result, many small colleges and universities have been unable to provide excellent programming and hence it is within this group that most campus closures occur.

Structural Characteristics

The smaller the campus, the less structure there is. Basic bureaucracy may exist (in admissions, class scheduling, registration, and student services), but it is normally kept to a minimum. Everyone tends to know everyone else, and this allows much more open decision making. A sense of community and family is a hallmark of a small campus, and engaging the student in the academic process is seen as a crucially important goal. Connections to alumni, business leaders, and other campus constituencies (such as parents) are open and sometimes well-publicized.

Faculty members are generally PhD qualified, though their degrees may well come from second and third tier doctoral-granting institutions (though the excellent schools will attract top tier 1 PhDs with the promise of top pay, solid research support, and reduced teaching assignments). Administrators will be few (depending upon the size of the campus) and many faculty will also serve in positions that have administrative duties. Staff will be small and usually from the community. The president or chancellor will normally be someone who comes from another college or university, often from highly dynamic settings and looking for a more peaceful, less complex world. These people must ascribe to and enact the vision of the institution in order to win over the campus and become its leader.

Power sharing can take on a number of forms. On some successful campuses, there is a strong president or chancellor, a person who has been successful in building the campus and has been responsible for the completion of major projects, both academic and physical in nature (such as a successful drive to build a new field house, or arts center). This person tends to be the stylized president of years gone by—mature, warm but stern, approachable but revered, respected, and believed to be fully in charge. On other campuses, a senate of the whole faculty makes major decisions, with representatives of the student body and the board of trustees in attendance. So although structural governance can take a variety of forms, certain characteristics are constant: Campus governance takes place in a unified setting, some element of governance is strong, and the entire campus is marked by a single strong culture.

Placement on the Model

The low level of resources places the family of small colleges and universities in the right half of the model, as explained above (Figure 2.2). In terms of philosophy, however, they are placed in the center of the vertical dimension. They are placed here because of the interesting requirement of these institutions having to be very responsive to a small number of students while needing to maintain a single strong culture. The more well-managed small colleges and universities do an excellent job of recruiting—seeking out students who will blend very well into their culture and then providing them with the attention and services that they will need to perform well within that culture.

As the model indicates, this placement is precarious. Those who have smaller resource bases and tend to be more provider-driven are found in Zone 1, the riskiest part of the model. Those who have solidified their position with a larger resource base and more excellent programs that appeal to a broader student body are found in Zone 2, which is still risky but not nearly as risky as the position of institutions that have been unable to build up their resources or meet the needs of their current and future customer base.

Community Colleges

A lot of people in higher education don't consider community colleges to be in the same industry as senior colleges and universities. This is unfortunate because community colleges—institutions that offer lower division courses and grant associate degrees and certifications—are a major factor in higher education today. In fact, community colleges offer learners a clear alternative to senior institutions and usually at a lower price. Community colleges also provide a viable alternative to a growing problem of overcrowding in lower divisions of public comprehensive institutions in fast-growth states.

The future of community colleges is unclear today. Some more aggressive campuses seek accreditation to become four-year institutions—an option that some states are looking at favorably, given the relatively lower costs of operating a community college as opposed to a traditional four-year institution. Where such a change might occur, there would be little movement to staff new upper divisions with the type of faculty found in their senior counterparts; rather, these institutions would probably continue their current staffing patterns in order to keep costs low. Other community colleges seek to find a special niche somewhere between high school and the four-year institutions, or a niche in providing certification programs to a variety of professional groups whose needs don't fit with the academic format of the senior institutions.

Basic Description

Most community colleges are publicly funded (although there is a growing number of private and proprietary two-year institutions) and serve a variety of community educational needs in an accredited setting. Some sit on impressive campuses, whereas others exist in small buildings tucked away in an industrial park. Some are small, and some are impressively large. They all tend to offer a wide variety of classes that include traditional college courses found in a liberal arts and business curriculum, as well as a variety of courses that serve special interest groups and community citizens who want to learn a new skill or learn more about a particular interest. Many work on an open-enrollment basis, whereby anyone can sign up for classes regardless of their prior academic record; others require an application for admission. The usual degree programs achieve an associate's degree that may or may not be transferable to a senior college based on the types of accreditation and transfer-articulation agreements that may be in place.

In some places, community colleges augment or substitute for high school courses. They may also augment or substitute for four-year college courses. So although there is a great amount of versatility, there may also be a lack of a clear mission. This ambiguity helps make some community colleges appear to be less formidable than they really are in the general economy. For this reason, many community colleges are employing strategic planning as a method for better establishing themselves within a recognized competitive environment.

Structural Characteristics

The structure of the typical community college is hierarchical in nature, with a strong CEO (president or chancellor) and a relatively small faculty base. One way of keeping costs down is to employ a minimum number of PhDs and instead use as many adjunct instructors as possible. PhDs are usually employed as deans, department chairs, or as full faculty in some larger departments where a more permanent faculty presence is needed. The majority of faculty, however, are adjunct instructors who are hired on term contracts at low wages to support the teaching demand.

Most classes are on a contingency basis, which means that adjunct instructors may not know whether they will be employed until attendance is taken the first day of class. This is good for the institution, because it helps keep costs down, but it can be maddening for both the learner and the adjunct instructor.

A bureaucracy exists, but mostly in the administrative and staff side of the institution. These are the folks who are there on a more permanent basis than the bulk of the faculty. Again, as a function of size, this bureaucracy can range from formidable to relatively nonexistent.

Placement on the Model

The number of community colleges across the United States is huge. This is demonstrated within the model by the family's relative size (Figure 2.2). Community colleges have a steady resource base (mostly from county districts and some state revenues), though they are expected to do more with less money than their senior college and university compatriots. This places them just left of center on the horizontal dimension of the model.

In terms of philosophies, community colleges exist to meet specific community learning needs. Just the notion of having classes on a contingency basis recognizes this. If there are enough learners who want to take a particular class, it will be held. If there are not enough learners who want to take the class, it won't be held. As a result, a community college will usually offer more courses than a four-year institution of approximately the same size, because the community college attempts to provide a sufficient choice of classes to attract a significant number of learners.

Another significant factor is tuition. At community colleges, tuition is usually significantly lower than at four-year institutions, and this gives them a low-cost competitive position that definitely supports their market viability. Another positive advantage is that community colleges do not have to worry about large student service departments, such as housing. Balancing the offerings with the demand, and doing so within restrained resource bases, is the mark of a well-run community college campus. For these reasons, community colleges are at the lower side of the philosophical dimension of the model.

Specialty Colleges and Universities

The specialty college or university is coming full circle to gain prominence once again. A hundred years ago, the specialty college was fairly common; perhaps the teachers' college was the best example. Then with the dawn of Sputnik, the general tendency of higher educational institutions was to become more comprehensive in nature to provide broader-based programs to educate a much broader spectrum of the population. So specialty institutions generally became less influential in terms of budget allocations and tended therefore toward becoming clones of the R-1s. As we have already described in this chapter, however, the need for learning alternatives is once again opening up a niche for specialty colleges and universities, and the niche is being filled by institutions that never dropped their specialties and by those who have decided to pool their resources into particular programs of excellence, developing them more fully as they let other programs purposefully wither and die.

Basic Description

The specialty college or university capitalizes on one particular discipline or set of related disciplines and creates centers of excellence that have a supportable marketing appeal. These centers of excellence often include highly distinguished research activities. The Colorado School of Mines is a good example of this. This particular college concentrates its programming in engineering and mathematics. It has developed an international reputation for its programs. It is in high demand by potential students and has a high demand for its graduates. Engineering schools (for instance, Polytechnic University in New York) all fall into this category. The U.S. military academies and institutions such as the Virginia Military Institute (VMI) and the Citadel are examples of colleges that specifically graduate people for the military, maritime industries, aviation, and aerospace.

The basic requirement is to choose a discipline or set of related disciplines that have a substantive marketing appeal and then create true centers of excellence. For institutions that have been specialized for their entire existence, this is a familiar strategy. For those who are finding that they cannot become a quality research institution and are going to have trouble being a high-quality comprehensive institution, the challenge of moving back into a single specialty is both structural (as we discuss in the next section) and philosophical. The philosophical issues include changing their offerings from a broad range of disciplines that, at least for the comprehensive institutions, requires a fair amount of consumer-orientation, to becoming more provider-driven, known for their centers of excellence (which, of course, they must continually support and up-grade) with a definite research component. For colleges and universities deciding to become specialty colleges and universities (many of whom must drop the name *university*), these are harsh challenges. Some of these colleges find it extremely difficult to close down particular schools, fire tenured faculty, and develop a new campus culture that supports the focused strategy.

Structural Characteristics

Specialty colleges and universities, almost by definition, become one-dimensional. The functional structure applies best to this type of situation and also allows for higher levels of centralization and bureaucracy, as everyone in the administration, faculty, staff, and student body is associated with the institution for the same reason. A unified culture is important, and although the long-time specialties will form one rather naturally, developing a unified culture is one of the major stumbling blocks for institutions who decide to change (or in some cases have the decision made for them by a governmental body) into a specialty college or university.

Faculty and administrators tend to be closely allied and all PhD-qualified from like institutions, the top-tier institutions, and even from within the institution itself. Staff members tend to be highly bureaucratic in nature yet do understand they are part of the same program and are regulated to assure high levels of performance and quality research.

Placement on the Model

There are a fair number of specialty colleges and universities around the world, perhaps more outside the United States than within. Due to their limited marketing appeal, however, they are not a large segment of the industry, so the size of this family is perhaps best described as smaller than the average (Figure 2.2). The philosophical positioning, as described above, places specialty colleges or universities in the upper half of the model. However, because they must always be conscious of their market and must make certain that their graduates meet market expectations, their placement tends toward the lower part of the top half of the model. Finally, in terms of resources, specialty colleges generally tend to have solid state, government, or industry support, so they seem to be on fairly solid ground. Nonetheless, because individual institutions tend to be small as well as highly focused toward a single discipline—even though the resources per capita may be better than what one might see for the comprehensive institutions, let alone successful research colleges and universities—resources are only slightly better than adequate. This places them toward the middle of the resource dimension.

As the model indicates, the rationale we have used for placement indicates that specialty colleges and universities are in both the high-risk Zone 1 and the moderate risk Zone 2. We believe this is appropriate due to the drive toward a more provider-driven philosophy and the relatively small size of individual campuses as a general finding in this family. Again, as we have seen with other families, the risks can be reduced by increasing the resource base and by complying with market realities. This might also apply to specialty schools such as the U.S. military academies, where continual decreases in federal financing could conceivably consolidate the three major academies down to two, or even one. Although this consolidation is unlikely at the moment, over time, as government shrinks and revenues decline, it is unreasonable to assume that the excellence of the three major academies would not be endangered. Their inclusion in the model as being moderately risky to highly risky is therefore appropriate.

Porter's Classifications

In preparation for the three-dimensional model we will present in Chapter Four, it might be useful to compare the five families of colleges and universities we have developed to Michael Porter's generic strategies (Porter, 1985). Table 2.2 represents where the five families might fit, based on the discussion we've presented in this chapter.

Table 2.2. Porter's Generic Strategies for the Traditional Forms.

	Broad Market Approach	Narrow Market Approach
Low-Cost Provider	Public R-1s, R-2s, D-1s, D-2s, Public comprehensive institutions, Community colleges	Public small colleges and universities, public specialty colleges
Differentiator	Private R-1s, R-2s, D-1s, D-2s, private comprehensive institutions	Private small colleges and universities, private specialty colleges

It is interesting that the major divider between the strategies of low-cost provider and differentiation is that of public versus private. Certainly the forces we described in Chapter One that are forcing most public institutions to do more with less are forcing all the public colleges and universities we have described in this chapter to look at ways of becoming low-cost leaders. This means simplifying administration practices and costs, forcing older, nonproductive faculty members out through early retirement, and hiring new faculty members and staff at the lowest rate possible, while increasing the demands for productivity (larger classes, for example). All these activities are going on. In the meantime, private colleges and universities must develop reputations of high quality and excellence in order to compete. No potential learner is going to spend $17,000 a year for a mediocre education at a so-so private school, particularly if there is a public institution nearby that provides the same or better educational opportunities for 50 percent, 33 percent, or even less of the cost. The reality of competition forces the private college and university to center its resource attentions on the programs in which they can develop (or sustain) excellence, and then let the community know about it.

Why Is Any of This Important?

In this chapter, we have described the types of colleges and universities with which we are all familiar. What is new is that we are treating these types or families of similar types of colleges and universities as strategic choices (also known as strategic groupings). Although an R-1 university may never aspire to become a community college, it may well find it appropriate to align itself with one or to even incorporate one within its large strategic design. Understanding how a community college is different from an R-1, therefore, may become part of a strategic plan that creates a new alliance or a new relationship between different institutional types.

The more likely and bigger strategic choice is that of many comprehensive institutions that find themselves stuck in the middle, with a tradition of trying to emulate the R-1s and a resource base and external environment that call for something else. These colleges and universities need to be aware that they have choices and need to devise a workable strategic plan that will help transform them into something that is more in line with the demands of their environments.

The next chapter expands these choices by looking at some of the newer forms of academic program delivery. This further broadening of the field of possibilities may not necessarily mean that a traditional college or university will change altogether to one of the new forms (though some are doing just that), but it may mean that significant growth and resource accumulation can result from becoming involved with a new approach to learning. All of this should be good and exciting news for the strategic direction of the campus.

Chapter Three

Extending the Model to Nontraditional and Alternative Educational Providers

It is fair to assume that most readers of this book are higher educational leaders from the more traditional types of colleges and universities we described in Chapter Two. However, there many new forms of higher educational institutions that are emerging and defining themselves as the twenty-first century begins. These newer types of higher educational institutions have evolved to fill newly identified needs of specific populations, businesses, or conditions that the traditional forms have not met. These "new breeds" have grown to become part of the landscape of higher education and so have also become competitors of the more traditional colleges and universities.

Further, some of these forms also demonstrate strategic opportunities that some of the more traditional colleges and universities we describe in Chapter Two may decide to pursue. This chapter profiles ten forms of nontraditional colleges and universities that currently exist as stand-alone entities or exist within other higher educational institutions but have the promise to emerge as stand-alone institutions in their own right.

Why is understanding these new-breed institutions important? What can the traditional campuses possibly learn from these new forms? There are two reasons we believe it is important for college and university leaders and planners to be aware of them. First, as we have stated before, these institutions represent additional competitors to the traditional institutions. Second, they represent opportunities in the sense that they can provide examples of how to expand current planning horizons through potential strategic alliances that benefit both parties and through complete institutional transformation. Before we go further, we want to be clear that we are not suggesting that a major R-1 university might want to transform itself into a company university or that this is a real strategic option. However, an R-1 might want to become involved with a cooperative alliance, say with an institution in another country, or it may want to add a virtual component to its offerings. It is even possible that a research college or university might set up a special program within a company setting or even a remote campus that is there only to serve the needs of that company. By taking advantage of these opportunities, the research institution may be taking advantage of specific strategic choices that can further strengthen its strategic position. This option is also open to the other four types of more traditional campuses we discussed at length in Chapter Two.

The other issue, however, is that these new providers have different combinations of the two dimensions we developed in the last chapter as well: prevailing organizational philosophy and the strength of the institution's resource base. Therefore, if a research college wants to participate in a virtual university situation (either independently or in cooperation with other colleges and universities) there is both a resource and philosophy requirement that the research college will have to reconcile if it hopes to be successful in its continuing role as a strong research institution while developing a successful virtual presence. This may mean creating a new structure, either a multidivisional (where the virtual operation works independently from the traditional campus), a matrix (where both operations would be considered independent projects that vie for the resources they need to be successful from independent departments throughout the campus), or a strategic business unit (a completely separate organization from the institution). In any event, understanding what is involved with the success of the new breed of higher educational institutions provides important competitive information as well as a guideline for taking advantage of the new opportunities that traditional campus leadership needs to understand better.

The New Breeds

In this section, we briefly describe the general models one can find today that represent the new breed of colleges and universities. We discuss how these institutions are characterized, what general purposes they serve, how they are structured, and how they fit in the model we developed in Chapter Two. Where appropriate, we list the names of actual examples the reader may wish to know more about. Figure 3.1 identifies where these additional college and university types fit on the model we developed in Chapter Two.

Cooperative Colleges and Universities

Rowley, Lujan, and Dolence (1998, p. 251) said of cooperative ventures: "One college or university cooperating with other institutions of higher education on the educational and research activities that benefit both of them and their learners is not a new idea—it is a rare one." Certainly this stance is understandable for traditional colleges and universities who were all modeling themselves after the Research One institution—what was there to be cooperative about? However, in the Information Age, cooperation between institutions is becoming more common as individual campuses recognize their lack of resources in trying to provide wide ranges of academic programming.

Basic Description

A coop college or university is, almost by definition, a cooperative effort among two or more campuses. The type of stand-alone institution that would be the result of cooperative alliances between other institutions would be a special-interest institution, a resource-sharing arrangement, or perhaps a foreign campus (which several American campuses have already developed with colleges and universities in foreign countries, primarily in Europe and Asia).

The Auraria Campus in downtown Denver, Colorado, is an interesting example of three institutions, the University of Col-

**Figure 3.1. Strategic Positioning of the
New Breed of Colleges and Universities.**

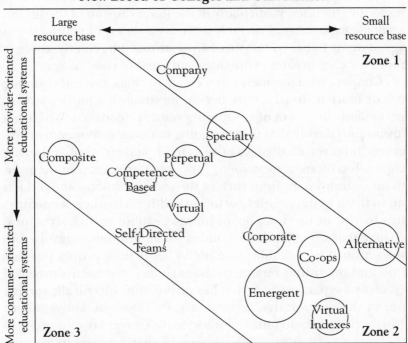

Copyright © 2000 by D. J. Rowley.

orado at Denver (UCD), Metropolitan State College (MSC), and the Community College of Denver (CCD), developing a cooperative campus. Although each of the three schools maintains its own program and identity, they each share a common library, lab facilities, classrooms, student center, bookstore, and campus services. There is no plan to create a single campus. It is interesting that the three institutions have relatively different missions that have the potential to complement each other: CCD provides a wide range of lower-division classes and training programs that lead to either an AA degree or certification (standard community college fare), MSC operates as a full undergraduate liberal arts college with specialized programs, and UCD operates as an undergraduate comprehensive university that also offers master's level and doctoral level programs. On the surface, the reader can see lots of room for synergies, particularly in the lower division of the undergraduate experience. Currently there are a variety of matriculation agreements between the three institutions, but clearly, there is room for even greater economies and areas of cooperation.

Cooperative agreements that create or share programs among two or more institutions are becoming somewhat more popular, particularly in an era of continuing resource concern. When two institutions decide that they are going to develop cooperative programs, however, challenges arise as to implementation and sovereignty. Too often, responsibility for cooperative programs is given to single individuals from each of the two institutions, and it is left up to them to figure out how to work with each other. Sometimes this works; in the long-term, however, some sort of structural change that affects both institutions (or all institutions involved in the venture) is probably more useful in creating proper jurisdiction and providing service to the various constituents involved (such as a separate office that has jurisdiction specifically spelled out in the cooperative agreement). In 1998, the University of Northern Colorado and Colorado State University entered into such an agreement to look for ways of sharing campus services (such as printing and design), as well as faculty, academic programs, and even some facilities. Both institutions believe that this cooperation will lead to reduced expenses for each, greater economies of scale, additional support for several smaller (but excellent) programs, and better service to learners on the two campuses, which are thirty miles apart in a rapidly growing area of north-central Colorado.

Structural Characteristics

The structural imperatives of the cooperative institution very much depend on the type of cooperative effort that has created it. If the cooperative institution is a stand-alone (such as a domestic-foreign cooperative campus), then a traditional functional structure (single purpose) may suit its needs—though with the continuing involvement of the parenting institutions, a modified matrix structure might be more useful.

If the cooperative venture is based on resource sharing, such as the Auraria example described above, a divisional structure that includes all academic entities as well as the coordinating administrative offices would be appropriate. For a cooperative venture that is sharing services or programs, a coordinating office is needed. Finally, if the cooperative venture is short-term in nature and limited in scope, home campus individuals need to be given clear assignments and clear jurisdictional limits to be as effective as possible.

Placement on the Model

Figure 3.1 places the co-ops in the lower right-hand quarter of the model we developed in Chapter Two. In terms of resource placement, today most campus administrative and faculty leaders see cooperative ventures as peripheral to the primary activities of the campus, so funding for such efforts is low. In terms of philosophies, most campuses are developing cooperative programs to meet current and emergent needs. Therefore, the criteria place cooperatives in the lower end but solidly in the boundaries of Zone 2, which suggests moderate risk. As major stand-alone operations emerge (such as the Auraria Campus example), where major resource bases are dedicated to the project, the sector could move laterally more toward Zone 3 and provide longer-term levels of stability.

Composite Universities

What we refer to as the composite university is a move to treat traditional colleges and universities more like business operations from a financing viewpoint. The Association of Governing Boards has identified three major universities in the United States that are moving in this direction (1996). The University of Southern California, the University of Michigan, and Indiana University have created *responsibility centers,* which link performance to funding. The University of Florida has created a similar approach to performance and funding. This is a model worth noting, particularly given the call for more accountability by state legislatures, state governors, and federal officials. The philosophies involved are repugnant to many academic faculties because they enforce a pure business model of financing on academic performance, which many argue is inappropriate. Appropriate or not, the fiscal realities of tying performance to compensation is a trend that appears to be gaining momentum in the United States and elsewhere, and the day when several traditional colleges and universities (both public and private) convert to a pure business model of administration and funding may not be too far off.

Basic Description

At the heart of this model is the elimination of the traditional method of allocating resources by universally increasing or decreasing them based on revenue accumulation (tuition, state appropriations, grants, gifts, interest income, reduction of either the capital or endowment base). Instead, individual programs are responsible for achieving certain goals and are rewarded appropriately. Programs that do not demonstrate high quality or do not achieve their goals have their allocations reduced. Programs that do demonstrate high quality and achieve their goals have their allocations increased (the program is rewarded). Clearly the drive here is to identify and support excellent programs and identify and either reengineer or eliminate nonexcellent programs. The overall goal would be to have a series of excellent programs that act to enhance the reputation of the institution and thereby attract a greater resource base. This model closely follows the basic business model whereby profit determines whether certain products or services survive. Academics are neither generally cognizant of this approach nor particularly amenable to it once it is explained.

Structural Characteristics

There is very little structural difference between a composite institution and a traditional one. The real difference lies in budgeting philosophies and funding formulas. Over time, of course, as programs emerge or wither away, the overall structure of the institution might change, but there would be no significant change in the basic functional or multidivisional structure that served the institution before.

Placement on the Model

We have placed the composite university in the upper left-hand quadrant of the model as seen in Figure 3.1. Accumulating more resources is a major issue for the composite college or university, so the successful composite institution would tend to accumulate and maintain a large resource base. In terms of philosophy, one can identify a strong market function at work here that supports more popular and higher-quality programs and does not support less popular or lower-quality programs. It is interesting that most of the institutions we gave as examples earlier in this section are still more concerned with their academic advancements than consumer needs, so though we would place them lower than the traditional research institutions, they are still in the upper quadrant regarding philosophy. (Please note that all four of our examples were of R-1 institutions who are becoming composite institutions.) This may change to some degree over time as the market becomes even stronger and begins to use its own resource base to influence the composite institutions toward being more consumer-oriented without giving up their primary research activities.

Perpetual Learning Colleges and Universities

The perpetual learning college or university is clearly emergent. As far as we know, there is not a major stand-alone institution today that offers true lifelong learning, though more traditional colleges and universities are talking about it and claim to do so through their continuing education programs.

As Rowley, Lujan, and Dolence (1998) describe, higher education is moving into the Information Age right along with the rest of society. One of the most significant changes between the Industrial Age and the Information Age is the learner's need to have continuous exposure to up-to-date and applicable education for the foreseeable future. This is the heart and soul of lifelong learning. Two primary requirements of continuous learning impact colleges and universities: to provide high quality, up-to-date educational opportunities, and to be able to update graduates when the disciplines develop new knowledge through both basic and applied research.

What we do see today is a growing number of colleges and universities offering "meet the professor" sessions where current learners and graduates are invited to attend a seminar or work session with someone who is on the leading edge of the field. Other campuses are providing "renewal weekends," or special longer-term sessions for their graduates where those graduates are invited back to campus to engage in seminars or work sessions that bring them up-to-date with the developments in the discipline. From here, we look forward to more campuses offering more formalized lifelong learning programs as part of their marketing appeal. With the growth of distance learning and the virtual university (discussed later), the basic methods for conducting such a program already exist. It is entirely probable that several more traditional colleges and universities (R-1s, R-2s, D-1s, D-2s, comprehensive institutions, and polytechnics) may reengineer their entire programs to provide lifelong learning contacts and opportunities.

Basic Description

Within a perpetual learning college or university, the learning process is continuous rather than discontinuous. Learners and institutions have lifelong relationships. The relationship begins when the learner enters the college or university and can identify a career goal. At that point, the learner and the institution work together to achieve a degree or certification (whatever the educational goal is). Whereas at this point most colleges and universities graduate that learner and both move on in different directions (except perhaps from an occasional mailing from the alumni association), in a perpetual learning situation the relationship is not severed but continues into the foreseeable future. This ongoing contact is discipline-specific and may occur as periodic seminars on campus, through distance learning, e-mail, the Internet, or (in the future) other means of interactive educational methods.

Structural Characteristics

Most campuses already have alumni offices, ranging from small to large. In the perpetual learning setting, these offices would expand to include communications capabilities within discipline areas. This would provide educators and learners a continuously updated database that would allow easy contact between both groups. The academic department itself would need to add an additional function of ongoing alumni contact and program preparation for updating sessions. By providing an interactive, regularly scheduled learning forum, the college or university would also benefit by being able to discover first-hand what is happening in the outside world and conduct joint research between faculty and alumni in a much more immediate and direct fashion. Funding for these structural additions could come from user fees, participation fees, membership fees, or from grants and endowments.

Placement on the Model

The placement of the perpetual learning college or university is near the middle of the model presented in Figure 3.1, but in the upper left-hand quadrant. Its ability to generate additional revenues would place it toward the larger resource base area. However, since fees would need to be market-driven and competitive (in such a world, the graduate of one institution could easily join the perpetual learning program of another institution, and would most likely be recruited to do so), it would not necessarily be a windfall for the institution (it should pay for itself and generate some profits, but would most likely not produce profitability beyond that of the competition in the area). In terms of philosophy, the driving force of the new information is developed by the institution and then offered to alumni and others who wish to be involved with the program. This must be information that is immediately useful to the learner, however, so the institution cannot be completely provider-driven. This brings the perpetual learning college or university close to the center of the philosophy continuum.

Virtual Universities

Virtual colleges and universities are the result of the emergence, growth, and sophistication of the Internet. As the World Wide Web has developed, and particularly as interactivity has been refined, the ability of educators to put their courses or portions of their classes on the Internet has flourished. Initially, individual faculty members spurred on this virtual world of learning by independently developing Internet course offerings and putting them on line. As is generally the case with most materials found on the

Internet, there was little control or organization for these offerings, and it was completely up to the consumer to take or not take what was there and judge its worth. There were few guarantees of quality, timeliness, appropriateness, or value. Costs ranged from free to whatever the market would bear. Institutionalizing these otherwise random offerings was an opportunity many organizations (both academic and nonacademic) have seized upon in creating the virtual college or university.

As we write this book, there are hundreds of programs available on the Internet that are associated with virtual colleges and universities. These numbers are growing steadily. Some of these programs are associated with an already existing college or university, while others are start-ups and stand-alones. Michael G. Dolence maintains a listing of several of these institutions on his Web site (http://www.mgdolence.com) where the reader can find several "tours" of many of the virtual university Web sites (2000).

Perhaps the most ambitious virtual university is the Western Governors' University (WGU). As of the year 2000, there are some forty colleges and universities from twenty-two U.S. states, along with the Territory of Guam, participating in the WGU (WGU, 2000). The courses that are currently offered at WGU are programs that come from the forty colleges and universities that have been developed for Internet application (Van Dusen, 2000; WGU, 2000). Eventually, WGU wants to offer all the programs (degree, nondegree, and certificate) available through their academic partners, including master's and doctoral level offerings. In 1998, the WGU signed a strategic alliance agreement with the Open University (OU) of the United Kingdom (which has also incorporated as the Open University of the United States) to bring the programs of OU into the U.S. market and the technology developed in the U.S. into the United Kingdom (and European) markets.

Basic Description

The purpose of the virtual university is to provide learning on demand that is Internet based. Learning opportunities can be either degree based or nondegree based. Most course offerings are open enrollment, allowing casual learners to decide that the course meets their present needs, sign up for the course, take it, and move on. Getting credit for the course is optional. Along side this open-ended format, the virtual university is a full-blown alternative to traditional education. Learners can acquire their entire college degree online. Currently, most such courses follow university-imposed scheduling. However, more and more are providing cafe-teria-style learning, which allows learners to decide when to take a course and when to complete it (though there may well be dead-lines for bringing closure to a course so that neither the learner, the university, nor the professor can extend the one course offer-ing beyond a reasonable period of time).

There is understandable criticism of the virtual university, par-ticularly from more traditional educators and quality education interest groups. The primary concern is for the lack of social inter-action among the learner and instructors or other students taking the course. The other is the concern for security in making certain that the person who is taking courses and submitting materials (including examinations) for evaluation is the person signed up for the course. In response, the providers of virtual university courses are developing more interactive learning methods, such as classrooms and see-you-see-me video linkages, as well as better security methods to overcome the criticism.

There are also some very appealing positive aspects of virtual universities that help explain their rapid growth as members of the higher educational community. For one, the cost of providing qual-ity education can be minimized (very few new facilities, minimal staff support, greater economies of scale, and greater overall effi-ciencies). Learners benefit from much greater convenience, greater control of their educational process, and greater freedoms to choose the specific courses. We believe that the positive appeal of this highly customer-centered approach is and will continue to be one of the driving factors of the burgeoning virtual university segment of higher education.

Structural Characteristics

For the university that is only a virtual university in its mission and activities, the appropriate structure it should adapt is known as a virtual structure. A virtual structure is highly organic in nature, with a central administrative control system supported by a wide variety of other institutions that provide the products and services on a contractual basis to the organization. The WGU is an excellent example of a virtual structure. Here the central administrative office contracts with a variety of colleges and universities that the WGU then offers to learners as WGU courses. This relationship provides tremendous flexibility to the WGU, in that it can always renegotiate contracts to assure that the academic partners provide exactly what courses WGU decision makers and WGU learners desire.

Institutions that have added a virtual university component to their traditional academic programs would most likely adopt a matrix structure. The matrix structure works here because the basic institution needs to support two separate programs—the traditional program and the virtual program—equally well. It needs to do so by using the same academic, service, and administrative resources. In this case, the college or university sets up two academic entities: the traditional campus and the virtual campus. Each campus has its own administrative head. As the traditional campus and the virtual campus each develops its own academic plans, the head of each campus negotiates with campus departments (academic, service, and administrative) for the specific programs and services each campus needs to provide its particular programs. Department heads need to change their orientation from the traditional academic approach to curriculum development and delivery to a resource-oriented approach, one that gets its resources from the two campuses to develop specific content for the two modalities of delivery. A departmental system similar to that of the Open University (OU) of the United Kingdom is appealing here. At the OU, there are no undergraduate students on the University's main campus in Milton Keynes and only a few graduate students. Rather, the campus houses all of the major academic departments of the university, along with a branch of the British Broadcasting Corporation (BBC), who together develop high-quality academic programming and academic materials for the several degree programs of the OU's primary distance-learning structure.

Placement on the Model

We place the virtual university segment in the lower, left-hand quadrant of the model in Figure 3.1. Virtual universities require fairly large resources that generally parallel the resource needs of their academic providers. Yet the amount needed is not as significant as that required by the research or comprehensive colleges and universities (one of the major benefits we suggested above). Virtual universities are also much more sensitive to the market than are more traditional colleges and universities. Because most virtual universities are still dependent upon those same colleges and universities for the actual academic content of the courses they offer, however, there is still a major component of the course that is provider-oriented. As virtual universities such as WGU become larger and become more intimately connected with their learners, they may well find that they can be more demanding of the academic providers and contract for courses that the virtual university knows meets a specific market demand. Over time, this should pull them down even further toward the bottom level of the model in Figure 3.1 and into Zone 3.

Virtual University Indexes

Another type of organization has emerged in the 1990s that provides the learner access to information in a completely nonaligned form. These are organizations that index a wide range of courses available from traditional and virtual colleges and universities around the world that can be accessed by learners from any part of the world who have access to computer technology. The learning process is digital in nature and responds completely to learner-consumer demands with large databases of courses and other learning opportunities. Dolence (2000) lists three such organizations on his Web site: the Globewide Network Academy, the World Lecture Hall, and New Promise Online Education. Each one of these has thousands of courses that are provided by hundreds of academic providers. Globewide Network Academy has over 17,000 such courses, the World Lecture Hall lists several thousand (though a large number of these are offered through the University of Texas, the site's sponsor), and New Promise has over 3,700 open enrollment courses listed.

The importance of these index services is that they open up a huge variety of learning opportunities to learners who have the power to choose for themselves what they want to get involved with, where they want to do this, and what it will cost. The consumer-learner (in many cases) can decide whether to take the course for credit or not (though not all courses are available for credit) and to a large degree when the course will be taken. Here the university or college course is available to just about anyone who wants the information contained in the course, and the level of ongoing connection between the academic institution and the learner is at the discretion of the learner. In an extreme theoretical example, a person might take individual courses from individual colleges and universities, all leading to a single degree (from an institution that allows huge transfer credits and no long-term residency requirement). Many changes would need to occur, however, before this could happen—including the changing of several accrediting standards that presently would be highly critical of such a practice.

Basic Description

The virtual university indexes are simply data bank resources available to anyone who has access to the Internet. The courses that are listed in the indexes are independent from the indexes. The consumer-learner chooses a course from the course description available from the index source, contacts the college or university, makes arrangements to take the course based on the policies of that institution, and then takes the course. If that one course is all the learner needs or wants, that is the end of it. The learner has learned the information he or she was seeking and goes on. The institution has delivered the needed knowledge and perhaps has made itself a long-term customer.

Structural Characteristics

All three examples listed by Dolence above are not-for-profit offices, most often associated with a major academic sponsor. Although it is likely other such indexes will join this list, it appears that most indexes in the future will depend upon other entities for their basic support. What resources that are provided by the host institution must be augmented by sponsorships in order to support the growth and activities of these index organizations. At best, these index organizations are a department of their host.

Placement on the Model

The consumer-learner is all-important here, so we place the virtual university indexes at the bottom of the model. At the same time, resources are scarce and it is important to keep overhead and administrative costs low. It appears that the three examples discussed here have good support, but it is also apparent in viewing their Web sites that more resources are needed. So we place them in the lower right quadrant of the model and into Zone 2, which suggests moderate risk associated with any college or university deciding to develop its own indexing service.

Self-Directed Teams

The use of teams in academia is not a new idea. Departmental teams, team teaching, and students working in teams are all common practices. These activities have been pretty much contained to the micro level of colleges and universities. What we are seeing now, however, is taking the notion of teams and applying it to the entire institution.

The primary purpose for creating self-directed teams is to look at the various activities of the college or university and the needs of the body of learners as a series of projects. Faculty, staff, and administrators are assigned to these projects and given the time and resources needed to complete the project. Once the mission is completed, the project goes away. When applied to the entire campus, this approach is not only novel, it is revolutionary. This campuswide approach challenges the traditions of academic departmentalization and further challenges the basic tenet of teaching as a process wherein a single professor teaches students. Self-directed teams, which very likely are cross-disciplinary in nature, create an all-channel learning environment where groups of professors work with groups of learners to create and transfer knowledge. This is fairly revolutionary even for the business world, where cross-functional and self-directed work teams have only been a recent phenomenon.

In terms of colleges and universities, Rowley, Lujan, and Dolence (1998) reported that at Evergreen State College, the campus has organized transdisciplinary teams that function in lieu of departments. They use this structure to promote flexibility, deal with problems, support research interests, and develop new fields of knowledge. Another example is the University of Denver, which uses thematic groups to integrate their curriculum. Their dedication to teams is so great that the new Daniels College of Business building (opened in the fall of 1999) was designed with glass-walled conference rooms that are just off the main hallways and close to faculty offices. The objective is to encourage students and faculty to meet spontaneously as they work on a variety of projects. Internationally, the experimental University of the Highlands and Islands treats each new incoming learner as a project. As each new learner enters, a team of faculty, staff, and the learner create a unique and flexible program suited specifically to that learner. Then the learner is integrated into a series of learner teams and learner-faculty teams to achieve both learning and research objectives. Roskilde University in Copenhagen uses a full interdisciplinary approach in all of its degree programs and is architecturally designed to support it (Roskilde University, 2000). Learners are attached to houses, each with approximately a hundred students, four to six tutors, and a secretary. Groups of approximately ten house members form project groups in "home bases," which are physically located among faculty offices also in the house. Each house has a classroom and a kitchen. Currently there are seventy such houses at Roskilde University.

Still another example is the University of Maastricht in the Netherlands, which has adapted problem-based learning as the primary learning methodology of the entire campus. Here small groups of learners are presented a problem related to a learning block they are about to study. The technique is based on the theory that learners actively construct their own knowledge base (Gijselaers, 1996). It is up to the learners to apply their own knowledge to solving the problem, decide among themselves what needs to be done to obtain a better solution, and then use university resources to develop an educated solution to the problem both individually and in groups (University of Maastricht, 2000). This method, developed at McMaster University in Canada in the 1960s, has been adopted by many other colleges and universities around the world but usually only in a single department (several medical schools use this approach), not campuswide (Wilkerson and Gijse-laers, 1996).

Basic Description

A college or university structured around self-directed teams does so to create flexibility, reduce costs, flatten the organizational structure, and improve the learning and research capabilities of the campus. Centrally and locally, campus leaders define objectives and then divide campus personnel into teams, each assigned one or more projects. All projects have a sunset mandate (defined ending dates), so faculty, staff, and administrators are constantly facing new challenges and opportunities. The learners are included in the teams where appropriate, and the vibrancy of the learning and research environment are enhanced to the benefit of all involved.

Structural Characteristics

Once again a matrix structure seems ideally suited for a self-directed team setting. The working core comprises the various academic projects, and the disciplines and administrative and service units support the matrix.

Placement on the Model

Self-directed team colleges and universities would have the funding patterns typical of most traditional comprehensive or small university campuses, thus placing them nearly in the middle of the resource continuum in Figure 3.1. Their approach, however, is clearly more consumer-learner oriented, thus placing them near the bottom line of the model. Also, since it is likely that the growth in the ranks of these types of colleges and universities would come from the comprehensive colleges and universities, their positioning on the model would tend to mirror the same perspectives.

Assessment and Competency-Based Colleges and Universities

Assessment and competency-based colleges and universities are emergent. Spurred on primarily by external calls for assessment and outcomes-based education by external constituencies, this model is to a large degree being forced upon many comprehensive and small colleges and universities across the United States and around the world. As we write this, the Colorado Commission on Higher Education is working to implement a two-tier assessment system for all public colleges and universities in the state. Assessment would be given to all sophomores to test basic reading and computational skills, and a second round of assessment would be given to all juniors or seniors to test writing, oral, and other higher-level skills.

Beyond this, however, we see a model coming out of assessment centers currently operating in the K–12 level. For example, the Sylvan Learning Centers offer a valuable educational service for primary and secondary education learners that is based on achieving a desired competency level through a variety of learning modalities. Sylvan takes an incoming learner, assesses that learner's current level of competence in a subject area, establishes with the learner (or learner's family) what the level should be, and then works directly with the learner to achieve that competency level by choosing learning methods that best meet the learner's learning style. Assessment is done at the beginning and at several points along the way, finally confirming that the learner has achieved the desired level of competence. Sylvan is beginning to experiment with these methods at the college level.

We think it only a matter of time before this model works its way more fully into higher education and begins to be an acceptable form of knowledge transference for an entire campus. Again, with the already-existing external pressure for assessment and quality assurance, the assessment-competency based method of learning shows a great deal of promise. It is particularly appealing to the so-called nontraditional student, a person who in the Information Age is seeking to shore up competencies or learn new ones. For colleges and universities who develop effective lifelong learning relationships with learners, the assessment-competency model could prevent redundancy of materials, zero in on what the learners need, and have a method of measuring whether the learners have achieved their goal after a regimen of directed study (individually, or as part of a group).

Basic Description

In an assessment-competency environment, learning is assessed rather than graded, and the learner is a major evaluator in determining when competency is reached. Grades are irrelevant, and since the learners make the final determination as to whether they have mastered a topic or an entire course, the quality of the educational experience is greatly enhanced. Individualized learning programs would drive up the costs, but the inclusion of newer technologies, particularly those that can assist both in expanding the methods of knowledge transference and providing assessment on an ongoing basis, should help keep costs reasonable over time. Again, since the learner is the primary evaluator, most of the institutional costs are up-front and the economies of scale would help bring the average costs down to a level where this type of education could be available to anyone who wants it.

Structural Characteristics

A college or university that adopted a full assessment-competency model would probably take on the characteristics of a traditional campus, with academic departments primarily in charge of developing and delivering their programs. Depending on size, either a functional structure or a multidivisional structure would be appropriate.

Placement on the Model

The model we describe is heavily resource dependent. That places successful assessment or competency-based colleges and universities in the left-hand side of the model. While such campuses would still be primarily responsible for developing and delivering the materials, there still needs to be a mechanism in place that forecasts what the needs of learners will be enough in advance that the institution can adequately respond. This places competency-based colleges and universities near the middle of the provider-oriented versus consumer-oriented continuum.

Corporate Universities

One of the fastest growing segments of higher education is the for-profit learning institution—and this is not limited to trade schools. The University of Phoenix is the best known of this particular brand of higher education, and it currently boasts the largest student body of any college or university in the United States: 76,000 current students on seventy-nine campuses.

Many traditional academics scoff at the quality of education that institutions such as the University of Phoenix (UP) provide, but they shouldn't. UP, for example, has several nationally recognized accreditations, including the North Central Association. It offers undergraduate, graduate, doctoral, and certificate programs. It has classes in classrooms and online. It readily accepts transfer credits from traditional accredited colleges and universities, and works with learners individually to create personal learning tracks. It is extremely consumer-oriented. Also, it competes for traditional college and university students. One of us recently lost one of his advisees directly to UP, due to his own university's inability to resolve a grade dispute and UP's willingness to accept all other college credit to date. This student will graduate on time, not from the author's university, but from the University of Phoenix.

Our point in discussing the corporate colleges and universities—and around the country, there are hundreds, if not thousands of them—is that some of them are directly competing with traditional colleges and universities, even if the traditional colleges and universities choose not to recognize them as equals. As shown by the UP example above, this may be a mistake. These corporate colleges and universities can produce high levels of quality graduates (and because of the strong influence of the market mechanism, they must maintain high levels of quality in their products and graduates) and may use their marketing clout to begin to skim off high-quality students whom the traditional colleges and universities heavily recruit.

Basic Description

Corporate colleges and universities are run strictly as businesses. They produce programs for which their marketing departments tell them there is a lucrative demand, and they do it via low-cost leadership tactics (see discussion under Low-Cost Leadership in Higher Education in Chapter Four). They form alliances with businesses to help assure a steady flow of students, and also work with those businesses to develop programs in which companies see real value. Their faculty members are primarily practitioners as opposed to academics (which is one of the reasons the traditional academy scoffs at the for-profit sector), and they do no research. They simply deliver the education the consumer wants. Their program areas tend to be more professional in nature, though UP also offers a smattering of nonprofessional programs.

Structural Characteristics

Corporate colleges follow standard models of hierarchical structure. Depending on size, they will use either a functional structure (for smaller, more narrowly developed program areas) or a multidivisional structure (for larger, more broadly based program areas). These colleges and universities are very much top-down in decision-making patterns, and there is no such thing as shared-governance in the for-profit sector. It's all strictly business.

Placement on the Model

As is true for most businesses that must generate a profit, corporate colleges and universities must utilize low-cost leadership strategies to make that profit. This means that success (profit) is carefully controlled and measured. Given the high number of for-profit institutions, that profit is squeezed, thus putting the entire niche in the right half of the model found in Figure 3.1. As for provider- versus consumer-oriented status, there is little doubt that the for-profits depend upon the consumer and must be sensitive to the consumer's needs and wants. Otherwise, they face delivering products no one wants, and in a for-profit setting, that signals disaster. This places them near the bottom of the model. They are in Zone 2, which is the zone of moderate risk, and can stay there as long as they provide the products and services their consumers want.

Company Universities

Many companies around the world have had educational and training programs for their employees for many years. The need for these programs has been primarily to socialize and educate employees in the specific technologies, cultures, and operational methods of the company. Because this training or education was specific to one company or perhaps to an industry, it was not available from traditional colleges or universities.

However, there has been a dramatic change in several of these educational programs. Certainly there is still the need to provide employees with knowledge that is company and industry-specific, but some of these programs have grown in response to a general concern that students who graduate from traditional colleges and universities do not have the basic skills one would expect them to have, and that the companies have to provide some of this basic education themselves. With both forces at work, many companies have created what they call universities and have developed major educational organizations within their own structures to organize and administer the academic programs. Some of these new universities act as full-fledged colleges or universities. The more highly developed ones are Motorola University, Arthur D. Little School of Management, and IBM University.

The reasons traditional college and university leaders need to be concerned with the company university include missed opportunities in strategic alliances and missed opportunities in program contracting to provide companies education and training for their employees. Some of the corporate programs are even starting to look more like a direct competitor. For instance, Motorola University has a strict admissions policy and is seeking traditional academic accreditations (Motorola, 2000). Others, such as IBM's PC Institute, have developed programs that are offered not only to employees, but also to other interested people outside the company (IBM, 2000).

The faculty in such universities are generally in-house trainers and educators. However, many company programs also hire more traditional academics to provide both full-time and adjunct educational services.

Basic Description

Company in-house educational programs range from simple course delivery to accredited degree programs. They meet the specific needs of the companies that sponsor them but are broadening to provide education in many basic skill areas as well. Their company sponsors can provide major resources and can often provide access to the latest technological and effective pedagogical tools, thus making the educational experience top quality and highly effective.

Structural Characteristics

Company colleges and universities are part of the multidivisional structures of the host companies. They exist at the will of the company and are therefore extremely sensitive to the needs and wants of the company's management. The hierarchical structure of the company probably extends to the functional structure of its university. Faculty members are purely employees and have no research or service requirements.

Placement on the Model

Because company colleges and universities serve the needs and wants of the company, their orientation is strictly provider-driven. In terms of resources, company universities are generally well supported by their company hosts (as long, of course, as the company can see benefits from them), though these resources are specifically dedicated to company objectives. This places company colleges and universities in the upper left-hand quadrant in Figure 3.1 and into Zone 1, the most risky zone. This level of risk is probably quite accurate, since these colleges and universities are completely dependent upon the company that supports them. Therefore, if the company loses its willingness to support the program or has financial problems and decides to cut auxiliary expenses, these institutions would wither and die.

Alternative Colleges and Universities

Throughout the world, there are a wide variety of free-form, nonaccredited, usually not-for-profit institutions that provide educational opportunities at the college level. On the surface, many appear to be highly disorganized and spontaneous. Individuals will develop a class and then teach it. In some cases, a group of people who want instruction in a particular area can petition the institution to find someone who will provide the class. Tuition is low, and is divided between the instructor and the institution (for administrative expenses). There are no rigid requirements regarding the qualifications of the faculty, no entrance requirements, and no credit given to learners. The major controlling factor is the market—if someone offers a course and no one signs up for it, it is simply dropped.

One example of such an institution is the Colorado Free University (CFU). CFU has been in existence for over twenty-five years and continues to grow (CFU, 2000). CFU publishes quarterly catalogs of courses that are offered in a variety of locations in the

Denver area. Each catalog contains hundreds of popular-interest courses on nearly any subject from basic skills to gardening to foreign languages to computer science.

Why should traditional college and university leaders be concerned with the alternative institutions? The answer is because such institutions offer yet another form of competition to the programs of the traditional campuses. The alternative institutions also offer a flexibility that can make their programming even more up-to-date and leading-edge than what might be available on most traditional campuses.

Basic Description

The alternative colleges and universities offer people who want to provide education and those who want to obtain education in a free-form setting the opportunity to do so. Overhead is minimal. Advertising is the greatest expense. There is very little record keeping. There is usually a minimal staff (for either administration or support). The focus is on the subject matter of the course and the ability of the instructor to deliver the promised knowledge. The market mechanism is the most powerful control feature of course scheduling and the institution's very existence.

Structural Characteristics

Alternative organizations such as the CFU have as simple a structure as they can maintain. Resources are few, and activities such as administration and advertising must be done within a simplified functional structure. Such institutions are by nature highly decentralized and subject to external pressures and opportunities.

Placement on the Model

The lack of resources places the alternative colleges and universities on the far right-hand side of the model in Figure 3.1. The philosophy is tempered by the facts that people who want to teach develop most classes and that the class will not survive if there is no market for it. To have a successful class, the instructor needs to develop material that fills a marketing need. This places alternative institutions in the lower half of the model in a mixture of Zones 1 and 2—essentially a risky venture.

Emerging

New models will continue to evolve as societal needs become evident. Looking at the fifteen models we have described in Chapters Two and Three, the sheer variety tells us that a single model of higher education is not only no longer the rule, it is inadequate to meet the needs of today's learner. The later stages of the Industrial Age, the emergence of the Information Age, and the growing sophistication of today's learner have forced the academy to redesign itself. This redesign is not yet complete and perhaps it never will be. As a result, those of us in higher education can look forward to still more models of how to research, develop, and disseminate the knowledge base of the third millennium.

Placement on the Model

We place this model in the lower right-hand quadrant of Figure 3.1. We believe most new models of education in the future will be responsive to the needs of society and will be much less provider-driven (we'll always have the research institutions to fulfill that important role). We also feel that resources spent on educational needs in the future will be tightly controlled. It is unlikely that any government, grant-giving agency, or private concern will give new educational institutions a blank check. This reflects the values of today's efficiency-driven world, and we see nothing to suggest a lessening of the austerity that currently marks the world of education.

The Wide Variety of Strategic Choices in the Change Model

Combining the types of institutions we describe in this chapter (seen in Figure 3.1) with those we developed in the previous chapter (as represented in Figure 2.2), we get a more complete understanding of the domain of higher education. We represent this combination in Figure 3.2.

We now see an idealized model of where any college, university, or higher education delivery institution fits within the general domain of higher education. Figure 3.2 also indicates where different types of institutions begin to intrude on the traditional

Figure 3.2. Strategic Positioning of All Information Age Colleges and Universities.

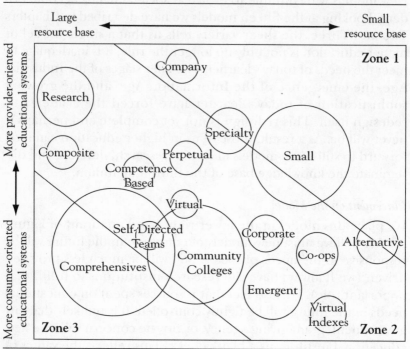

Copyright © 2000 by D. J. Rowley.

domain of others, as well as how far apart certain types are from other types.

The model in Figure 3.2 also suggests different sizes of niche classifications. This is representative of both current institutions and emerging types. For example, though some individual Research One institutions are quite large (University of Michigan, and the Ohio State University, for instance), there are not that many of them in the United States or around the world. The majority of state colleges and universities are in the much larger niche of comprehensive institutions. Also, there are a large number of small colleges and universities that dot the landscape around the world, including some excellent liberal arts colleges and other smaller private and state institutions.

The smaller circles in the model depict newer academic types. For example, the company universities—some of which are highly academic in orientation, such as IBM and Motorola Universities—are becoming more and more a part of the higher educational scene. Some of these are even seeking accreditation. Others are strictly trade-oriented, such as McDonald's University or Burger King University. This is still a relatively small niche and is completely dependent upon company support, which for business reasons could be withdrawn at any time.

The other smaller niches—composite, competency-based, perpetual, corporate (for-profit), self-directed teams, and virtual colleges and universities—command a relatively small portion of the overall industry. As their particular missions become more refined and known, however, it is quite possible that these niches will increase in size. As of this writing, the corporate or for-profit institutions seem to be on a fast track as they use aggressive advertising campaigns and strategic alliances with businesses to increase their presence and enrollments significantly.

The size of the emergent niche indicates that the other fifteen niches depicted in the model are not the final set of strategic choices. Just as more recent educational niches have been created to serve learner needs in a unique new way, such as the virtual colleges and universities, it is certain that other methods of participating in what Dill and Sporn (1995) describe as the knowledge industry will emerge. Given the speed of change typical of the Information Age, it is likely that new models and niches will emerge sooner rather than later.

The Important Continuing Role of Strategic Planning

As many others in the field have argued elsewhere, the role of strategic planning is unquestioned as the best method currently available to help any organization achieve a better fit with its environment (Pearce and Robinson, 2000; Miles and Snow, 1984). It has been widely argued by many that the future of higher education is both an exciting and fearful place and that no one is completely insulated from its threats and uncertainties. Many colleges and universities have come to understand that their role in society may need to change substantially in the Information Age. Many who have recognized this fact are beginning to shape the industry in new and dynamic ways. Yet no institution is immune, and all colleges and universities throughout the world must prepare to examine their current role and determine their adequacy for meeting the needs of the new century.

Strategic planning continues to be the best method of attaining positive outcomes. The strategic choice typology we have identified in this chapter, along with the model of strategic choice and the discussion of implementation strategies found in the rest of this book, are all intended to provide academic strategic planners with additional tools to define the appropriate roles their institutions will serve in the future.

Chapter Four

Refining the Model for Enhanced Competitive Positioning

In the previous three chapters, we developed a model that describes the typology of higher education in today's world based upon the crucial attributes of relative available resources and relative provider-consumer orientation. The model also describes a variety of strategic choices for colleges and universities and provides some advice on implementation in terms of appropriate structures needed to carry out the chosen strategy. One of the useful features of this model is that campus leaders and strategic planners can use it to assist them in better defining their competitive position in the marketplace in terms of the niche their type of college or university fills. This "niching" by type is what Porter (1980) called the formation of a strategic group.

In this chapter we will introduce two additional elements or attributes in the model that can also help campus leaders and strategic planners more clearly position their college or university within the larger strategic group and thereby help define more exactly their institution's overall competitive strategy and their strategic approach to the marketplace. We do this keeping in mind that the world of higher education (more properly referred to as the industry of higher education) is quite unique in that the large presence of both public and private institutions in the marketplace has created a two-tier system of competition. Nonetheless, further understanding of the implications of various methods needed to develop a competitive advantage successfully and the implications of establishing a particular strategic approach to the marketplace are crucial issues in developing and implementing a successful strategic plan on any college or university campus. Furthermore, although private and public colleges and universities may claim to have the same target market in terms of potential student profiles, in practice their overall strategies to garner these students will differ dramatically.

Methods of Creating Competitive Advantage

To understand better why developing a strategic advantage and establishing a particular strategic approach to the marketplace is so important for colleges and universities, let us briefly revisit some of the basic theory involved. In what many consider some of the seminal works in the strategic management literature, Michael Porter (1979, 1980, 1985) suggested that organizations can only obtain a competitive advantage (a distinctive competency that would produce a somewhat unique position in the market relative to its competitors) in their market niches by making a specific selection about the strategy whereby the organization would compete in its market. Organizations cannot survive if they try to be all things to all people because very few organizations would have the resources necessary to outperform their competitors in all market segments. Organizations that have tried to pursue this all-encompassing strategy have had at best mediocre performances and no competitive advantage (Porter, 1985, p. 12).

This finding has been widely documented in business, but there are also some very interesting examples in higher education. In the early 1980s the New Jersey State College system had one flagship university (Rutgers) and numerous secondary colleges. At the same time, New Jersey was experiencing a high export rate of students to out-of-state colleges and universities. They seemed not to be able to counter the trend. Further, many of the state colleges had similar academic programs, such as business schools, and found that those programs floundered because there were no substantial resources available to invest in a particularly distinguished set of faculty or facilities. New Jersey State colleges had similar tuition rates and, therefore, students experienced little price sensitivity when selecting a particular state college. From this example, it appears that the state colleges had tried to be all things to all people, and therefore they experienced mediocre performance.

Porter also postulates that organizations can seek a competitive advantage in the marketplace by selecting a particular method of competition and by choosing a specific scope of that competition. He concludes that organizations can create a competitive advantage by being the *low-cost producer* within its target market, or they can *differentiate* themselves from their competitors through specialized products or marketing campaigns. For the academy, one major determinant that influences the strategies of choosing either low-cost provider or differentiation is that of being either a public or a private institution.

Low-Cost Leadership in Higher Education

Porter has defined low-cost leaders as organizations that are capable of charging lower prices than their competitors to obtain a similar profit (or surplus for not-for-profit institutions such as colleges or universities) or organizations that can charge similar prices and obtain larger surplus margins. Low-cost leaders have specific skills and capabilities not shared by their competitors, including having a dominant market share, being highly capitalized, and having secured needed resources.

Porter (1985) notes that the skills and resources that foster cost leadership include

- Process management and engineering skills
- Low-cost distribution and delivery systems
- Close supervision of labor or the technical core (reminiscent of Thompson, 1967)
- Products and services designed for easy distribution
- Continued capital investment

Organizational requirements that support and sustain low-cost leadership activities include a structured organization with clearly enumerated responsibilities, frequent reporting, continuous improvement of the operation (including the process of instructional delivery), benchmarking, strict cost control, and incentives based upon specific targets. For colleges and universities, low-cost advantages specifically include having access to external sources of funding (public or private) to supplement the revenue derived from tuition, including endowments, grants, and public support.

Low-cost producers usually stand out in creating efficient operations that focus on cost reduction. They employ cost-cutting technologies, maximize economies of scale, reduce product frills, and minimize overhead and administrative expenses. For colleges and universities, these techniques may include online registration, increased employment of adjunct instructors and teaching assistants, large classroom sizes, reduced elective classes, large academic divisions rather than departments, large spans of management with few administrators, basic (or traditional) majors, and various forms of distance learning.

Further, by employing a low-cost leadership strategy, organizations can increase market share by lowering their prices below competitors' ability to produce a profit (or surplus) or to help them withstand a price war from new entrants or existing competitors. In higher education, for example, distance learning provided by senior colleges and universities will only be a threat to community colleges when the tuition for distance learning courses is relatively close to what community colleges charge (factoring in ease of use may actually allow distance learning tuition to be slightly higher than community college tuition). In general, low-cost organizations with relatively high market share (community and state colleges in rural, low-density areas for example) can then generate additional surplus or reduce price to sustain their competitive advantage (Miles and Snow, 1984).

Unfortunately, there are always risks associated with a specific strategy. Pearce and Robinson (2000) have suggested that organizations pursuing a low-cost strategy may find the following risks:

- Cost-savings activities are easily duplicated. Many colleges and universities are following market innovators by jumping on the distance-learning bandwagon as a method of reducing instructional cost and increasing their distribution channels.
- Zealous cost cutting can reduce the quality of key product and service attributes. Although increasing the number of adjuncts employed or reducing the number of courses offered may cut costs, these actions potentially threaten quality of instruction

and the breadth of course offerings (affecting the quality of the programs).

* Cost-leadership may become a trap. Colleges and universities may find continued pressure from students to maintain low tuition regardless of the increasing cost structure of the industry.

Therefore, colleges and universities that wish to pursue a low-cost strategy to obtain a competitive advantage in their market niche should analyze their cost structures (including the process of delivering course instruction). They need to decide which activities in their operations produce cost advantages over their competitors (especially any sustainable advantages, such as large endowments), consider the risks associated with cost leadership, and then implement the strategy.

Differentiation in Higher Education

The other available strategy Porter (1985) identifies is that of differentiation. He states that differentiators achieve a competitive advantage by offering consumers special product attributes that are beyond the basic product function but still deemed below the real value by the consumer when compared to competitors' products. It is customers that judge these attributes to be critically important to them in justifying paying a premium price for the product or service. Organizations often obtain a differentiated strategy by offering higher-quality or technologically superior products or services (prestige, high college entrance requirements, nationally known faculty, or excellent academic programs), a broader distribution channel (distance learning or multiple campuses), better customer service (personalized attention), and widespread promotion. In academia, many small colleges and universities have marketed low faculty-student ratios, the ability to know everyone on campus, and courses taught by full-time faculty (rather than adjunct instructors or teaching assistants) as value-added benefits to students that differentiate them from their counterparts.

The purpose of a differentiated strategy is to build customer loyalty through an image of excellence regarding the organization and its products and services. This loyalty creates a barrier between the organization and its competitors (especially new entrants) and ensures that customers see real and important product and service distinctions. In higher education, many faculty members in the field of business administration might note (with some envy) that Harvard's School of Business has successfully differentiated itself from other colleges and universities through its internationally recognized faculty and programs, its historic prestige, and its extremely loyal (and generous) alumni base.

Customers are also less likely to switch by transferring to other schools if they perceive distinctive quality in the organization's product or service. Porter (1985) states that the skills and resources that foster differentiation include

- Product and service engineering skills
- Exceptional marketing and promotional skills
- Reputation for technological leadership or high quality
- Long industry tradition
- Creative flare or strong capability of basic research
- Unique combination of skills "borrowed" from other organizations
- Strong cooperation from suppliers and others in the market channel

In general, organizational requirements for supporting and sustaining differentiated activities include working conditions and benefits that would attract highly skilled labor and creative individuals, strong internal coordination between those involved in product and service development and marketing, and relatively subjective measures of performance tied to incentive packages, a history and culture that reinforces staying close to the customer, and highly skilled individuals in operations and sales.

Differentiators usually add value to the product or service by altering one or more activities associated with the value chain (the process by which resources are converted into finished goods and services, delivered to the customer, and serviced by the organization). In colleges and universities, for example, unique methods of course instructional delivery (contract learning, online instruction, home-based instruction), when desired by the customer, will help create a competitive advantage.

Another example may be that of offering potential students unique majors that are not easily replicated and tied into unique resources or the college's location. For example, Southampton College, which is located on New York's Long Island, offers a unique program in marine sciences and creative writing. The sustainability of that advantage will be determined by the ability of competitors to duplicate these programs and the continued desire of the customer for the value-added services.

As with the choice of following a low-cost leadership strategy, there are also risks associated with a differentiation strategy. Organizations pursuing such a strategy may encounter the following risks:

- Product differentiation is difficult to maintain given the emergence of imitators. Rival colleges and universities might easily duplicate innovative programs and majors, especially if the fixed costs (in particular, capital costs) associated with developing those programs are fairly low. For example, weekend college programs are usually very easy to duplicate given the idle classroom space at other campuses with traditional day and evening class times.
- The cost difference between low-cost competitors and differentiated organizations becomes too large to sustain brand loyalty. As private colleges and universities' tuition rise (both relative to each other and the public sector), these organizations will either need to add additional value as perceived by the customers or greatly discount their standard tuition price. This may be quite difficult for some smaller colleges and universities who already have limited resources with which to reinvest in their operation or support increased tuition discounting. At worst, many students may opt to go to colleges and universities with similar programs without the premier image or, at best, select to go to a two-year community college or public four-year college and look to trade up (transfer) to a differentiated, private institution. Either way, these actions by the students will reduce the value gap and artificially lower the educational cost of these institutions. (The *value gap* refers to the difference between the actual tuition rate and the perceived value derived for that tuition.)

- Technological changes may nullify or minimize past investment or learning. Many colleges and universities have invested heavily in computer laboratories for students. The increasing rate of product turnover in the personal computer market has made many of those laboratories obsolete, requiring large and expensive upgrades. This has reduced the competitive advantage of early adopters of computer laboratories while placing a profound expense on any college looking to maintain computer laboratories. Some colleges have responded to this technological change by wiring their classrooms and dormitories (presumably a one-time, fixed expense) and requiring students to purchase their own personal computer or laptop and have them then plug in to the college's central computer system.

Colleges and universities wishing to pursue a differentiation strategy should analyze their own academic and support operations to determine any advantages they might have over their competitors (through benchmarking). They can then determine whether they have the in-house capabilities and skills to deliver value-added products and services desired by their customers. If so, they can work to mitigate the risks associated with differentiation and then implement the strategy.

Breadth of Competition: Broad versus Narrow

Porter (1980) adds a second dimension to how organizations can compete in terms of low-cost and differentiation: colleges' own particular definition of their competitive domain (scope of operation). Here, the term *breadth of competition* refers to the relative range of market segments in which an organization chooses to compete. For example, a college or university competing in a broad range of market segments will most likely have a plethora of degree programs (undergraduate, graduate, doctoral) across many disciplines and will offer students an extensive array of courses and on-campus services. Such educational institutions position themselves as the one-stop shop for all students' educational and extracurricular needs. To be successful, colleges and universities pursuing a broad strategy such as this must possess a strong resource base to keep up with educational trends, such as additional courses, programs, related equipment, and services. As we discussed in Chapter Two, this strategy is not possible for the majority of colleges and universities.

Most colleges and universities, therefore, will pursue some form of a focused or narrow strategy. A focused strategy concentrates on the particular needs of a market segment, usually a segment that is atypical of the normal customer and has specialized requirements and needs. An organization that follows this strategy may service isolated regions, have unique service delivery systems, or modify their product to meet a specific customer group.

For example, community colleges predominately service students from the local community who do not wish a residential experience, may not have high academic high school records, or may be older and seeking nontraditional programs. These colleges usually have strong evening and weekend programs to accommodate their part-time, adult students and offer programs that either prepare students to transfer to a four-year institution or prepare students for immediate entrance into the workforce. Many of their programs are very professionally oriented, such as paralegal studies or laboratory technician, and are vocational in nature.

Smaller organizations are usually better at focused strategies given their ability to be more responsive, more rapidly to customer needs. By having a smaller target market, these organizations can develop an expertise about how to service the peculiarities of their particular customer market.

However, focused strategies are not without risk. The specific risks may include the following:

• The focused strategy is easily imitated. Small private colleges may find that their regional, friendly environment with small class sizes is being imitated by large universities with their satellite campuses or that new entrants emerge to service the same population, such as proprietary colleges.
• New entrants further segment the market. The emergence of new instructional methods and technologies has created colleges and universities that not only cater to the nontraditional student—for example, university-without-walls programs such as Union Institute or Walden University—but have further segmented the market by means of differing instructional

delivery, such as the University of Phoenix, which uses both classroom-based and Web-based instruction, and Regents College, which gives course credit through testing.

• The target segment becomes structurally unattractive because demand has dwindled and the market segment has disappeared. Enrollment in foreign language programs and courses slightly declined from 1990 to 1995. Western foreign language courses experienced major declines: Russian by 45 percent, German by 25 percent, French by 25 percent, and Latin by 8 percent. (Only Spanish experienced an increase of nearly 14 percent.) Non-Romantic languages such as Arabic and Chinese increased 28 and 36 percent, respectively (Modern Language Association, 1995). Colleges and universities that have focused on the study of Romantic languages and have committed resources and tenured faculty in those disciplines have been negatively impacted by these trends and undoubtedly are experiencing enrollment downturns.

• Broad competitors overwhelm the market by reducing the differences between the segments and thus increasing their competitive position. Universities can offer focused programs (such as engineering, pharmacy) as part of their broad program offerings, thus blurring the distinction between themselves and specialized institutions, while simultaneously offering more traditional programs. This may attract students who desire specialized instruction and a liberal arts education or who desire specialized training in unrelated areas, such as engineering and music.

Putting It All Together: Porter's Four Generic Business Strategies

All thriving organizations (including colleges and universities), whether through deliberate planning, accident, or emergent actions, create for themselves an overall competitive strategy of either (1) low-cost leadership, (2) differentiation, (3) low-cost focus, or (4) differentiated focus (Mintzberg, 1987). Further, much of the research literature demonstrates that most organizations that do not have a clear strategic position in the marketplace (or organizations that are simultaneously pursuing low-cost leadership and differentiation, that is, stuck in the middle) will be less successful than their competitors.

There is an interesting precedent for employing Porter's approach as a methodology for analyzing colleges and universities' strategic positions. Groves, Pendlebury, and Stiles (1997) examined British higher education as a background and rationale for the use of institutional strategy. Intrinsic and structural difficulties were then considered in managing universities strategically before adapting Porter's (1985) generic strategies and placing these strategies within a stakeholder focus group framework. Their findings reinforce the need for colleges and universities to have an unambiguous strategic position based upon their ability to compete as a low-cost producer or differentiator in a broad or narrow market segment.

Strategic Approaches to the Marketplace

Whereas Porter's generic strategies describe the *position* of the organization in the competitive market given an organization's general strategy, a second influential work, Miles and Snow's (1978) four business strategies, characterizes the organization's *strategic approach* to the marketplace. This additional strategic dimension to an organization's overall strategic posture is also critical in determining how any organization, including colleges and universities, can compete successfully within its market niche. This particular strategic approach also identifies the consequences of an organization's behavioral and attitudinal perspective as well as its general orientation to competition (Mintzberg, 1987). Together, Porter defines the *content* of competition, while Miles and Snow identify the *context* of competition.

Miles and Snow's Strategic Approaches

One can view Miles and Snow's four business strategies as a continuum of possible actions that organizations in general can take to implement their chosen competitive strategy and integrate it successfully into the organization's general culture. Like the competitive strategies of Porter, Miles and Snow's strategic approaches also have application in higher education. To understand better how this works, we begin by defining each of the four strategies.

Prospectors

When an organization chooses the strategy of being a prospector, or innovator, it means that the organization has chosen to pursue a dynamic, proactive approach to its market. Prospectors compete mainly by creating new products and services that establish new markets, or market niches, and take advantage of perceived opportunities. They are able to respond rapidly to changing market conditions, including competitive actions, and strongly value being the *first mover* or *pioneer* in new markets regardless of possible profitability. These organizations also tend not to maintain key competitive positions in all their markets because they focus their resources on product and service innovation rather than product or service maintenance.

Successful prospectors either enter the market in large scale or with a high-quality product, have a broad product line, and heavy promotional expenses. Kerin, Varadarajan, and Peterson (1992) suggest some of the advantages associated with first movers:

- The ability to define the rules of the game. By creating markets, prospectors set the standards for the competition in terms of price, promotion, distribution, product, and service quality. Other organizations will have to try to enter the same market at a higher level in order to attract customers. In the academy, for example, any college or university that has not entered the distance learning market will have to provide services equal to (if not greater) than organizations already in that market.
- Economies of scale and experience. Prospectors gain market knowledge (both in terms of customer service and product improvement) and can use this knowledge either to lower costs or further differentiate their products. To pursue the earlier example, Southampton College, as an early entrant into the marine sciences educational market, has been able to utilize its experience in marine sciences to develop a strong spin-off program in the psychology of biology. This program combines the expertise of Southampton's marine scientists with newly hired animal neurologists to create an innovative program for students interested in studying marine mammals but who prefer a less hard science–intensive experience.

- First choice of market position. Prospectors, because they are first to market, not only set the standard for the market or market niche, but also have the luxury of choosing the most opportune strategy or market segment in which to place their products and services. For example, a public university opening a unique doctoral program may find that they can simultaneously maintain high entrance standards and small class sizes due to the university's commitment to innovative programming and growth. Other colleges and universities (public or private) wishing to offer the same or similar degree might have to target lesser-prepared students and have lower entrance requirements in order to attract students.
- High switching costs for new customers. Because prospectors offer a unique product or service, customers will have a difficult time finding substitutes or switching to competitor products or services. Colleges and universities with unique degree programs (and therefore unusual courses), such as sports administration, may find that students in those programs are less apt to transfer to other educational institutions because of these students' inability to find comparable programs or receive course-specific credit.

Defenders

When an organization chooses to follow the strategy of being a defender (also known as market leader), it chooses a highly insular approach to its market. Defender organizations tend to ignore changes in the marketplace that do not directly impact their operation and tend to be laggards in new product development. They protect their market domain by offering higher quality and better service or lower prices to their customers, and they do so by offering a limited product or service line as compared to the competition. Defenders seek out relatively stable markets and attempt to lock in their position through operational excellence, product leadership, or customer intimacy (Treacy and Wiersema, 1995).

Successful defenders usually focus on either continuous improvement of product and service processes to create greater operating efficiencies and better service delivery, or continuous improvement of the product or service to increase product-service quality. Advantages associated with a defender strategy include

- A simplified strategy. Defenders, because they have already carved out a niche or position in the market, can fortify their position by merely improving customer satisfaction and repeat business. In an academic example, a college or university with a well-known name, such as Harvard, can offer new advanced degree or certificate programs that piggyback or dovetail their more traditional undergraduate and graduate programs to their alumni. They do this believing they will see excellent results.

- Low or limited investment needed for new product or service research and development. Unlike prospectors, defenders have limited expenses associated with new product development. These funds can then be employed (at lower levels) to focus on improving customer retention through measurement of customer satisfaction (customer perception of how the organization is meeting their expectations and preferences) and improvement of service delivery. Student retention has become an important issue for many colleges and universities in that marketing and scholarship dollars (or tuition discounting) have been already expended for these students—what accountants would call a *sunk cost.* Any actions that a college or university can take to increase their retention rate will increase their competitive advantage and their return on their previous investments.

- Minimal risk strategies that take advantage of core competencies. Defenders, since they continually sell the same product or service to the same customer group, build upon their core competencies rather than try to expand those competencies (Peters and Waterman, 1982). Defenders wring more business from their market through market penetration and product-service extension (finding new uses for the product or service). These are particularly low-risk strategies in that current and potential customers are already familiar with both the organization and its product-service lines while the organization expends little on product marketing and development. For example, Southampton College now markets its new five-year BS-MS in accounting degree to its traditional four-year accounting students through faculty advisement and continued tuition discounting. The only resources spent in terms of program development were faculty time and the hiring of an outside consultant to evaluate the program proposal (as required by the New York State Education Department, Professional Division).

Analyzers

When an organization chooses the strategy of being an analyzer, it finds itself somewhere between the positions of prospectors and defenders. Analyzers try to maintain a strong position in their key product-market but also try to grow their operation by expanding into related markets. These organizations are hardly ever first movers into a marketplace and would much prefer to wait for other organizations to create markets that they can enter either with lower cost or with higher quality, a follower strategy. Analyzers make less frequent and slower market and product changes than their prospector counterparts yet are more often classified as more stabile and efficient than defender organizations. Furthermore, these organizations try to preserve key product lines and services. However, they cautiously follow a specific set of interesting new developments in their industry.

Successful analyzers have superior product technology, quality, or customer service or employ a larger market entry as compared to prospectors. Advantages associated with a follower strategy include

- Taking advantage of prospectors' positioning, product, and marketing errors. Analyzers have the luxury of studying a prospector's strategy, learning from their mistakes, and then entering the right market with the right product or service and the right marketing campaign. For colleges and universities, studying the success or failure of their competitors' new products and services, such as a new degree program, could save the organization time and resources. For example, by studying their local rivals who offered traditional MS degrees in management, Southampton College determined that the product that they could successfully enter the market with would be an accelerated format generic MBA. (Graduate students in their area wanted a quick degree with high-powered market recognition.)

- Employing the latest technology. Analyzers can leapfrog prospectors by using the latest technological advances to either improve the quality of the product or service or lower the production costs. Although Union Institute was one of the first universities to enter the university-without-walls market (in 1964), other nontraditional colleges such as Walden University and most notably the University of Phoenix have employed Internet technology in order to increase student access to educational resources and therein competitively reposition their organizations.
- Utilizing superior resources. Many analyzers want to enter the market big and therefore garner their resources in order to outspend prospector competitors. Certainly public colleges and universities, as well as those private universities with large endowments, may be able to support new programs and services heavily. For example, the Open University (OU) in the United Kingdom with nearly 250,000 students and a $300 million budget has been using distance learning since its inception in 1969. They possess both the student base and the resources to move heavily into the Internet education market and garner a large market share. (Note: as of this writing, the OU uses distance learning pedagogies rather than Internet delivery, but a strategic alliance with the Western Governors' University in 1998 has perhaps laid the groundwork for the OU to make just exactly such a move.)

Reactors

One does not choose to be a reactor. In the absence of a meaningful strategic choice, one simply is. Reactors are usually dysfunctional organizations in that they have no clearly defined or deliberate strategy. Their strategy is emergent at best (Mintzberg, 1987) and imposed by the marketplace; that is, they respond only when forced to by environmental pressures. Reactors do not competitively market their products and services and are not willing to assume any risk associated with the new development of products or markets. Furthermore, reactors do not have a clear position or identity in the market but instead have an inconsistent product-market mix—they neither compete on low-cost nor on product quality.

One can equate success in reactor organizations with survival. In order to survive, these organizations inhabit secondary and less profitable target markets or niches that have been left over by prospectors, defenders, and analyzers. They become the scavengers of the market. Once these markets do become viable, prospectors and analyzers will flood the market with more competitive products and services and reduce or even chase out the less competitive reactor organizations.

An example of a reactor college or university would be any organization that has not consciously confronted the impact of Internet and computer technology on instructional delivery. Although their faculty may employ Web pages, e-mail, chat rooms, and Internet-based assignments, there is no collegewide strategy or policy dealing with technology-based distance learning. The college's position in the market on this issue is therefore haphazard and is defined relative to its competitors rather than to its own plan of action.

Similar to Porter's generic strategies, there is an abundance of research that clearly demonstrates that reactor organizations underperform rival prospector, defender, and analyzer organizations. Woodside, Sullivan, and Trappey (1999) replicated previous research and found that prospector, analyzer, and defender strategic types more often exhibit higher levels of distinctive marketing competencies than reactors.

The Competitive Environment of Higher Education

Many colleges and universities have difficulty talking about competition, particularly when the term applies to them. The long history and prestige that colleges and universities have enjoyed tends to suggest that colleges and universities have a right to exist. However, as Rowley, Lujan, and Dolence (1997) have pointed out, no single institution can ignore the reality of competition. Today, some smaller colleges and universities understand full well what competition is, particularly the private schools. They compete with the bigger institutions for students, grants, endowments, and faculty, and they often lose. This is not a situation faced only by smaller colleges and universities, however. Resources simply can't spread as far as most colleges and universities would like, and so even larger schools, both public and private, find themselves in competition. It is therefore a wise practice for college and university leaders and planners to understand competitive dynamics and develop strategic plans that take them into account.

As we identified previously, Miles and Snow (1978, 1984) described the types of approaches to the marketplace in a manner that could best be characterized as a continuum of aggressive behaviors, with prospectors being the most aggressive and reactors being the least aggressive. Michael Porter described the actual method of competition. The context of competition, the competitive environment, is a determining factor in deciding the types of actions colleges and universities will take to implement their strategic plan. Here we must be concerned with two particular environmental dynamics: those that occur in the college's specific niche (or type; see our descriptions in Chapters Two and Three) and those that occur in other niches that could affect the focal institution. The first type of competition is referred to as *intraniche competition,* and the second type is referred to as *interniche competition.*

Intraniche Competition

Also known as *level of rivalry* or *direct competition,* the level of competition within a college type or niche is strongly correlated with the level of profitability or surplus of the organizations in that niche. As competition increases, surplus or profit decreases. Therefore, it is imperative that colleges and universities understand the competitive nature of their niche and determine a strategy that will reduce competitive pressures or allow the college to operate with a less confrontational, competitive approach to the marketplace.

The motivation for greater competition in any market segment or niche is derived from an organization's perception that their position in that segment is weak or vulnerable to external market conditions (political, economic, social, and technological forces), or that the organization perceives opportunities for growth in that sector. Organizations employing competitive strategies see their loss of surplus or profit as short-term due to increased competition but assume that they will experience a long-term gain by capturing larger market share through low-cost competition, or increased profit margins through differentiation. Organizations with greater resources also increase competition in order to eliminate in the short term the fringe competitors and reactor organizations with no clear strategic approach to the market and in the long run reduce overall competition (Cohen and Zysman, 1986). Rivalry is a determinant of several factors:

- The number of competitors in the market niche or segment. As the number of competitors increases, the probability increases that new and innovative strategies will change market segment conditions and heighten competition. Distance learning has increased competition for regional and small colleges and universities because this delivery method has removed one competitive advantage of these organizations, namely location (ease of access).
- The relative size and capabilities of competitors. When rival colleges are more equal in size and resources, the chances are far greater that competition will decrease due to the inability of one organization to outspend another.
- The fixed costs of competitors. When fixed costs (campus grounds, buildings, etc.) are high and marginal costs are low (courses are under-loaded or classrooms are empty), low-cost educational providers are under strong economic pressure to fill classroom space. They will therefore intensify competition through increased advertising and greater tuition discounting.
- The level of differentiation. When students perceive education in certain market segments or niches as a commodity, the selection of the college or university is determined predominately by price, resulting in increased competition. For example, the small college and university market segment has offered small class size and personalized attention as their raison d'être—their competitive advantage. If students interested in that niche market cannot differentiate between colleges and universities in that niche, they will assume that those market attributes are a given and shop for price or other differentiating attributes.
- Switching costs. The easier it is for a student to transfer from one college or university to another in the same market segment, the more competitive that segment will become given the ease or lack of penalty associated with exiting behavior.

Southampton College has historically had a very liberal transfer policy (will accept up to ninety-six credits and will allow students to take summer courses at other academic institutions) but is reconsidering this policy in the light of increased competition and decreased retention.

- The stake in achieving success. If numerous single-unit colleges and universities (a single campus) exist in a market segment, it is quite likely that the level of competition will increase due to an organization's dependency on that site and the need to keep the site open. However, industry sectors with multiple campus colleges and universities may have less competition due to the ability of these organizations to sacrifice a site for survivability.

- Exit barriers. Exit barriers are impediments that inhibit a college or university from going out of business and include the inability to liquidate assets, the actual fixed costs associated with exiting, emotional barriers, and government and social restrictions. When exit barriers are high in a particular market segment, organizations will intensify competition although they will experience low surplus (if not negative surplus). This will deflate the overall viability of the market segment because less efficient and effective colleges who might otherwise cease to exist will attract students who might otherwise have gone to more viable colleges. These more stable colleges will now be forced to lower costs or increasingly differentiate their products and services to maintain their enrollments.

- The potential of new entrants. New entrants introduce new capacity and the motivation to secure a position in the market segment, and they sometimes possess substantial resources with which to compete. Just how serious a threat they are depends upon two factors: barriers to entry and expected retaliation from existing organizations in the niche. Entrance barriers include government policy such as accreditation, access to distribution channels, capital requirements, and industry-sector knowledge. Expected retaliation is the perception that the market niche has or has not historically taken aggressive action against new entrants (Porter, 1980; Sherman, 1989).

Intraniche competition requires that the college or university clarify its position in the market segment in such a way that separates the organization from the segment mean. For example, if a public college is a comprehensive university, it is competing with other public institutions predominately through fairly broad low-cost programs and employing a fairly defensive approach to the market. This college can clarify its position relative to its competitors in the niche in one of two ways:

- By becoming a lower-cost producer or a greater differentiator than their competitors
- By becoming more aggressive in terms of their strategy (analyzer or prospector) than their competitors

Intraniche competition therefore requires that colleges and universities clarify their position in their market segment relative to their competitors and simultaneously not get caught in the middle of the continuum of competitive strategies in their niche.

Interniche Competition

Another form of competition that affects colleges and universities in a particular niche is indirect competition. Colleges and universities in different market segments or niches compete with other types of colleges and universities that are relatively close to their type of college and do not compete with their more distant peers. For example, research-driven private colleges and universities—colleges with large resources—are provider-oriented, compete by broad differentiation, and have a prospector orientation to the marketplace. They do not compete with public two-year colleges, which have fewer resources, are consumer-oriented, compete on narrow low-cost, and exhibit analyzer characteristics. However, they certainly can and do compete somewhat with the much smaller niche, composite private universities who are slightly less provider-oriented, more analytical in their approach to the market, and mix their broad generic strategies. Going back to Figure 3.2 then, interniche competition tends to naturally occur between college and university types that are in relatively close proximity to one another as compared to those that are far apart.

The relative rate of competition between niches is also a function of the success of a particular market segment and the competitiveness of that segment. Colleges and universities in intense competitive niches may opt to try to reposition themselves in less competitive market segments. This requires long-term planning, an understanding of the other market niches, and a commitment to at least partially shifting the mission of the institution.

For example, small colleges and universities have experienced a decline in enrollment because increased tuition costs have driven many students to enroll in public institutions. Some small colleges therefore have attempted to attract students through increased focused differentiation by dropping their generic programs and competing more directly with specialty colleges. Other small colleges have formed strategic alliances with public two-year colleges in order to reduce the overall cost of their tuition artificially (focused low-cost) and thereby compete with cooperative colleges and universities. These small colleges and universities have adopted an analyzer's approach to the market by studying the other market segments carefully and then at least partially entering those niches. If successful, these small colleges and universities will eventually move their market position from one niche to the other.

Integrating Porter's Generic Strategy and Miles and Snow's Strategic Approaches with Strategic Planning for Colleges and Universities

In the general study of strategic management, several authors (Walker and Ruekert, 1987; Segev, 1989; Treacy and Wiersema, 1995) have integrated the competitive aspects of both Porter and Miles and Snow into a single strategic framework for analysis. In a similar vein, we have added these two additional dimensions to the strategic choice model we developed in Chapters Two and Three. We do this in order to further define the strategic niche of each type of college and university and to provide a set of guidelines for selecting and implementing strategic options relative to a college's and university's overall position in the typology.

Figure 4.1 builds on the model we developed in Figure 3.2, with the added dimensions of Porter's generic strategies and Miles

Figure 4.1. Strategic Positioning of Information Age Colleges and Universities: A Three-Dimensional Model.

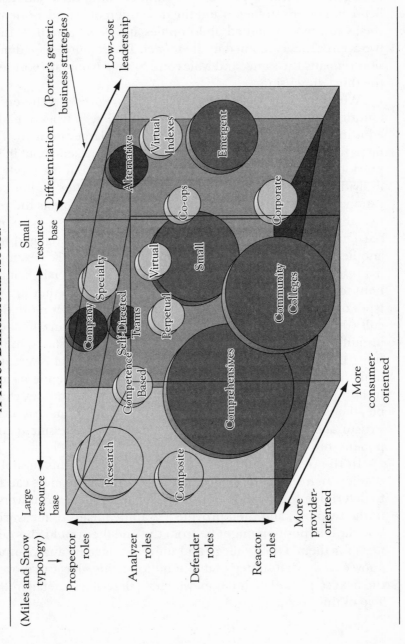

and Snow's typology to produce a three-dimensional model. Since we argued to some degree in this chapter about the relationship between Porter's strategies and the dimension of provider-oriented versus consumer-oriented philosophies, it is possible to have these two approaches combined in the model. The resource-base dimension remains the same, and Miles and Snow's typology represents the third dimension.

What one can now see is a space that represents the entire industry called higher education, where the sixteen types of higher educational organizations coexist within the larger domain. This helps further identify the idea of niche we have talked about in the previous chapters and demonstrates the position in the model of individual colleges and universities relative to other higher educational institutions. This idealized model also suggests the relative difficulties involved in developing a strategic plan if a particular college or university wants to become engaged with another segment of the higher educational industry. For example, if a research university wanted to add a virtual university component to its academic offerings, this model suggests that the two types of education are rather far apart, thus making it more difficult (though not impossible) to develop a structure in which one institution could operate both types of educational systems. In pursuing this strategy, the university might find that it must create a multidivisional structure within which to place independent structures for the research and virtual components. In another example, the same research university might not have to make as many structural changes to infuse a competency-based assessment component into its academic program.

In the next chapter we will use the basics of this model to develop an instrument that college and university leaders can use to determine the position of their particular college or university in the typology, and then provide a graphic means of measuring how far that position might be from the one they would choose as ideal for them. Once college and university leaders and planners know exactly what strategies they want to pursue, they can move to the next step, implementation, which we describe in detail in Part Two of this book.

Chapter Five

Tools and an Instrument for Applying the Model

In this chapter, we introduce a simple tool to help college and university leaders and planners position their organizations on the basis of the two-dimensional model we presented in Chapters Two and Three. We developed this instrument to provide campus leaders and strategic planners with a straightforward method of calculating where their particular college or university fits within the model. In this chapter we provide guidance as to what actions may be taken if that place on the model is not where they want their institution to be. The instrument does this by measuring important institutional resources and by evaluating the intangibles related to the provider-driven versus consumer-driven philosophies.

We then present an abbreviated case example to help readers better understand how the instrument can be useful to administrators and faculty leaders as they begin to analyze their own data. We then go on to discuss what the results mean and how they might be used to determine institutional direction and prepare colleges to implement their strategic plans. Finally, referring back to the advanced three-dimensional model we presented in Figure 4.1, we then discuss what it means to place one's institution in a position that is not consistent with the institution's perception of its appropriate typology or market niche in the model, and what it takes for the strategic planning process to move the institution toward its desired position or niche in order to minimize risk.

An Instrument That Measures
Institutional Resources and Philosophy

This instrument has two parts. First, a questionnaire contains a series of questions that call for the person (or group) filling it out to draw conclusions about a variety of aspects of the campus. The instrument also provides a simple scoring guide so that when all the data for the instrument have been properly recorded, the results are immediately known. This instrument is found in Exhibit 5.1 on page 112.

The second part of the instrument is based on Figure 3.2 (the two-dimensional representation of where the sixteen types of higher educational institutions are within a domain defined by resources and philosophies), with the addition of two axes, resource base and institutional philosophy. Once a person or group has determined the institutional score from completing the instrument found in Exhibit 5.1, the results are transferred onto the model according to where they fall on the numeric lines (axes) that appear on the side and bottom of the model. This instrument is found in Figure 5.1.

Drawing lines perpendicular to the two points across the table will identify a point of intersection that represents the campus's current location, based on the data entered into the questionnaire. With this information, the analysts can then determine how closely this position coincides with their preconceptions, as well as the type of institution their campus most closely resembles. Finally, once the analysts have determined the location of the institution in the model and have decided where it ought to be, planners can begin to ask, how do we get there from here?

Many of the answers are already in the model: adjusting or acquiring a greater resource base, challenging the academic philosophies of the college or university, establishing whether or not cost leadership or differentiation is right for the campus, and determining with what form of strategic opportunism the campus is most comfortable. Once campus leaders know where the campus needs to be headed, they must decide how to implement the plan, a topic we begin discussing in the next chapter.

Figure 5.1. Strategic Positioning of All Information Age Colleges and Universities: Measuring Institutional Resources and Philosophy.

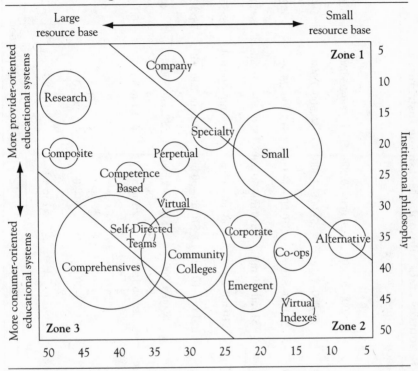

To show how the two instruments work, we now look at an actual case and then go through the completion of the instruments based on the facts of the case. This exercise should help readers better understand how the instruments should be applied, and how they help campus strategic planners move toward the next steps. The case we present here builds on the vignette we offered at the beginning of Chapter One. It is the case of a real university in the United States, but because it contains some negative information, we have altered all the names associated with the case.

Exhibit 5.1. Institutional Resources and Philosophy Measuring Instrument.

Instructions: Circle the one best response for each of the following:

Institutional Resource Base

	1	2	3	4	5
1. Size of the institution (no. of students; bodies not FTE)	<1,000	1,000–5,000	5,000–10,000	10,000–25,000	>25,000
*2a. Yearly tuition (public, in-state rate)	<$1,000	$1,000–2,000	$2,000–3,500	$3,500–7,500	>$7,500
*2b. Yearly tuition (private schools)	$<5,000	$5,000–10,000	$10,000–15,000	$15,000–25,000	>$25,000
3. Grants generated each year	<$1 mil	$1 mil–10 mil	$10 mil–50 mil	$50 mil–200 mil	$>$200 mil
4. Size of institutional endowment	<$10 mil	$10 mil–50 mil	$50 mil–100 mil	$100 mil–500 mil	$>$500 mil
5. Annual giving (alumni, others)	<$1 mil	$1 mil–10 mil	$10 mil–50 mil	$50 mil–200 mil	$>$200 mil
6. Faculty travel allowances (yearly)	$<500	$500–1,000	$1,000–2,500	$2,500–5000	>$5000
7. Ratio of full-time to adjunct faculty	1:3 or more	1:2 to 1:1	2:1 to 3:1	4:1 to 5:1	6:1 or less
8. Teaching load for FT faculty	4 or more	3	2	1	none
9. Average class size (in your department)	>100	99–50	50–30	30–10	<10
10. Ratio of students per computer	10:1 or more	9:1 to 7:1	6:1 to 4:1	3:1 to 2:1	1:1

Total all circled items _____

Total all items in this section: _____

*Choose one or the other

Institutional Philosophy

	1	2	3	4	5
1. Institutional emphasis on research	very high	high	medium	low	none
2. Institutional emphasis on teaching	none	low	medium	high	very high
3. Average advising load per faculty	>50	49–35	34–20	19–10	<10
4. Level of institutional bureaucracy	overwhelming	extensive	reasonable	some	minimal
5. Importance of research for tenure	only importance	very important	half and half	some	none
6. Importance of teaching for tenure	none	some	half and half	very important	only importance
7. Student impact on curriculum changes	none	very little	student evaluations	committee help	intensive
8. Alumni and business impact on curriculum changes	none	very little	program review	committee help	intensive
9. Level of contact with alumni	none	random	once a year	2–3 a year	more than 3 per year
10. Most changes in curriculum generated by	outside govt.	univ. faculty	college and school	departs.	independent committee

Total all circled items _____   Total all items in this section: _____

Case Study: ABC University

ABC University is a sixty-year-old private liberal arts college that started as a teachers college with a hundred students. The university has grown over time into an eight-thousand-student university with an annual budget of $100 million and a broad range of traditional undergraduate and graduate programs, including several doctoral programs. Several guides to colleges and universities rate the university as competitive, and local newspapers have included a number of articles about it.

The university's mission is to provide students with a well-rounded education that will lead to not only an appreciation of lifelong learning and personal growth but will also lead to career opportunities. The university also views itself as a social, educational, and cultural center, so its mission also includes fostering community and artistic, political, and economic activities critical to a free society. The university clearly considers itself a liberal arts institution and prides itself on having a strong liberal arts component in all majors. The largest programs on the campus are professional studies, including business, education, law, and engineering. Together, however, the programs generate less than $5 million a year in research grants.

Demographics and Location

ABC's campus is located in a suburb of a major city in northeastern United States (about twenty miles away from the urban center) and covers nearly two hundred acres of property along a major feeder highway. Most people consider ABC a local university in that it serves the students from the surrounding community as well as some students from adjacent states. Less than 10 percent of the students come from outside the Northeast, and there is a minimal presence of international students.

Housing on campus can accommodate approximately three thousand students (approximately one-half the undergraduate enrollment); an additional one thousand students live locally off-campus. Many students commute from home or from work and enjoy the elegant campus grounds and the Ivory Tower feel of the university. The student body comprises about 40 percent men and

60 percent women; it has a very small percentage of minority students, though the proportion is equal to that in the surrounding community.

Several other colleges surround ABC University, including a technical college, a state-funded four-year college with over five thousand students (with some graduate programs), several two-year community colleges, a proprietary business college, and several other private colleges that range in size from fifteen hundred students to eighteen thousand students. The area is considered a hub for colleges and universities and provides local residents with a plethora of choices. ABC is in the high price range of local colleges and universities in that the estimated annual cost for tuition is slightly under $20 thousand. However, ABC deeply discounts this rate through scholarships, graduate assistantships, and work-study programs and has managed to remain somewhat price-competitive with equivalent institutions in the area.

Given the concentration of other two-year and four-year colleges in the vicinity, ABC has been able to develop articulation agreements with several community colleges as well as two private colleges that only offer bachelor's degrees. ABC also has developed several reciprocal tuition agreements with the local technical college and the local college of music and arts.

The Administration

Effective strategic campus leadership has been a major concern for the board of trustees at ABC. For some years, the campus has seen its student numbers decrease, its top faculty leave for greener pastures, its endowments shrink, and its reputation come into question. With this deteriorating situation, the board has sought leadership that could successfully turn around the campus and begin to build toward a more stable and secure future.

The most recently dismissed president, Dr. James T. Hilliard, came to ABC with a PhD in philosophy from a Midwestern public university. The search committee considered him a good fit, as did the board of trustees, since he had developed several strategies for turning around similar institutions on the West Coast, where he had also served as president. Dr. Hilliard brought with him not only his vision of what a private liberal arts university ought to be but also several influential contacts in Washington, D.C., grant-funding institutions and private foundations. ABC generated less than 10 percent of their annual budget through grant research and foundations, and the search committee perceived Dr. Hilliard as a "cash cow."

Dr. Hilliard was also well known for his charming personality and his ability to develop a rapport with donors and alumni. People who were asked to provide job references for him raved about his ability to secure endowments from the business community and the well-to-do, and continually referred to his ability to placate disgruntled alumni. The selection committee and board considered this skill a real plus, particularly since annual giving amounted to slightly more than 5 percent of the university's annual budget, with the total endowment fund equaling one-half the annual budget.

Unfortunately, after two years of dreams and promises but no substantive results in terms of fund-raising, endowments, and increased enrollment, the board of trustees decided that they could not afford to keep President Hilliard and decided to conduct yet another search.

As for the rest of the administration, many had spent several years moving up through the administrative ranks of the university. For instance, the provost (who also acted as the chief financial officer and the chief operations officer) started as the director of the registrar over fifteen years ago. She was considered a highly competent individual, although all her academic work experience was gained through the university. Other key administrators (directors of academic advising, public relations, alumni affairs) were also home-grown or had long-time relationships with the provost or members of the board of trustees prior to being hired.

The organizational structure of the university is fairly typical of most American universities. Reporting to the president (who is also a member of the board of trustees) is a management group comprising four vice presidents (academic, development, operations and finance, and student affairs) and legal counsel. Campus governance is top-down in the nonacademic areas; the faculty employ a senate and committee structure to manage academic issues (curriculum, instruction, personnel).

The academic component comprises schools of arts and media, business, humanities, natural sciences, social sciences, and library services. Faculty regularly make recommendations to the academic vice president and the president in areas related to budgets, program development, and student retention, though the administration retains full authority in those areas.

Administrators flatter themselves on running a student-driven operation; many of the office personnel will go out of their way to assist students in dealing with problems relating to student finances, class registration, and other personal issues. Many students often comment positively on the family feel of the university and the fact that they are known by their first names by both the faculty and administration. The procedures that have been established for handling student issues, including admissions, registration, advisement, and housing, have been highly standardized and are predominately paper-based, although students may apply and register over the Internet.

The office of alumni affairs coordinates contact with alumni and reports to the vice president of development. This office publishes quarterly newsletters and an annual giving report. It also contacts alumni via telemarketing and surveys and also notifies them of upcoming special events such as Alumni Weekend and other on-campus proceedings. Alumni have their own independent board and work with the alumni office to facilitate alumni-related events.

The Faculty

Over 80 percent of the members of the faculty possess terminal degrees, and the average faculty member works at the institution for nearly ten years. Nearly 80 percent of the faculty members are tenured, although nontenured faculty members find it very difficult to obtain tenure given departmental caps on tenured faculty numbers. At least 20 percent of the senior faculty are scheduled to retire within the next five years.

Faculty course loads are four courses per semester (two preparations), with the possibility of one course release per semester, providing the faculty member is actively engaged in funded research. Although ABC has the reputation of a teaching institution, the university expects the faculty to publish at least one article per year, advise students, serve on several university committees, be involved in professional and community organizations, and of course provide excellent course instruction. The university is consistent in awarding tenure and promotion based upon the above criteria and terminates nontenured faculty members who received less than very good teaching evaluations regardless of their publishing record.

Student-teacher ratios vary from program to program; however, the university average is twenty-five to one. Full-time faculty members regularly teach classes, and the university seldom uses graduate students in this capacity. Recently, however, the university has relied more and more on adjunct instructors, who now teach approximately 50 percent of all courses. In the professional programs, more than 70 percent of the courses in some subject areas are taught by adjuncts.

ABC considers academic advising a critical component of a student's experience. All new instructors attend training and orientation workshops to learn the advising system. The university expects tenured faculty members to attend refresher workshops that include not only content instruction, but also sensitivity training and counseling. Faculty members advise at least twenty students per year, and university administrators and several full-time academic advisors provide additional advising services. ABC has developed a freshman counseling program, including a one-credit College 101 course, in order to increase retention and provide a softer transition for the traditional student from high school to college. Several faculty members participate in this program, although involvement is voluntary.

The university allocates faculty members $250 of discretionary funds and provides additional opportunities for them to obtain up to another $250 annually for conference attendance and travel. Institutional research on faculty workload noted that the average faculty member devotes fifty-five hours each week to working; the largest portion of their time is dedicated to research.

Technology and Curriculum

The campus has managed to keep up with technological trends in library facilities with online searches and in course instruction. All classrooms and dorms are wired to their local area network (LAN) and the Internet. However, there are no specific plans to take advantage of these facilities. Some faculty members have independently ventured into online instruction and distance learning, but there is no organized effort to move faculty into this instructional methodology. The campus boasts six separate computer labs around campus, with approximately six hundred personal computers available to students at any one time.

In general, individual faculty members drive curriculum and course development by proposing new courses or new programs (majors and minors) based upon their personal assessment of changes in their fields or changes in the leading academic institutions' curricula. Curriculum changes go through a series of academic reviews: department, school, curriculum committee, faculty senate, and eventually to the administrative offices of the vice president for academic affairs and the president. There is no requirement that students, alumni, and local organizations be consulted regarding changes to the curriculum, and rarely, if ever, are these groups included in the approval process.

Recent Trends at ABC University: Background

Enrollment at ABC University has declined by 3 percent annually for the past ten years. This decline, combined with the substantial negative cash flows that the university had experienced under university President Hilliard's administration (its third president), has created some panic in the budget committee of the board of trustees. The university's endowment has declined from $75 million to $50 million during the last four years, and annual giving has now declined dramatically over the same period from a steady $5 million a year to just under $4 million. Over the past nine years, the board of trustees has reacted to the decline in enrollments and the deteriorating financial situation by hiring new presidents to try to turn the situation around and get the university back into the black. The board has asked each president to

- Introduce cost cutting measures to reduce overall costs as well as the cost of delivering course instruction
- Increase nontuition revenues (such as endowments, grants, alumni giving)
- Develop instructional programs or methods that will expand the student base (increase enrollment) and allow the university to reach out to new students

- Establish a strategic plan that will improve endowments and annual giving

During the past nine years, the university, under various presidents, had tried various approaches to meeting the demands of the board. The first president had focused on the cost issues and had hired a long-range planner who analyzed class enrollment patterns to weed out courses that historically were under-enrolled. Classes with less than ten students were immediately canceled, and courses with a history of having less than fifteen students were placed on a program review list. Furthermore, the university cut course offerings 10 percent (regardless of department) across the campus and froze adjunct budgets.

Predictably, faculty members and their respective academic deans had reacted very negatively to these changes. Many of the senior faculty became irate because they were not consulted about these changes and felt that the administration was micromanaging their operation. Academic deans believed that the academic integrity of the university's programs were being jeopardized because of their inability to offer certain courses required for their majors. A small group of students protested the changes by holding an old-fashioned sit-in in the president's office, which unfortunately made the local and regional news media. As a result, a significantly higher number of students transferred to other universities with programs that were perceived as stable. After three years of declining enrollments and no real plans for bringing in new students, the board had decided to search for a new president.

The board had hired the second president because she had a long history of working well with students, faculty, and staff in her former positions as academic vice president. She also had a reputation for being very analytical yet highly consultative in her work. Upon her appointment as president, she immediately met with the administrative and academic deans, both individually and as a group, and also attended school and department meetings to understand the faculty and staff better and their perception of organizational problems. These activities increased the morale of the university's personnel. However, the board became impatient with her inability to produce meaningful plans to deal with declining enrollments, reduced revenues, and increased costs. The board removed her after her second year as president because she failed to understand that immediate action was needed.

The board tried to be especially careful as they set out to select the third president, Dr. Hilliard, and they filled the position after more than a year's deliberation. They even used a nationally known, academic headhunter to facilitate the process. Dr. Hilliard had seemed the perfect president. He appeared to understand the immediacy of the problems. Even with a strong liberal arts background, he seemed to understand the need for high quality professional programs, had a vision for the university, and had excellent external connections. Hilliard was a definite charmer, and the board believed he would work well with all of the university stakeholders.

Dr. Hilliard's initial plan, which resonated well with the faculty, staff, and the board, was to create premier and specialized applied liberal arts graduate programs to augment the current traditional graduate programs that ABC had built upon the strong reputation of their undergraduate programs and community resources. For example, in the School of Humanities, he worked with the faculty to develop a master's writing program and brought in prestigious local writers to work as adjunct instructors and also hired a nationally recognized writer to showcase the program. The university considered graduate students prime customers for this program because they required very few student services and usually required little tuition discounting. Several of these "boutique" graduate degree programs emerged during Dr. Hilliard's administration and demonstrated several impressive results both in terms of increasing enrollments and bringing national recognition to the university.

President Hilliard spent top dollar to secure experts for his new degree programs, stating that quality programs required quality faculty and personnel. He also felt that his office and his university home should also look the part if he was going to entertain potential large donors, grant administrators, and key politicians. Against warnings from the provost that he was "murdering the budget," Dr. Hilliard spent extravagantly on cocktail parties and other university events and became a popular personage in the local community.

In the end, however, Dr. Hilliard's plans resulted in neither overall increased enrollment nor increased contributions and grants to the university. The board removed him after his third year in office.

Moving Forward

The board understands that their selection of the next president is the key that will determine success or another failure in the development of an effective strategic plan, as well as in the proper implementation of that plan. Maghroori and Rolland (1997) remind us that a new president will need to provide dynamic strategic leadership and guidance for the various members of the university family by translating the vision and mission of the board into action plans (strategies) for goal achievement. Furthermore, the president must be able to oversee the implementation of these action plans by aligning the internal processes of the organization, such as structure, reward system, skills, systems, style, staff, and shared values (Kotter, 1978; Peters and Waterman, 1982) to match the opportunities or threats from the external environment.

Before the board of trustees conducts another search for a president they need to assess their university's position (or university type) in the marketplace and assess the risks and opportunities associated with that position. They also need to determine their overall competitive strategy and their strategic approach to the marketplace in order to develop a strategic management plan. Having done this, they should then be able to search for a president who understands the current situation and can help the university better position itself in the marketplace. Further, they need to work closely with the new president to devise a method of implementation, clearly different from what the three previous presidents have done, that will successfully move ABC University from where it is to where it needs to be.

Exercise: Positioning ABC University on the Two-Dimensional Model

To demonstrate how ABC might begin this process, we turn to the institutional resources and philosophy measuring instrument that we introduced in Exhibit 5.1. By applying the facts of the case, the instrument should be useful in allowing the board to get a sense of where ABC University might be located on the model presented in Figure 5.1. With this information, the board should also be able to get a sense of what it will take to get ABC to a different position on the model, if they feel that is the appropriate strategic goal for the university to pursue. Let's examine how someone might complete the instrument and then interpret it. To do this, we will first determine ABC University's relative institutional resource base and, second, its prevailing institutional philosophy.

Step 1: Institutional Resources (X-Axis)

For item 1 of Exhibit 5.1, ABC University has eight thousand students (a score of 3). For item 2b (for private versus public university), the annual tuition per student is nearly $20 thousand (a score of 4). For item 3, annual grants amount to less than $10 million per year (a score of 2). For item 4, the institutional endowment is currently $50 million (a score of 3). For item 5, annual giving is approximately $4 million (a score of 2). For item 6, faculty travel allowances are $250 per annum (a score of 1). For item 7, the ratio of full-time faculty to adjunct faculty is 1:1 (a score of 2). For item 8, full-time faculty members have a four-course teaching load (a score of 1). For item 9, the average class size is twenty-five (a score of 4), and for item 10, the campus has a student-computer ratio of over 10:1 (a score of 1). The total score for ABC University in terms of its resource base is 23. When one enters this score on the bottom of Figure 5.1, the result is that ABC must be considered as having a less than average resource base.

Step 2: Institutional Philosophy (Y-Axis)

It is harder to gauge institutional philosophy than institutional resources because some of the factors are more qualitative and therefore require judgment calls. These factors include the institution's emphasis on research; emphasis on teaching; average advising workload per faculty member; level of institutional bureaucracy; importance of research for tenure; importance of teaching for tenure; impact of students, alumni, and businesses on curriculum changes; level of contact with alumni; and source for curriculum changes.

In going over ABC's case and applying the information there to the second part of the questionnaire, we note that for item 1 of Exhibit 5.1 ABC University most likely scores a 3. The campus appears to have a medium emphasis on research given the fact that the majority of the faculty's time is devoted to research and that they are expected to publish at least one article per year. Faculty do have additional duties (such as academic advising and community service), however, and a heavy teaching load that detracts from their research endeavors.

For item 2, ABC's emphasis on faculty instruction seems high in that the administration expected excellent course instruction and considered itself a teaching institution. Nontenured faculty members who did not receive very good evaluations were not renewed regardless of their publishing record. The faculty, nevertheless, spent most of their time doing research and neither the administration nor the faculty had developmental programs to assist faculty to deal with instructional issues (including new instructional technology) or curriculum development. As noted by Kerr (1975), rewards for good teaching are usually quite limited (little remuneration and prestige), whereas rewards for research are usually quite high (besides internal rewards such as promotion, there is external recognition and resume bolstering) and transferable to other institutions. Therefore, it is logical for faculty to concentrate on research even when an institution claims to desire teaching excellence. One might therefore conclude that the emphasis on teaching at ABC was medium (a score of 3).

For item 3, the average advising load per faculty member at ABC is thirty students (a score of 3), and it is interesting to note that administrators also shared in the advising function. The level of institutional bureaucracy seemed reasonable given the highly standardized and predominately paper-based procedures coupled with a student-driven operation "where everybody knows your name." The lack of emphasis on computerization and Web access to the administrative services, however, reduces the overall quality of the service (hence the score of 3).

A comparison of the structure and bureaucratic processes at peer institutions reveals that the level of bureaucracy at ABC is relatively excessive, so in item 4 ABC University scores a 2.

In terms of the relative importance of research for tenure and teaching for tenure, the case shows that the university is very consistent in awarding tenure and promotion based upon research and instruction. As noted above, nontenured faculty members are terminated regardless of their publishing record if they receive less than "very good" teaching evaluations. Therefore, both research and instruction seem important criteria in making a tenure decision (item 5 gets a score of 3 and item 6 also gets a score of 3).

The impact of students (item 7), alumni, and local businesses (item 8) on curriculum seems negligible, since most changes in the curriculum are faculty-based or derived from benchmark colleges and universities (a score of 1 for student impact, 1 for alumni and business impact; a score of 5 for item 10, source of curriculum change). There seems to be fairly heavy contact with the alumni on other issues nonetheless (certainly more than three times per year), via published quarterly newsletters and an annual giving report. Alumni have their own independent board and work with the alumni office to facilitate alumni-related events (a score of 5 for item 9). The total score for ABC University in terms of its philosophy is 29, which places it in the slightly consumer-oriented area of the model when located on the vertical axis of Figure 5.1.

ABC's Position Among Information Age Colleges and Universities

After placing the scores for resource base and institutional philosophy on the model in Figure 5.1, one notes that ABC University, with a score of 23, 30, occupies Zone 2 and just left and slightly below the niche of small colleges and universities. Placement in Zone 2 (and we might note fairly close to Zone 1) denotes a moderate market risk. This risk is exacerbated, however, by the long-term decreasing enrollments, decreasing endowment, and poor fiscal management, all of which threaten to shift ABC back into Zone 1, a high-risk category.

Analyzing the Board of Trustees Strategy Options

The above analysis gives the board of ABC several important areas of crucial information. First, it's out of sync with its market niche of small colleges and universities. On the positive side, ABC is in better shape than many of its counterparts, but its operations may well draw it into a more risky position.

Second, ABC is floundering. This is partially demonstrated by their misaligned position. Since it is probable that ABC would not be well advised to move to the more risky position of general small colleges and universities, it's unclear where ABC belongs. The two obvious choices that would require moderate adjustments of one sort or another would be to move toward being more of a specialty university (capitalizing on centers of excellence and developing a market reputation in those limited areas of expertise) or move toward becoming more of a comprehensive university. In order to make either move, however, ABC would need to make strategic changes. To become a specialty university, ABC must improve its research capabilities and zero in on specific centers of excellence, while reducing or eliminating other programs that do not support the centers. ABC must also improve its resource pool, particularly in the area of grants and endowments, in order to support both a more highly distinguished faculty and an improved research capability. To become a comprehensive university, ABC will need to significantly improve its resource base and turn its attentions more directly to the needs of learners in its service area, particularly in light of Information Age societal needs. This may mean shifting the focus of whatever basic research it is engaged in and building pedagogical programs and learner-professor interfaces that improve learning and support applied research activities.

Third, the board should be able to see that ABC simply isn't large enough or distinguished enough to continue its pseudo practices that emulate several research institution standards. The research demands upon faculty members seem out of place at ABC, especially when a faculty member can be terminated so easily for not performing well in the classroom. Instead, ABC needs to adapt its academic philosophies one way or the other, and not try to emphasize both research and teaching. With a clearer vision of how they view academics and their learners, ABC should be able to solidify its approach to resource accumulation as well.

Therefore, in beginning the search for a new president that will help establish an appropriate strategic direction and lead the campus in the successful implementation of the strategic plan that will define that direction, the board now knows where the campus stands relative to its market and its competition. Before it begins its search, however, the board should also reexamine its own earlier recommended goals and strategies to see how they could impact the direction of ABC University in the future and perhaps revise them according to some of the information it now has as a result of completing the instrument.

Introduce Cost-Cutting Measures to Reduce Overall Costs and the Cost of Delivering Course Instruction

It seems strange that the board would target course instruction for cost reduction. Normally, colleges and universities understand the importance of supporting their academic efforts, since the transference of knowledge is one of the primary missions on any campus. Some campuses do reduce course offerings, however, believing that certain faculty or adjunct salaries are excessive (for example, eliminating a full professor and high salary and hiring a new PhD for much less). Of course, what these types of activities do to faculty is decrease trust, loyalty, morale, and motivation—all of which prove to be additional costs to the institution in the long run.

Cost cutting measures must be carefully orchestrated to prevent cutting activities that actually build reputation, quality, and future enrollments. For example, a cut in the adjunct budget may require the college to offer fewer sections of a given class offering, but in so doing will increase section size. The potential negative impact of this move might be a decrease in reputation for being learner-centered, decreased quality through reduced interaction, and lower faculty morale resulting from an increased workload. These are all dangers that campuswide could help shift the position of the college into a more risky zone.

Cost-cutting tactics also tend to shift the philosophical orientation of the college away from the consumer and toward the provider. In the case of ABC, the university could save money by increasing the faculty-advising load and reducing the number of staff members providing advisor services. The cost for advisement would go down of course but so might the quality of advisement given the additional workload burden to the faculty.

Also, cost-cutting actions tend to bureaucratize the organization by introducing an excessive number of procedures for controlling costs. Again, ABC may become less consumer-oriented if these cost reduction methods reduce the family feeling that the students have about the administration and faculty. In summary,

cost reduction strategies tend to shift colleges away from consumers and may in fact reduce the college's resource base if the
funds are not reinvested in the university's operations. This emergent strategy (Mintzberg, 1987), based upon the board's desire to
reduce operating costs, would seem inadvertently to shift ABC University toward a specialty university model, although that was certainly not their intention. This would only be the case if cost
cutting resulted in a reduction of cost liability to the institution
along with a reallocation of resources from inferior programs to
programs of excellence. In the model of specialty colleges and universities, only a few premier programs would house the majority of
the students in the university. In ABC's case, its professional degree
programs might constitute such programs.

As we pointed out in Chapter Two, specialty colleges reside partially in Zone 1 and Zone 2 because of their focus of offering limited programs to a portion (or niche) of the total market. This may
be an acceptable short-term option for ABC. However, in the long
term, this strategy may result in increased risk by shifting the college into the more precarious Zone 1.

Increase Nontuition Revenues (Endowments, Grants, Alumni Giving)

This is clearly an important goal and directly confronts the issue
of increasing the resource base of the university. It also focuses on
some of the weaknesses in ABC. Our analysis of ABC noted that
they scored low in the three resource areas of endowments, grants,
and alumni giving (a 2.33 average per area), both giving and grants
being quite low. The big question for ABC is what kinds of strategies will they need to help them more successfully attract more
research grants, large endowments, and increased giving—providing that their proper strategic choice is to move toward being
more of a specialty university?

The impact of this philosophy shift is huge. Not all faculty
members are successful grant applicants, and in teaching institutions, many faculty don't even want to be involved with grants.
Grantsmanship is an art, and any successful research college or university will testify to the fact that it takes a particular type of professor who is interested in grant-worthy research, has a reputation
for doing grant-worthy research, and is familiar with and successful at writing grants and having them funded. Furthermore, such
professors command premium salaries, and will naturally expect

market standards or better if they decide to come to a particular college or university. These issues clearly demonstrate that if a college or university is going to move toward a new strategic position that requires new skills and new academic orientations, it will have to change its structure substantively (and this isn't going to happen overnight).

Endowments and annual donations are a different issue. Individuals, groups, and corporations give to colleges and universities because they deeply believe in the quality and worthiness of certain of the institution's academic programs. They tend to support only areas of excellence, where the institutional guarantee of continuing growth and support is already a given. This is a clear example of a market force at work in colleges and universities. For the institution to be successful in strengthening its giving programs, it must establish a strategic plan that marries these market forces to programs that exemplify the institution's strategic intent.

Giving may also increase the consumer-orientation of the university by increasing the level of contact between the university and its stakeholders (alumni, students, local businesses). But by asking for funds from the community, the college or university may have to give up some power to that community by allowing them to have a say in the typically sacred areas of curriculum development. Unlike grants, giving may shift the institution more toward a consumer orientation while increasing its resource base.

As the case suggests, however, ABC is closer in mission and philosophy to the comprehensive university than to more research-oriented institutions. It is not evident that the board is conscious that their second strategy includes two inherently different positions in terms of the marketplace. If ABC is to reduce their risk in the market, the board must understand that they must clarify how grants and endowments fit the mission of the institution by defining in their mission and overall strategy the university model they wish to emulate.

Develop Instructional Programs or Methods That Will Expand the Student Base (Increase Enrollment) and Allow the University to Reach Out to New Students

At first, this goal seems at odds with the first goal, introduce cost-cutting measures. ABC can reconcile the apparent confusion, however, if it follows the tactic of reducing or closing ineffective programs and using the savings to grow effective programs or develop new ones. This goal and its resultant strategies should help ABC increase resources and also address the negative enrollment trends at ABC. Potential strategies are two-pronged. The first part requires increasing the number of academic programs, degrees, majors, and minors to appeal to a new audience of students. The second part requires developing new delivery systems for instruction, such as distance learning and satellite campuses.

In terms of new program development, ABC has the opportunity not only to increase their resource base but also to become more consumer-oriented by including alumni, students, and the local community in the development of the new curricula. Since the board is now altering the process of curriculum development—from a normally bottom-up process to one that will start with a top-down directive—the source of most of the curriculum changes may shift from the individual faculty member and the closest person to the consumer to the department, school, or universitywide committee, thus reducing ABC's consumer orientation. The board would consequently be well advised to rethink their strategy.

In terms of new program delivery systems, ABC can directly impact their resource base by

- Expanding their usage of the current physical plant (although not mentioned in the case, class scheduling could be expanded to include off-hours or days such as weekends, early morning, or late night classes)
- Increasing their physical geographic domain such as satellite campuses or classrooms, perhaps including the use of distance learning technology
- Employing technology or alternative instructional methods to reach learners asynchronously, such as Web-based instruction, contract learning, and credit by examination
- Forming a joint venture with other colleges and universities to offer ABC's programs at their partners' campuses
- Developing backward and forward integration methods by working with high schools and local businesses to offer college courses at their facilities, possibly including tailoring courses and programs to meet these particular consumer needs

Most, if not all, the above actions may increase ABC's consumer orientation (particularly because ABC is already emphasizing its teaching) by increasing the importance of instruction, increasing the external stakeholders' impact on curriculum delivery, and potentially reducing the level of bureaucracy by getting closer to the customer. In summary, increasing breadth and delivery of academic programs may increase the resource base for ABC as well as potentially increase their consumer orientation.

Program development and expansion can lead ABC closer to the comprehensive university model. ABC, however, would have to develop strategies that would increase capital resources to fund expansion and might need to rethink some of the cost-cutting plans mentioned earlier.

Still another strategic option for ABC would be the combining of program development and new instructional delivery systems that could potentially drive ABC toward more of an emergent university model. In this kind of exciting possibility, ABC could create a hybrid university by integrating one of the classical university models, on-campus chalk-and-talk instruction, with innovative off-campus or technology-driven programs. The more traditional elements of the university could remain the core of the operation, as Thompson (1967) has suggested, while the more avant-garde elements could act as self-directed teams. Overall, this strategy would require fewer resources than becoming a comprehensive university and would allow the board the freedom to select which programs would remain part of the traditional liberal arts university and which programs would become detached spin-offs, or what a business conglomerate might call a strategic business unit.

Conclusions About the Impact of the Board's Strategies

The board's goals and strategies handed down to the preceding presidents of ABC University were doomed to fail because they *did not clearly move the university toward one specific university model, niche, or strategic direction.* Although the board did not realize the true impact of this situation, it is clear that the three suggested goals include contradictory actions when viewed from the perspective of how these changes would move ABC's position in the market.

Further, apparently the first and third presidents they hired tacitly understood this paradox because each chose to follow just one tactic.

The irony of this case is that President Hilliard purposively chose a strategic direction for ABC that unwittingly moved the university toward a more consumer-oriented model, perhaps even one of the emergent or market-driven types described in Chapter Three. His introduction of liberal arts graduate programs took advantage of the strong reputation of ABC's undergraduate programs and community resources and increased the reputation of the university. His success in increasing enrollments was marred by his inability to control costs simultaneously. As noted earlier, program development requires investing resources, and Dr. Hilliard could not achieve both objectives concurrently. In strategic management terms, growth requires investment in infrastructure and human capital and therefore cost-cutting measures (unless one focuses upon frivolous items, such as Dr. Hilliard's office) run counter to growth strategies.

Determining Competitive Strategy and Strategic Approach in the Marketplace

In Chapter Four, we introduced the notion that colleges and universities compete on either low cost or differentiation in a broad or narrow market segment and that their relative approach to the market varies from highly aggressive (prospectors) to passive (reactors).

We also introduced the notion that colleges and universities compete both within and between market niches based on their relative position and the level of competition within their niche. Colleges can clarify their position relative to their competitors in the niche via one of two methods:

Determining Competitive Strategy

1. Becoming a lower-cost producer or a greater differentiator than their competitors
2. Becoming more aggressive in terms of their strategy (analyzer or prospector) than their competitors

Determining a Relevant Competitive Strategy at ABC University

Stage 1 of this process begins with the development of a list of direct competitors in a college's market niche, or those closest to one's position on the two-dimensional chart. To develop this list, a college or university must begin by defining its competitive domain. The domain within the market niche may be defined through a combination of variables, including geographical boundaries or proximity, premier programs, relative reputation (perhaps as defined through an external college guide), financial resources, mission, customer psycho-demographics, breadth of programs, and age of facility.

Once campus planners have identified the domain, a college or university is ready to identify its competitors. Pearce and Robinson (2000) suggest that administrators consider the following factors when distinguishing the competition:

- Determine how other colleges or universities in the niche define their market.
- Decide the relative similarity of benefits that students receive from other colleges' and universities' programs and services.
- Establish how dedicated other colleges and universities are to the niche market. Are their long-term intentions and goals to stay in the niche (that is, do small colleges wish to remain small or change their market position?) or are they planning to shift their position?

Pearce and Robinson also caution not to make the frequent errors that many executives make in identifying competitors. These include focusing on known competitors while failing to search for new competitors and potential entrants into the market niche, overemphasizing large competitors while minimizing small ones, excluding international or national competitors, expecting competitors to maintain their current strategies and misreading changes in those strategies, focusing on tangible resources of competitors (financial assets, number of students) while disregarding intangibles (quality of personnel), and presupposing that all colleges in the niche are equally affected by the external environment, meaning that they have the same threats and opportunities.

Once planners have identified competitors, Stage 2 of the analysis involves the development of a spreadsheet that includes competitor information of nearby or competing colleges and universities including tuition, a short description of the college or university, enrollment, number of degrees, highest degrees, and other information deemed pertinent by the student to distinguish colleges based upon either a low-cost (such as rate of tuition discounting) or differentiation strategy (admissions requirements, housing, quality of degree programs, extracurricular activities) (Comte and White, 1999). See Table 5.1 as an example.

Stage 3 is the diagnostic phase of the positioning analysis and involves making a determination as to where the college or university fits in terms of relative cost and differentiation. Although Table 5.1 is incomplete for a full analysis, it is apparent that Northern Kentucky University is the low-cost producer in the group, since it offers the least number of degree programs, has the lowest tuition rate (assuming that out-of-state tuition for these institutions is comparable to their in-state rates), and has lower fixed costs, given its predominate commuter orientation. It is harder to determine which of the other two universities is the greatest differentiator given this limited information. The University of Cincinnati has the broader breadth of degree programs, whereas Miami University caters to the residential student.

Note that the positioning question, from Miami University's perspective, would then deal with the nearly 31 percent difference in tuition between the two institutions. Are Miami's services to residential students superior to the University of Cincinnati's in order to justify the tuition differential, or are there other tangible or intangible factors that warrant a higher tuition in the eyes of the students? Do they possess greater resources or have a more consumer-driven orientation? Since Miami is not competing as the low-cost producer in its market niche, it is necessary for the university to distinguish itself clearly from its other competitors.

Determining ABC University's Competitive Approach

In order to determine the college or university's approach to the marketplace, campus leaders and strategic planners must determine its characteristics relative to the four strategic types described

Table 5.1. Greater Cincinnati Comprehensive Public Universities and Four-Year Colleges, 1997–1998.

	Description	Enrollment	Number of degrees	Highest degree	In-state tuition
University of Cincinnati	4 yr + graduate, professional, residential, commuter	34,526	445	PhD	$3,918/yr
Miami University	4 yr + graduate, professional, primarily residential	19,562	270	PhD	$5,660/yr
Northern Kentucky University	4 yr + graduate, professional, primarily commuter	11,473	73	Master's	$1,800/yr

Source: Comte and White (1999). Used by permission.

by Miles and Snow (1978) that we identified in Chapter Four. A complete listing of the variables can be found in Resource A. However, the areas that planners need to consider include

- Domain establishment and surveillance
- Growth
- Operational problems and solutions
- Dominant coalition and management succession planning structure
- Control
- Coordination and conflict resolution
- Performance appraisal and maintenance

Campus leaders and planners can employ information from the table found in Resource A as a checklist to determine the overall strategic orientation of the college or university. Please note that although no college or university will be a perfect fit with one particular strategic approach, there should be a predominance of characteristics that borders defender-analyzer or prospector-analyzer. Institutions that find that they have a combination of defender-prospector characteristics, and perhaps some analyzer characteristics as well, should accept that they possess reactor traits.

Once the strategic approach is established for the college or university, data should be gathered on the niche competitors via method 1 in the earlier list, Determining Competitive Strategy. By using the checklist developed in part A, a judgment should then be made as to the overall approach of each competitor. This information should then be added to the competitor spreadsheet found in Table 5.2.

Determining Competitive Strategy and Competitive Approach for ABC University

ABC University considered itself a local university and therefore defined its domain geographically. Because ABC's strategic position fell just outside the small college designation, we need to gather data on local private colleges that also seem to have a larger resource base than small colleges but would not be considered truly comprehensive universities. The case does state that several

Table 5.2. Competitive Strategy and Approach of Greater Cincinnati Comprehensive Public Universities and Four-Year Colleges, 1997–1998.

	Description	Enrollment	Number of degrees	Highest degree	In-state tuition
University of Cincinnati	4 yr + graduate, professional, residential, commuter, *differentiator, defender*	34,526	445	PhD	$3,918/yr
Miami University	4 yr + graduate, professional, primarily residential, *differentiator, analyzer*	19,562	270	PhD	$5,660/yr
Northern Kentucky University	4 yr + graduate, professional, primarily commuter, *low-cost, prospector*	11,473	73	Master's	$1,800/yr

Based on Comte and White (1999). For demonstration purposes, assumptions were made about the strategic approach of each university not evident from the case material in Comte and White (1999).

other private colleges surround ABC that range in size from fifteen hundred students to eighteen thousand students. Since ABC has an enrollment of eight thousand students, one might exclude from analysis institutions that are much smaller or larger in size, such as under five thousand and over fifteen thousand, or that do not offer the same relative range of degree programs (exclude colleges with only bachelor degrees or universities with a plethora of doctoral programs).

There is not an abundance of competitor information in this case, but we do know that ABC is considered to be in the high price range of local private colleges yet it discounts this rate to remain somewhat price competitive. In terms of spreadsheet information, ABC has a balance of commuter and residential students, and the largest programs on the campus in the areas professional studies (business, education, law, and engineering). The beginnings of a competitive spreadsheet would look like Table 5.3.

With limited information, we can determine that ABC University is not the low-cost producer in this group and seems to be more of a differentiator, given its focus on professional programs and "boutique" liberal arts degree programs. We do not yet know how these programs align with their competitors' programs, so we do not know which university is the most differentiated.

In terms of ABC's competitive approach to the market, one could generally conclude that given the turbulence in the presidency and the lack of a clear strategic direction for the university from the board, ABC has been reactive in nature. One can discern the following strategic characteristics about ABC University:

Domain Establishment and Surveillance (Analyzer)

- ABC has generally maintained a stable set of programs yet, through President Hilliard, has ventured into new boutique degree programs that connect them with the community.

Growth (Analyzer)

- Though minimal, growth has occurred through new program development in current markets—again, the boutique degree programs.

Table 5.3. Competitive Spreadsheet for ABC University.

	Description	Enrollment	Highest degree	Tuition per year
ABC University	4 yr + graduate, professional, boutique liberal arts degree, residential, commuter	8,000	PhD	Under $20,000
Competitor A	4 yr graduate, science, primarily residential	5,000	Master's	$15,800
		12,000	PhD	$17,800
Competitor B	4 yr + graduate, professional, primarily commuter			

Based on Comte and White (1999). For demonstration purposes, assumptions were made about competitors A and B that were not presented in the case.

Operational Problems and Solutions (Defender, Prospector)

- Technology is updated to keep up with current trends (prospector); however, it is not employed for program development (defender).
- Technology is not employed to improve efficiency. Registration and other systems are paper-based. Staff drive the quality of the systems such as having friendly relations with students (defender).

Dominant Coalition and Management Succession (Defender)

- Administrators below the president come up through the ranks and stay in the organization for a long time.

Planning (Reactor)

- Although Dr. Hilliard had a vision, it was not evident that any of the three approaches to planning were employed.

Structure (Defender)

- Functional organizational structure with extensive division of labor.

Control (Defender)

- Budget-driven and top-down, although it is not clear exactly what control systems are in place.

Coordination and Conflict Resolution (Defender)

- Decisions made through chain of command, either vice presidents or president.

Performance Appraisal and Maintenance (Defender)

- Budget and enrollment driven as compared to past performance.

Overall, it is clear that ABC has primarily defender characteristics, although in terms of market domain and growth ABC exhibits more analyzer traits. Going back to Table 5.3, we would first include the information that ABC is a differentiator-defender and then attempt to determine the competitive strategy and characteristics of its competitors (see Table 5.4).

An analysis of this additional information suggests that ABC University is best positioned as both a differentiator and a defender (score 23, 30) in Figure 4.1, the three-dimensional model of colleges and universities in the information age.

Evaluating the Current Market Position

In evaluating a college's current market position, campus leaders and planners have to ask themselves two questions:

1. Are we satisfied with our institution's general position in the market (as defined by our resources and philosophy) given the risk associated with that position?
2. Are we satisfied with our institution's position in the market niche given our position relative to our competitors (competitive approach and characteristics)?

Question 1 deals with a college's acceptance of its position in the market given the specific university type that it is aligned with and the danger related with its particular position. Institutions must assess their own risk tolerance, regardless of their position in their market niche, and determine whether they are comfortable with their current position. Defender organizations tend to be the least risk tolerant whereas prospectors seem to thrive on chaos (Peters, 1987). In our case, ABC University finds itself fairly close to the small college sector and getting closer every year as student enrollments continue to drop. This decreasing resource base increases its peril by shifting ABC toward Zone 1. As a competitive defender institution, ABC's board seems to have a low tolerance for risk and has tacitly decided that this additional risk is not warranted, although they have not examined the potential benefits derived from competing in this market niche. The board should therefore move onto the next step, which is repositioning the university in the marketplace.

Question 2 is posed when the college or university is comfortable with the risk associated with their market position and

Table 5.4. Competitive Spreadsheet for ABC University Including Competitive Strategy and Approach.

	Description	Enrollment	Highest degree	Tuition per year	Strategy
ABC University	4 yr + graduate, professional, boutique liberal arts degree, residential, commuter	8,000	PhD	Under $20,000	Differentiator, defender
Competitor A	4 yr graduate, science, primarily residential	5,000	Master's	$15,800	Low-cost, analyzer
Competitor B	4 yr + graduate, professional, primarily commuter	12,000	PhD	$17,800	Low-cost, reactor

Based on Comte and White (1999). For demonstration purposes, assumptions were made about competitors A and B that were not presented in the case.

addresses the institution's competitive approach and characteristics as compared to the market niche. If ABC's board had a greater tolerance for risk, the board could then examine the possible benefits and costs related to competing as a small differentiator-defender university. ABC may then discover that in its new domain it has the broadest number of degree programs. This would allow ABC to become the greatest differentiator in the market niche and thereby create a sustainable competitive advantage that could be easily protected, given ABC's defender characteristics.

If ABC felt that its programs were too costly to maintain, it could shift its strategy to a low-cost producer, given its larger resource base and the fact that defenders focus upon cost-cutting measures. Regardless of its competitive approach in the niche, ABC would be accepting its market position at the cost of increased risk, thus becoming the "big fish in the small pond."

As we describe in Chapter Four, intraniche competition requires that colleges and universities not get caught in the middle of the continuum of competitive strategies in their niche but create a distinct position among their competitors. ABC would then determine its strategic position in the niche relative to its competitors by using the competitive spreadsheet and deciding how to clarify its position in the industry sector in a way that separates it from the other institutions.

Choosing a New Position

Colleges and universities that decide to reposition their institutions must study their position and determine which university models will reduce the institution's risk to an adequate level (move it from Zone 1 toward Zone 3). In terms of repositioning ABC, the board has several choices that will reduce ABC's risk given its current market position (move it more firmly into Zone 2 and perhaps into Zone 3):

- Increase its resource base and move toward the comprehensive university model or niche or even newer models.
- Dramatically increase its resource base and its provider-orientation and move toward an R-1 university model or niche or newer models.

• Increase its consumer orientation and become an emergent university model by creating a new niche.

The repositioning of ABC University, or any other institution, should be decided through a strategic planning process (see Dolence, Rowley and Lujan, 1997). This process identifies key performance indicators for the university, assesses their external and internal environments, matches strengths with opportunities, and selects the strategy or strategies, goals, and objectives that best fit the university's mission and market position. This methodology can be modified to fit any competitive type of college (defender, prospector, analyzer) because planning is a critical component of each type's characteristics. Reactor organizations will have the most difficulty, since planning is not the normal behavior pattern for this type of institution.

Once the institution has decided its alternatives in terms of the university types it could be, the next phase is to construct competitive spreadsheets (similar to Step 4) for the new niches (public or private) the college plans to inhabit. Shifting to a new niche may shift an institution's competitive approach and characteristics in light of its new competitors.

It is also quite advisable that institutions looking to shift their positions to a new niche ascertain, prior to the switch, which alternative would require the least amount of effort or be the most palatable in terms of the institution's competitive approach and characteristics. Successful implementation of a position shift is partially dependent upon the flexibility of the institution, its desire to change, and the amount of change required (Kotter, 1978; Peters and Waterman, 1982).

To apply this step to ABC University, if ABC decided to increase its resources and compete in the comprehensive university niche or the R-1 niche, ABC might find that its differentiation strategy is fairly plain as compared to larger private universities because these universities may have far more doctoral programs. ABC would therefore not be able to defend its market position and might have to become an analyzer in order to determine which strategy, low-cost or differentiation, would be most effective in the comprehensive university or R-1 niche.

Becoming an emergent or hybrid university type might be easier for ABC because it could remain a differentiator (specialty programs) but increase its consumer orientation through analysis. As an analyzer, ABC could adapt some of the more innovative instructional delivery systems employed by prospectors in the industry to their existing programs. Regardless of which alternative is selected, ABC will have to change at least part of its strategy in order to accommodate its new market position and make appropriate internal adjustments.

It is critical that institutions understand that they must make a choice in terms where they would like to position their university and what university model, niche, or general strategic direction they would like to follow. Without a clear choice, universities will become stuck in the middle (Porter, 1980) between various university models or niches and therefore not offer students a distinct choice.

Once the institution has decided where it wants to be in terms of the university type and its competitive approach and characteristics, the next set of processes deals with implementation issues—how does the institution "get there from here." In Part Two we focus on positive and negative forces for change and how the change process must align the college's mission, structure, and market position.

Part Two

Implementing Strategic Choices

Chapter Six

The Hard Facts of Implementing Change

Up until this section of the book, we have addressed the issues of what strategies colleges and universities have available to them to secure their position in the new millennium. In developing a clear understanding of which strategies make sense for a particular institution of higher education, campus leaders and strategic planners have accomplished a great deal. But this is only the first part of the strategic management process. What is needed now is the ability to carry out the strategic plan, that is, implementation.

In Part Two, we examine the difficult issues of implementation that challenge college and university administrators, faculty leaders, and strategic planners as they move from planning to managing the strategic direction of the institution. We begin by describing what implementation is and how it works. Then we look at many of the problems campus leaders encounter when they try to implement change or new programs.

When one looks at nearly any strategic management text, the discussion of implementation usually is one of implementing *structure*. The point the authors of these textbooks are making is that to achieve success in carrying out strategies, the organization must adopt a specific structure to carry them out. *Structure* is the pattern of how organizations arrange people to maximize their talents and skills within specific task groupings to accomplish goals and objectives. Most of these authors go on to describe a series of structural choices, which usually include *simple, functional, multidivisional* (or the *M form*), *conglomerate, matrix,* and *network* or *virtual structures.*

When an organization has decided upon a particular strategic plan, planners and administrators are then charged with altering or creating an organizational structure to best carry out that plan. Once an organization has chosen the proper structure, the implementation process moves on to identify specific people and tasks to carry out the intentions of the planning process. In Part One, we described sixteen strategic choices colleges and universities have, discussing what sort of structure the institution should adapt to carry out each strategy.

That's the theory—and we do not try to argue that the theory is not sound. However, as is true of any theory, the theory does not contain the detail that practicing administrators need in order to choose and implement a structure that will successfully carry out the strategic direction of the institution.

This is a problem that faces strategic planners in colleges and universities, just as it faces their counterparts in other sectors of the economy. As we described in Chapter One, one of the central challenges to the implementation process is developing the support systems with the organization that will sustain the institution's strategic direction, one that both the institution's internal and external constituencies support.

Implementing change is hard. Implementing change means that the framework that people throughout the campus have come to know and trust as part of the predictability of campus life may no longer serve the same purposes for them. Depending upon the severity of the change, jobs may be lost, departments may be rearranged or even eliminated, support services may change dramatically, relationships among faculty may change, programs may be reengineered or slowly eliminated, and the ways people on campus work together may be entirely different. These are not simply hard realities, they are scary realities for campus constituents. No wonder that resistance or apathy often accompanies the mere prospect of implementing change. In this part of the book, we examine these issues and attempt to provide some solutions to help the change process succeed with the least possible campus disruption.

To begin this broad discussion, we look in this chapter at several of the generic issues that many, if not most, campuses face in implementing changes that can lead to the traumas alluded to above. These topics include stratification of administrators, staff, faculty, and students in the change process; the pros and cons of top-down change; the pros and cons of bottom-up change; the process of consensus change management; the pros and cons of change leadership; the pros and cons of using outside change agents; the pros and cons of imposed change (generally); the costs associated with change; and the reality of environmental change. We conclude the chapter with a description of Lewin's force field analysis as a way of helping change managers determine the level of positive and negative forces prior to attempting to implement change.

The Variety of Campus Constituencies Involved in Change

Change on college and university campuses occurs in several different strata of campus life. Further, change in one area generally will have an impact of one degree or another on other areas. This is an important concept because when the strategic plan calls for changes that affect students, for example, that change will also affect faculty, staff, and administrators. As a result, it is important for implementers of change to understand that they are not operating in a vacuum. Change in one area might bring resistance from other areas of the campus where one might not have expected that anyone would be particularly interested. By taking this broader view of the impact of change, implementers will take greater account of the entire campus when developing change scenarios; be certain to include affected people, departments, and operations in the change decision; keep communication high and reciprocal with people who will be involved with or affected by the change; and seek to make the change experience a positive event as much as possible for everyone involved.

This, again, is hard. This is a time-consuming and costly exercise that involves a tremendous amount of grassroots activity. Certainly it is impossible to please all of the people all of the time. Modifications to the change will be suggested or even imposed as people throughout the campus have their say. This can be very frustrating, and although the political process of trying to reach a consensus can also be a political tool for stopping change, through perseverance and support from campus leaders the process can make the actual transition smoother and easier. To understand this at a deeper level, we now look at each of the constituent groups to develop a clearer picture of who they are, what they want, what they will tolerate, and what their relationships are with other campus groups.

Administration

From the president's office (or chancellor's office) through the vice presidents (or vice chancellors) through campus services department heads to academic deans, every campus has a plethora of administrators whose primary job is to make sure the campus runs smoothly. Most of these people look at the campus as a whole. They are aware of the many parts of the campus, but they make their overall decisions based on the overall good of the campus. This makes their orientation much different from the other groups we will discuss here.

As in business organizations, college and university administrators have a tremendous amount of responsibility and wield great power in making decisions about campus budgets, growth, external communication and relations, and internal structuring. The administrative part of strategic planning, therefore, needs to focus on these issues and explore what administrators can do to implement the campuswide aspects of the plan effectively.

Faculty

On most campuses in the United States, college and university faculty have a strong belief in shared governance. Already wholly in charge of the academic program of the campus, faculty members often feel that they should also have a voice in campuswide decisions, especially if those decisions affect the academic program. This is generally the area where faculty members and administrators encounter conflict, as one side may claim that the other side violated its rights given the nature of a particular decision. Shared governance, unfortunately, is not well understood by either side in a lot of cases, and this lack of understanding clearly adds to the problem.

The faculty of a college or university in the United States has sole responsibility for developing and delivering the campus's research agenda and academic program. Whether the institution is provider-driven or consumer-driven (as we discussed in Chapters Two, Three, and Four), this responsibility belongs with them. In most cases, the campus also grants faculty the power to carry out this responsibility. Shared governance issues arise when administrators question the academic program or unilaterally decide to alter or eliminate a particular program. In a perfect world, change in academic programming should begin with the faculty and then go through the academic and administrative channels to the governing board for approval. Sometimes, however, administrators might make a decision on a given academic program based on program review, concerns expressed by board members, budget-related concerns, or perhaps even the precepts of the campus strategic plan. The result is predictable—resistance from the faculty and charges of violation of shared governance by administrators.

When policy is imposed on faculty, the trust relationship between faculty and administration suffers. What is lacking is a thorough understanding by everyone involved regarding the nature and level of power the two groups actually have. In an environment of shared governance, the faculty has power over academics and the administration has power over the general well-being and management of the campus, yet both parties need to develop effective forums for communicating with each other and coming to consensus on issues that impact both areas. Without this, implementing a strategic plan can become nearly impossible.

Staff

Administrators and faculty members tend to overlook staff members in the decision-making process. Although faculty and administrators are highly dependent upon staff, rarely do they feel that staff should be included in campuswide decision making. The reasons for this include the feeling that as employees (very much as in a business concern), staff have little stake in the campus beyond their paycheck, that staff are not academically qualified as are faculty members and most administrators, and that staff really don't understand the complexities of the academic life. From a power perspective, most staff members have very little personal job power and may not have much group power, unless they are formally organized into a union. Even here, their power concerns salaries and benefits, never academic issues. Staff thus tend to be treated as peripheral to the general activities of campuswide issues such as strategic management.

This is, of course, a mistake. To repeat, both faculty and administrators depend heavily on staff to support their own activities or to carry out their decisions. If staff are truly not personally and emotionally involved with what is happening on campus, the level of support they provide will be minimal at best. If staff feel they have a stake in the decisions that academics and administrators make, however, the quality of their support will rise appreciably. It is also important to remember that staff control the quality of operations across the campus, from mowing the lawn to making sure that members of the board know where and when their next meeting will be. Involving staff in major issues such as a strategic plan is yet one more way of gathering support for the successful implementation of that plan.

Students

For most colleges and universities, students are the primary purpose for the institution's existence—even on research campuses. This understanding gives students a certain amount of power. Further, students pay tuition, which on every campus is a major source of revenue. This fact provides students with even greater power. In today's world, students are activists—perhaps not in the sense that they were in the 1960s and 1970s, but they are more involved with the quality and content of their education. They want to have a voice.

There is a love-hate relationship between students and other campus groups. For example, the student grapevine will identify whom they consider to be "good" versus "bad" faculty members, staff who are helpful and those who are problematic, administrators that try to work with students and those who seem to work against them. Nevertheless, students are much less complacent today than they have been in the past. Especially as tuition rates rise, more students want a say in the campus decisions that affect their education, and that often includes strategic planning.

The biggest problem in dealing with traditional students as a group is that their stay on campus is temporary and their passion for campus activities is fairly well confined to their residency. Some campuses are trying to extend that passion through more effective alumni and foundation relationships. Research One and smaller private institutions seem to do a good job at continuing the relationship than do most of the colleges and universities depicted on Figure 3.2. Regardless, it is a real mistake not to include students (and perhaps alumni) in major campus decisions, since this is the very group that academic programs seek to benefit. Further, the thought that students really don't know what they want from their college or university is a notion that often proves to be false once students are invited to participate.

Governing Board

The governing board of a college or university has a curious position on the campus. The board generally meets periodically and is made up of people who are mostly from businesses and other organizations that are apart from the campus. Their numbers change from time to time, based on the state regulations or constitution and bylaws of the campus. For the most part, college and university governing bodies have no sense of the day-to-day life of the institution, yet they hold tremendous power.

In state and county institutions, the board is really a board of trustees who act on behalf of the true owner of the college or university, the state or county, in protecting and enhancing the academic programs the state or county has mandated. For private institutions, the power remains the same, but instead of representing owners (governments), private college and university boards represent founders, major donors, alumni, and grant givers in preserving and enhancing the academic program of the campus. In nearly every instance, they have the power to do whatever they feel is appropriate to uphold their trust, including hiring or firing the president or chancellor, approving budgets, setting campuswide policy, approving or discontinuing programs and services, and literally anything they feel they need to do in the best interests of the whole campus.

Administrators tend to be much more familiar with board members than are the faculty. Faculty know who the board is and what it does, but they do not normally take an active interest in what the board is doing (with the obvious exceptions of when the board needs to approve or review a particular academic program, or when the board makes policy on, for example, a faculty salary model). The faculty know that the board's decision is final, so the relations that do occur between these two campus constituencies are formal and respectful.

Certainly there are pros and cons to all of this. Some of the pros are that there is no question as to where final authority resides, even in the issues related to shared governance; that as a mostly external body, the board can be presumed to be more objective; and that as representatives of major external forces, individual members of the board can bring great wisdom and strength to a major campuswide decision-making process. Some of the cons are that boards make final decisions on academic issues, and this potentially infringes on academic freedom; that by being temporal to the campus, some board members may not fully understand campus realities and academic issues; and that the often political nature of board appointments has the potential of allowing parochial external issues to affect decisions made about the campus.

External Forces

As Rowley, Lujan, and Dolence point out (1997), colleges and universities live within greater communities that have expectations for the activities of the academy. Understanding and being able to respond appropriately is one of the cornerstones upon which modern campus decision making must rely. How much of this response to external expectations, however, should be included in campus decision making?

We find it interesting that several accreditation agencies are becoming more concerned with how well individual colleges and universities are able to demonstrate that they are listening to their external constituencies, both in terms of the type of education they are delivering and how effectively their students are performing based on their educational experiences. This is accountability, something the academy has been somewhat slow to embrace. Nonetheless, there are a variety of trends that are pushing college and university campuses to develop paths of communication with crucial external constituencies to help assure that academic programs are needed and effective. We do not see these trends reversing themselves in the foreseeable future.

Again, however, how much should external forces be involved with decision making? Certainly there is no place in the micromanagement of campus life for external groups. On the strategic level, nonetheless, we believe there is room and that it is appropriate that a select number of well-positioned and well-informed external experts serve in an advisory capacity. Many campuses do this already, and many have several advisory committees assisting in strategic decision making at the college, school, department, and even individual program levels. This practice does involve the issue of appropriateness, and it is a trend that many academics may find disturbing and threatening. If the plan is properly managed and communicated, however, the integration of external constituencies into the planning process can be extremely beneficial to the campus in introducing new ideas, objective evaluation, and potentially strategic partnerships that can help develop new areas of resources. It can be a win-win situation.

How Decisions Are Made

Implementing change is not simply an issue of who the various groups are in a decision-making event, it also involves how decision makers make their decisions. Essentially, there are three choices regarding decision making: top-down, bottom-up, and consensus.

Top-Down Change

Top-down decisions that try to impact the change process of a college or university are those that strictly follow lines of power and responsibility. This can begin at the governing-board level. As we've already stated, most boards have the power to do whatever they feel is in the best interest of the campus, and because they have the power, their decision is final. In other instances, where a board has hired a strong chancellor or president, this is the person who might well make campuswide decisions. If this person has strong support from the board, it may be impossible to have her or his decision overturned.

Pros

Not all top-down decisions are necessarily bad. Certainly in a time of crisis, top-down decisions are much more effective than any other kind. When it is clear that the campus must make a dramatic change from traditional academic programs to newer programs, top-down mandates may be the most effective way of instituting change. Another positive situation might be that of a highly respected and benevolent president or chancellor being the person that the campus community looks to for guidance, particularly for campuswide issues. (We are fully aware that this depiction sounds like the storied college and university presidents and chancellors of a time gone by, but while this is not a common model in today's world, the model does exist in some places.)

Cons

The biggest problem with top-down decision making is that it is very difficult to gain lower-level support for it. People might tolerate it in a crisis, but they don't want it as a norm. Another problem is that these types of decisions tend to be unilateral in a multilateral world, and therefore the quality of the decision may be suspect. Still another problem is that these decisions tend to put the decision maker in a box; that is, once the decision has been made, there is no easy way of unmaking it.

Bottom-Up Change

A different approach to decision making is referred to as bottom-up. In bottom-up decision-making, people throughout the organization bring forward ideas, opinions, and potential actions in a sense of camaraderie and empowerment. People toward the bottom of the organizational structure have tremendous position power (which is true of most college and university professors, particularly tenured professors). They decide what areas need attention and then go about proposing what to do about them. When upper levels of management essentially act as pure administrators, making sure that resources and needs are well matched, and do little in terms of proposing changes themselves, this is a true form of bottom-up decision making.

Pros

Bottom-up decisions have the advantage of already having ground-level support, the place where decisions are implemented. Not only do people at the so-called "bottom" of the organizational ladder have the motivation to implement changes they have proposed, they also already have most of the knowledge needed to get the change actually accomplished. Organizations that facilitate bottom-up decision-making also have the advantage of being able to have flatter structures, structures that have a minimal amount of midlevel management. This can save the organization a great amount of money. Further, bottom-up decision making may work well in a very calm environment where the changes will have predictable results and cause very little disruption to the rest of the organization.

Cons

Bottom-up decision making is slow and cumbersome. There may be little coordination between decision makers, especially in larger organizations. For example, a department of computer science (located in a college of arts and sciences) may want to use university resources to build a campuswide network based on Apple's Macintosh technology while a department of computer information sciences (located in a college of business on the same campus) may want to use university resources to build a campuswide network based on Microsoft's NT platform. From another perspective, bottom-up decision making does not take appropriate advantage of upper levels of administrative expertise in coordinating, securing and distributing resources, and providing marketing or other external information resources. Finally, in a chaotic environment, the inability of top management to assert their strategic agenda is exacerbated by a structure that is not used to having decisions made in this manner.

Consensus Change In a Shared-Governance Environment

A plethora of organizational experts tell us that consensus decision making is the preferable decision method. Decision-making power is shared across the organization. In colleges and universities, this is the basis for the notion of shared governance. Major decisions are presented to the entire community through discussion, analysis, and compromise, and then the various groups reach a decision—the hope is that it will be a consensus decision. (What we mean when we talk about *consensus* is that everyone is able to agree on a common solution.)

Change affects everyone in the organization. By employing a consensus style of decision making, everyone has a say. Everyone is franchised. However, just as in a democratic election, some people may not be involved in the process. Also, people know that they can build coalitions and consequently may be able to have their side prevail in future decision-making events. This is a political atmosphere that has its own particular pros and cons, but it is one in which teamwork can flourish.

Pros

A consensus decision is the best because there is negligible dissent. A politically derived decision is still good because a majority of people have supported it and resistance is minimized. This type of decision making is more egalitarian and therefore more difficult to attack. With a consensus decision or a strong political decision, implementation is fairly routine.

Cons

A consensus is nearly impossible to achieve, and when one looks at the variety of opinions and passions that reside on most college and university campuses, developing a consensus might appear to be going after the impossible dream. Most campuses are therefore left with the political solution, and politics can be ugly. Rowley, Lujan, and Dolence (1997, 1998) spent a great deal of time talking about politics on the campus and the need for effective leadership (both administrative and academic) to help assure that the discussion and maneuvering aspects of campuswide change become a positive exercise and not an exercise in futility. The consensus and political processes are also time-consuming and can seriously damage opportunities that could positively benefit the organization.

What It Takes to Be an Effective Change Leader

Leadership is the key to effective change management. Here we are not just talking about the campus president or chancellor; we refer to academic leadership, staff leadership (to a fair degree), student leadership, and governing board leadership. Implementing change takes a campus from familiar territory to the unknown in a lot of instances, and having campuswide leadership that understands the importance of the change, the method of change, and the likely results of change is crucial for success. There is no other effective way of envisioning and implementing change.

The key to effective campuswide leadership is effective communication, and the keys to effective communication are openness of the process, honesty, building trust, listening, choosing the proper forms for discussion, and agreeing that it may be OK to disagree. If these were simple concepts, there would be no need for this book. As all campus leaders know, these are highly complex ideas that the pressures of a busy campus life make even more difficult. Personalities and egos get in the way. On one campus a president might decide that she has the only solution and ends up in endless battles with faculty and students over her dictatorial style. On another campus, the tradition of hostility between the faculty and the administration is infused with mistrust and dislike. On still another campus, a very large campus, people in one area don't even know people from other areas, and they don't care. These examples are all issues of leadership, albeit bad leadership. In these environments, shared governance is a battle instead of a format for building. What is needed is a *leadership turnaround* (which we will discuss at length in Chapter Nine) whereby campuswide leadership is able to turn down the rhetoric of mistrust and increase the atmosphere of cooperation and understanding. Also, this has to be truly campuswide. If campus leaders are unable to find common ground, there is little hope for success of any strategic change initiative.

The Use of an Outside Change Agent

We believe that there is enough expertise on most campuses that the need for an outside consultant is unnecessary. On some campuses, however, either the expertise to implement effective change is not there, or the problems are too difficult to overcome by an insider. In these cases, the campus might want to find a qualified outside consultant to help them through the difficult parts of developing and implementing their change process.

Who These People Might Be

Choosing an outside change agent is a risky business. One might say that the woods are full of wolves and one goes into those woods at one's own peril. Unfortunately, there are many people who hold themselves out as experts who in reality are not. There is no national accreditation for consultants, so it is truly a world of "buyer beware."

There are, fortunately, a number of people who have both the expertise and experience to be helpful to a campus. To find these people, campus leaders might want to talk with leaders on other campuses that have had positive experiences, talk with colleagues at national professional organizational meetings, or read the literature for articles about successful as well as unsuccessful change events. Though difficult, there are ways of finding effective consultants if that is the need of the campus.

Pros

The outside change expert or consultant may bring the knowledge, wisdom, experience, and tools that can help a campus move forward. Better consultants work under contracts that assure satisfaction. Being "external" means that the person will be much more objective than is true of people mired in the difficulties of the campus, and this can be extremely helpful. Finally, the consultant may be able to add a perspective to the campus discussion that may effectively provide a format for effective change.

Cons

Not all consultants are competent. Many outside consultants are unrealistic about their fees and the level of service they are willing to provide. When the contract is done, the consultant walks away and has little ongoing responsibility for what happens on the campus. As an outsider, the consultant may not adequately understand the roots of many of the problems with which local colleges and universities struggle. Also, many consultants run into resentment from campus leaders and campus constituents who don't like the idea of an outsider telling them how to solve their problems.

What is the bottom line here? If the campus is able to solve its own internal problems, it should do so. If a campus is unable to solve its leadership and communication problems on its own, however, hiring an external change expert makes good sense. We add the caveat that campuses need to select such a person carefully and meticulously.

Mandating Change

The mandate for change may come from a variety of sources, but when that mandate is unavoidable, campus leaders and strategic planners often struggle with deciding how to proceed in the implementation process. As we have discussed here, there are a variety of choices, including top-down, bottom-up, and consensus. Probably most campuses will become involved with the political process in trying to reach consensus, and this can prove to be very frustrating to campus leaders. From time to time, college and university leaders eye the tactics of business to see whether they can help them. There is very little from the analysis of business, however, that can be helpful.

The Difference Between Business and the Academy

The world of business is based on public ownership and depends on two strategic realities to survive: growth and profitability. Neither of these two strategic aspects necessarily applies to the traditional academy (though one could argue that growth is important in its relation to resource accumulation, but for most colleges and universities, there are physical limitations that mean that on-campus growth is not much of a possibility). These two strategic orientations affect everything: governance, operations, outcomes, accountability, staffing patterns, and decision making.

In terms of decision making and implementing change, businesses can easily mandate changes from the top. Chief executive officers (CEOs) are empowered by their boards of directors (who represent the stockholders) and normally held to high performance standards that assure meaningful growth and positive profitability. The CEO is a powerful person who answers only to the board and does not have to be concerned with issues such as shared governance (unless they choose to). Essentially, when the CEO says that a particular operation of the firm will no longer be performed, that's that. No discussion is necessary with the people involved with that operation, no appeal, nothing. The decision is final, and midlevel managers make it their business to implement the decision as quickly as possible. (However, many businesses have adopted a far more communicative process to implement their plans more smoothly.)

This is hardly the world of the academy. Although a board will select the president or chancellor and provide that person with certain mandates (as we demonstrated in the ABC University case in Chapter Five), because of shared governance, the president or chancellor seldom has the power to make broad sweeping decisions such as, "Let's get rid of the school of music," without encountering major roadblocks from the academic faculty.

Where Business Tactics Work

What is interesting is that, because not all of the campus is academic programming, there are portions of the campus where business tactics work. At the University of Northern Colorado, for example, the strategic plan called for some major revision in its enrollment management. Once the board of trustees signed off on this portion of the plan, the president and vice president for student affairs essentially told the registrar's office to put its plan in place. In the end, the registrar's office complied.

We are not implying in this example of pure top-down decision making that there was no one in the registrar's office involved in developing the plan; clearly there were several people from that office involved. They helped map out the problem, looked at a set of alternatives, and with the university's strategic planning committee mapped out the plan that the president then brought forward to the trustees for approval. The changes the plan called for, furthermore, were reached by consensus.

Where Business Tactics Don't Work

It is hard to find any area of the academic side of the house that would respond well to top-down mandates about the academic program. Both as a reality of shared governance and as a result of the faculty's ownership of the curriculum, decisions that involve the faculty can hardly ever be top-down. (The possible exceptions might be certain small private colleges or campuses dominated by paternalistic presidents or chancellors.) In the rare occurrence when a board of trustees might mandate closure, revision, or inclusion of an academic program, their authority may be strong enough to have it implemented. Nonetheless, such an event would not be surreptitious, but rather the result of many hours of negotiating with faculty and administrators before reaching such a momentous decision.

Identifying the Costs of Change

Another major aspect of the change process is that of cost. Even eliminating a program can't be done without incurring some monetary costs (severance, transfers, notifications, and perhaps legal bills) and prestige costs (loss of alumni support, decline of reputation, and demoralization of campus faculty and staff). These costs are one of the greatest deterrents to implementing change.

As suggested, there are two types of costs: monetary and prestige. It is possible for campus leaders and knowledgeable staff to determine monetary costs. This can be done well in advance of approving the change so that decision makers will know what they are and can budget for them (as we discuss at length in Chapter Seven) prior to approving the decision. What is more, this is a study a college or university *does* want to conduct. It is demoralizing to be planning for a significant strategic change only to discover that the campus does not have the resources to support it. It is also dangerous to go into a change process and discover that the costs associated with that change are beyond the ability of the college or university to provide.

Measuring the prestige costs associated with change, either negative or positive, is much more difficult. In a reductionist change, people will feel a sense of loss. To counter this, the college or university needs to be careful to let everyone affected know what is happening and why. This notification must include alumni, and the campus needs to go further here to offer assistance if the demise of a given program might hurt alumni professionally. In an expansionist change, it is nearly impossible to know beforehand how people inside and outside the college or university will respond. In academics, a new program is not necessarily perceived as a quality program. Many people believe that academic programs are like fine wines—they need to mature over time before they are ready to be consumed. Certainly marketing (another cost) and expanded communications (still another cost) can help, but as any marketing expert will tell you, the results of most marketing efforts are nearly impossible to predict accurately.

Keeping an Eye on the Environment

No planning or implementation process is going to be successful if that process is not imbedded in a thorough understanding of both the internal and external environments. Certainly, examining a college or university's environment cannot be a one-time event. As volatile as the present educational environment is, and as likely as it is that this environment will continue to become more complex, continual environmental checking is required. For example, if a given college or university were to choose to move toward a competency-based educational system, not only would it be important to know the capabilities of current technology and its ability to measure different aspects of competency, but it might also be important for that particular institution to be involved with the research that would make a competency-based system work more smoothly. Determining for which areas learners and employers are calling for more competency-based learning opportunities would also be important.

Force Field Analysis

Dealing with resistance to change can be frustrating and demoralizing to campus leaders and strategic planners in both the planning and implementation stages. To counter this resistance adequately, it is useful to understand where that resistance comes from, what it represents, and how strong it is. Force field analysis is one of the tools that campus leaders and strategic planners may use to discover the causes and strength of resistance. Further, force field analysis can also reveal tactics to reduce or even eliminate that resistance.

Kurt Lewin (1951a, 1951b), a well-known researcher and writer in the development of several organizational behavior theories, did research on the phenomenon of change. He developed force field analysis as a model for measuring some of the factors that push for change and those that push against it. Force field analysis involves three factors:

- The change event itself—understanding what the change is and who and what it affects
- Identification of a set of forces that support the change
- Identification of a set of forces that oppose the change

Describing the Change

In using force field analysis, the planner must first identify the change as completely as he can. Understand what the change involves, the people, the timing, the resources affected, and the reasons for the change. For example, let's assume that a smaller, but well-respected liberal arts college with a positive national reputation has decided to offer some of its courses over the Internet. In the short term, the college wants only to offer a few lower-level courses, but in the long term is interested in making an entire degree program available. According to Lewin, a planner must first describe and understand the change itself. The description might go something like this:

> Four professors who currently teach basic general education courses need to develop one of their courses for application on the Internet (release time, training, and program material costs total $225,000). The campus will need to build an interactive computerized classroom to conduct these courses (cost of the classroom is $350,000). The campus will need to hire an Internet administrator who will design and administer the Web site ($50,000 per year). The Web site program will need to be marketed (estimates of $40,000 per year). The campus's academic affairs committee, the faculty senate, and the provost

must all approve of the new program (four to six months time). A computerized program to facilitate online registration will have to be created and implemented (purchased registration program from a vendor will cost $125,000). Everyone on the campus will need to understand what the new program is all about, how it will work, and how it will affect them ($1,000 in materials, and 120 hours of meeting time, including coordination). If all goes well, the four professors will develop their four course offerings for the Internet (after training and working with the new Internet administrator); the new Internet administrator will have developed a high-quality Web site ready for putting up the class offerings and have interactive capabilities (including video); publicity will go out; students will register; and on the day of launch, the administrator will upload everything to the Web site, and it will work.

Beyond the hypothetical example we provide here, we will simply say that the planner needs to describe the change as thoroughly as possible, particularly making sure that those who will be involved with or affected by the change are considered.

Identifying the Forces that Support or Resist Change

Once the planner has identified the change, he needs to identify two lists: one that identifies all the important forces that support change, and a second one that identifies all the important forces that resist change. Let's look at the example. In looking at the change itself, we can identify several things that will naturally become positive or negative forces in this proposed change.

- The total estimated cost in dollars is $791,000 to produce four classes on the Internet. Some of these costs will recur year after year, so this is not only a one-time drain of resources, it will have permanent resource implications as well.
- A great amount of time will also be involved in training, developing, marketing, making decisions, and problem solving.
- New facilities need to be developed and built.
- Choice of four professors to develop the four courses could be a mixed bag—the college might find that no one wants to do it or that more people want to do it than are needed for the program.
- Campuswide support can also be a mixed bag. For this example, let us assume our active faculty make most academic decisions after heated and often political debate.

- An appreciable market must exist from which to draw students who will be willing to take up to only four classes, and there will be a cost to develop that market.
- An especially energetic member of the board of trustees pushed hard to develop this program.
- The new registration program could be expanded to cover on-campus registration, but it would cost an additional $500,000.

The point here is to look at all the various constituents who have a stake in the change or will be affected by it and determine whether they will support or resist the change.

From all these data, the planner can then develop the two lists. Here's a very brief example:

Positive Forces	*Negative Forces*
1. Increased institutional exposure	1. High cost
2. Strong board support	2. Negative faculty politics
3. New campus facilities	3. Highly time-consuming
4. One professor is enthusiastic	4. Program needs at least four professors
5. Initially, seventeen learners show interest	5. Program needs 120 students to break even
6. Campus can use the new registration program	6. Full registration program is expensive

Again, the list of positive and negative forces would be fairly extensive, with perhaps ten to twenty items on each list. Also, please note that it is not important that the two lists have equal numbers of forces, or that they necessarily oppose each other. In the preceding list, for example, Positive 2, strong board support, is not opposed by Negative 2, negative faculty politics.

Measuring the Positive and Negative Forces

With the two lists of positive and negative forces, the planner should next conduct a survey. Using a Likert-type scale, the planner would construct a series of questions designed to measure each of the items on the two lists. For example, for item Negative 2, negative faculty politics, a question might be, do you believe that faculty politics on this campus is destructive? The response might look like the following:

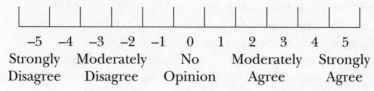

–5	–4	–3	–2	–1	0	1	2	3	4	5
Strongly Disagree		Moderately Disagree			No Opinion		Moderately Agree		Strongly Agree	

The planner would then give this questionnaire to everyone on the campus who would be involved with or affected by the change. They would be asked to complete the entire questionnaire and mark their responses by placing an X on the bar to indicate their answer. Assuming that the planner uses usual and accepted techniques to distribute and collect questionnaires, the results would provide the planner and campus leaders with a fairly graphic and empirical picture of what forces for and against change actually exist and how strong they are.

Let's assume that for item Negative 2 the results demonstrated a mean of –3.4 and a standard deviation of 1.7 (based on an 80 percent randomized response rate). Campus leaders can construe this information to read that the campus as a whole apparently perceives faculty politics as counterproductive, perhaps even destructive. The standard deviation would suggest that the level of agreement is diffuse, but that at least 66 percent of respondents scored this item on the negative side. Now we can conclude that politics is a strong negative force that the college will need to deal with effectively in order to move forward with the change.

Campus leaders would need to analyze the entire questionnaire and would find a variety of results. Some items that the planner had originally listed as potentially important might test out as insignificant (average score around 0 or extremely large standard deviation, say around 5) and can therefore be dropped from further discussion. Other items might prove to be much more of a surprise. Perhaps the results for item Positive 5, seventeen students have shown interest, demonstrates a mean of 1.5 and a standard deviation of 1.2. Campus leaders might conclude that these results indicate that no one is particularly concerned with the low initial numbers. Still other items might test out to be pretty much as predicted. Let's assume that item Positive 2, strong board support, demonstrated a mean of 3.9 and a standard deviation of 0.4. This would provide strong evidence to conclude that the campus views board support as very important and very strong (and we could perhaps infer from this that "if the board wants it, the board will get it").

Using the Results to Move Forward

Lewin tells us that once we have developed the force field analysis and are certain of its validity (in our case, following the analysis of the questionnaire data and the development of two final lists that contain all surviving items and their measures, or strengths), the analyst then knows what the organization is facing in terms of specific forces and their strengths. The next step is to work to reduce the negative forces and increase the positive forces. In our example, there would be little need to do anything about gaining further board support, since it is already seen as strong and significant. However, turning around negative faculty politics would appear to be a necessity.

What the Lewin model shows us is a practical, empirically based, logical, and straightforward method of examining change and moving toward implementation. This method holds a great amount of promise for college leaders and strategic planners in that it objectifies the process of change and provides a clear picture of the areas that need attention and those that simply need support. This is a powerful tool in developing an understanding of what campus leaders can do to implement strategic changes.

In the next chapter, we look at specific strategies that campus leaders and strategic planners can use to implement change. These strategies might be used within the force field analysis we presented in this chapter, or they might be used directly in situations where the pros and cons are already known and accepted.

Chapter Seven

Eleven Approaches to Implementing Successful Strategic Change

Implementing strategic change in colleges and universities can be accomplished in a variety of ways. In this chapter we examine several methods of effectively implementing change and discuss how each particular method works. Prior to choosing a method, however, make sure all the homework has been done. The plan itself needs to have been already adopted. The college or university's direction should be established and broadly accepted. Campus leaders and strategic planners should have completed a careful analysis of the factors surrounding change and should understand what elements on campus and off campus will impact the implementation process (through a tool such as force field analysis, described in Chapter Six). Only after all of this preparation is complete should campus leaders and strategic planners look toward implementation. Otherwise, leaders and planners risk being blindsided by the unknown and make success much more difficult to achieve.

The Eleven Methods of Effective Implementation

In the following discussion, we examine eleven approaches to implementing successful strategic change. Depending upon the campus involved, campus leaders and strategic planners may be successful implementing change with only one method. Or perhaps two or more methods might be needed to implement change, again given the type of campus involved, the amount of resistance in place, and the nature of the change itself. With good information about what the methods are and how they work, administrative and academic leaders and strategic planners should be able to determine what methods are best for the campus and move forward toward implementing the change that will help better align the campus strategically with its own particular environment.

Specifically, the eleven methods that campus leaders can use to implement strategic change effectively are

- Using the budget to fund strategic change
- Using participation
- Using force
- Establishing goals and key performance indicators
- Working within the human resource management system of the campus to plan for change and to create change
- Using the reward system to foster and support change
- Working with or changing institutional culture through faculty and staff development
- Working with or moving away from tradition
- Developing and using change champions
- Building on systems that are ready for or are easily adaptable to strategic change

The first eight of these methods are some of the strategies that most colleges and universities might consider for changing their existing structure as they consider which implementation strategies are most appropriate for their campuses. We refer to these as the immediate results options. The last three strategies are paradigm shifts and provide additional advice for campus leaders and strategic planners who need to explore issues that accompany implementation. These are the longer-term options.

In this chapter, we look at the first eight implementation strategies by developing a full description of what each strategy involves, how it is likely to work, and where it is appropriate. In the next chapter, we will look at the remaining three strategies and provide a more theoretical discussion of the challenges of implementation in general.

The Immediate-Result Implementation Strategies

People are naturally impatient, particularly when they want something to change. This is certainly true in strategic planning as in other decision-making activities. Beyond that, the situation often requires immediate action if opportunities are not to be lost or threats can be rapidly managed. Campus leaders and strategic planners need to know what implementation strategies are available to them. Based on the appropriateness of one strategy versus another, given the specific characteristics and needs of a campus, they can choose the strategy that will be most effective. In this section, we identify eight implementation strategies for leaders and planners to choose from and also give some insight about the appropriate use of each.

Budgeting to Achieve Strategic Change

A college or university's budget is the single most powerful controller of activity there is on a campus. If the campus does not provide resources to support a program or service, that program or service will not be carried out. If a campus allocates resources specifically for a particular type of program or service, however, the chances that that program or service will be carried forward increase significantly (though, unfortunately, not necessarily as effectively as planners may have hoped). Therefore, control of the budget is control of the strategic plan and control of the campus. Swain (1988) understood this as he helped successfully direct an early form of strategic planning at the University of Louisville, as did Roach (1988) in a later successful strategic planning effort at West Texas State University. Detweiler (1997) also tells us that a strategic commitment to improving technology at Hartwick College allowed an easy budget swing to support its strategic goal through a highly participative planning and implementation process. Based on its strategic plan, the University of Central Florida used a formula-based budgeting system to tie institutional priorities to resource allocation and resource management (American Association of State Colleges and Universities [AASCU], 1993). Finally, at the University of Southern Colorado, administrators used strategic goal priorities to free up $3.2 million (16 percent of its state budget allocation) to achieve twelve major strategic goals it had identified in its strategic plan (AASCU, 1993). To understand better how to acquire this control and use it properly, it is useful to look more deeply into the issues that surround an academic budget.

Understanding the Process of Budgeting

Although there are variations of how different campuses prepare their budgets, there are also several common practices. In this discussion, we confine ourselves to the more common practices. One very common practice is to use the previous year's budget as a starting point. Departments throughout the campus use the previous budget as a baseline and then request additional allocations based on a variety of economic and academic (or operational) needs: inflation, parity forces in faculty salaries, union salary demands, state-mandated expenditures, new programs, new faculty or staff, new technologies and technology upgrades, and new and replacement supplies of all sorts. Departments submit their budgets through the hierarchy of the campus up to the vice chancellors or vice presidents of the campus. The next step occurs when vice presidents or vice chancellors prepare their divisional budgets, which may mirror all the requests they have received (though this is very rare) or reflect realities and priorities with which the vice chancellors or vice presidents are constrained. The next step occurs when the chancellor and all the vice chancellors (or president and all the vice presidents) get together with budget officers and negotiate the campuswide budget. By this time, there will be fairly reliable data available regarding expected tuition income, grants and contracts income, state allocations (for public institutions), foundation income (including giving and interest earned), and other miscellaneous income figures (such as settlements, property sales, rollover resources, and so forth).

There are rarely ever enough resources to meet needs, even after the vice presidents or vice chancellors have massaged their own budget figures. This top-level body, normally chaired by the president or chancellor, consequently has the difficult responsibility of making requests match expected resources. The most common way of working through these issues is to prioritize campus needs, values, and programs. (For example, a campus with three recognized programs of excellence may prioritize requests from these areas over all other academic program requests.) The final step is to take a finalized budget and present it to the governing board for formal approval. Most boards recognize the importance of this part of their responsibilities and take a fair amount of time to review the budget and ask questions; of course, they have the right to change anything they wish. Upon their final vote of approval, the budget is adopted and everyone on campus then knows exactly what he or she will have to work with during the coming fiscal year—which also means that their programs or operations will operate for the upcoming period as mandated by the board. (State and county colleges and universities would have to then have their budgets approved by the appropriate legislature and signed by the governor or county executive.)

Another variation of the process is zero-based budgeting. Some colleges and universities are using this more severe technique as a way of instituting specific ending dates and criterion on any and all programs and operations across the campus. In zero-based budgeting, each department submits its budget based on absolute need. Further, departments must justify their budget requests. Then, as the budget moves up the hierarchy to the board, requests are compared based on justification. Many campuses find this type of process cumbersome and excessively time-consuming, but the general reputation of zero-based budgeting in business has proven to be a positive appeal to other colleges and universities who are trying to operate their campuses on a more business-like basis, or who have serious problems with resource allocation.

The first two methods of budgeting involve a bottom-up approach where the operating unit was asked to project needs and justify expenses based upon the unit's tactical plans. The third method for setting budgets, the use of a master budget, is a top-down method that is devised based upon the calculation of expected revenues, estimated expenses, and the desired level of surplus. This budgetary system starts with the identification of all revenue streams for the institution (that is, tuition, grants, gifts, government aid, etc.). Forecasts estimating revenue for the upcoming year are calculated based upon historical trends (enrollment patterns) and the probable impact of the strategic plan on revenue generation. Once total revenue has been calculated and a level of acceptable surplus capital agreed upon by the board of trustees, the chief financial officer adjusts the operating units' budgets to reflect both the priorities of the institution and the availability of funds. Operating units are expected to adjust their functions and objectives accordingly (Barfield, Raiborn, and Kinney, 1998).

Budgeting Strategically

As suggested above, there are several decision points throughout the budget process where budgeters can ask the question, how does this expenditure support the college or university's strategic plan? This is a clear advantage to zero-based budgeting, since budget requests from the ground up need to be justified. However, in the add-on method we first described, there are still several points at which budgeters can ask the question—obviously, the sooner in the process, the better.

A key to success for the strategic plan is to make certain that those who will be involved with the budget are also involved in the strategic planning process. Also, as planners develop the plan, they need to build budget considerations into it. For example, when a college or university decides to establish a virtual learning program on the Internet, they need to determine the budget requirements of the new program and be able to establish an appropriate priority for the program. When budget planners begin the budgeting process, they can then tie the strategic priorities directly into the budget and, like zero-based budgeting, will already have the justification in place as the budget moves on to the governing board. Over time, budget decision makers across the campus will be able to tie the entire strategic plan into the campus budget process.

Implementation Through Participation

Perhaps one of the greatest differences between strategic planning in business and strategic planning in colleges or universities is the importance of planning in the academy in a collegial and participative environment (Rowley, Lujan, and Dolence, 1997; Birnbaum, 1991). Participation means that everyone affected by a process is involved in the decision making that leads to a final decision. Participants are also involved with implementation. Many people believe that such an environment does exist in colleges and universities and are often particularly attracted to such institutions because of this quality.

In the academy, even the terms *collegiality* and *university* refer to a cooperative and positive environment in which knowledge is generated, analyzed, and disseminated. So one would think that when it comes to strategic planning, let alone the implementation of the strategic plan, that a participatory environment on any college or university would be natural and common. This is unfortunately not the case.

Based on our many personal experiences as well as the review of many case examples, not only does a participative atmosphere not exist on many campuses, in its place is a system of decision making that is riddled with parochial politics and bereft of significant cooperation. Further, it is the lack of participation and the resulting distrust and power struggles that lead to the failure of the strategic planning process in many colleges and universities. For example, Swenk (1999) found that the unsuccessful strategic planning process at Western University was primarily the result of the failure of administrators to encourage or even allow faculty to participate in the process.

All of this is regrettable. As Gilmour (1991) tells us, shared governance is not one of the unique features of colleges and universities; it is also part of what makes campus operations effective. By bringing together both the administrative and academic sides of the house to make major institutionwide decisions, the potential for assuring that such decisions accurately reflect the administrative and academic realities of the campus are significantly increased. But as one can see in the political systems that exist on many campuses, distrust between faculty and administrators is more natural and common (Dooris and Lozier, 1990).

Politics stems from the issue of the control of rare resources (Pfeffer, 1992). It's really an issue of power to make decisions about those resources. Foote (1988) also reminds us that power is shared in a university setting among administrators, faculty, the board, and even students in many cases. Since the boundary between who controls what is often confused or at least gray, conflict results, distrust grows, and true participation declines. When these issues become part of the strategic planning process, politics is inevitable (Marcus, 1999).

Participation, cooperation, politics, conflict, and implementation are all behavioral aspects of the strategic planning process. Bryson and Bromiley (1993) suggest that it is the behavioral side of the strategic planning process that explains why a planning event is either a success or a failure. A report by AASCU (1993) (based on a study of Cleveland State University) suggests that the primary obstacle to implementation of a good strategic plan resides in the people in the institution that resist change. In looking at the problems in strategic planning at the State University of New York at Geneseo, AASCU concluded that the major problem of implementing the plan was a history of nonparticipatory decision making about resources, which resulted in a highly reticent faculty. Controlling these behavioral realities and encouraging participation becomes one of the major determinants of success in the strategic planning and implementation processes.

In Chapter Nine, we discuss at length working directly with these behaviors and moving them into a positive direction to assure the best outcomes for individuals and institutions as a whole. We note here, however, in talking about the behaviors of participation, that people throughout the campus make personal decisions about how they will act or respond (behave) in certain situations. These decisions can then be a significant plus in moving the strategic plan forward, or they can spell its doom.

So, who's in charge of controlling these behaviors? Several authors tell us that the responsibility for assuring that participation occurs lies with the chief executive officer, the president, or chancellor of the campus (Farmer, 1990; Cyert, 1988; Keller, 1983; Steiner, Miner, and Gray, 1982). Once again, from personal experience and from a study of several cases on the successes and failures of strategic planning, the role of the president or chancellor, more often than not, is pivotal in learning what worked and what did not work.

We believe that one of the significant problems is perhaps the proliferation of the business model of strategic planning. Many college and university administrators, as well as a surprising number of campus strategic planners, do not understand that for them, strategic planning is different, that the business model doesn't work. For these administrators and planners, the mistake they make is to adopt the top-down approach, which is the common model for most business strategic management texts. As we have pointed out earlier in this book (and as Rowley, Lujan, and Dolence [1997] also pointed out) this may well be the primary reason planning fails. Understanding the crucial role of participation can reverse many of these problems. Here again, it is up to the president or chancellor not simply to recognize the imperatives of participation, but to enforce them.

Enlightened college or university strategic planners have recognized the importance of participative planning and have consciously sought to ensure it. For example, Cline and Meringolo (1991) tell us that in its successful planning event, Pennsylvania State University was so concerned about assuring participation by a broad sector of the campus constituency that it placed particular emphasis on developing participation within its strategic planning and implementation processes. Brown (1988) credits participation by both faculty and administrators at the University of North Carolina at Asheville and cooperation between faculty and administrators for the success of their strategic plan in taking a relatively new campus and building bridges between the campus and the community. Morrill (1988) thanks a highly collegial and cooperative group of faculty and administrators for the success of strategic planning at Centre College of Kentucky in reversing enrollment declines and budget deficits.

Participation is not without its problems. The more people involved, the more time will be involved. Cyert (1988) says it took him five years just to convince deans and department heads at Carnegie Mellon University to support the planning process. Further, the more people involved, the less likely that a top-down desired planning outcome will emerge unscathed. As Foote (1988) points out, the thirty-eight members of the strategic planning committee at the University of Miami represented the top administration, midlevel administrators, and faculty. This was an unwieldy group. Decision makers, nonetheless, believed that bottom-up and top-down planning needed to be combined if a successful plan was to be implemented. Foote tells us that the final plan was an amalgam of unit and program plans with overall campus plans. It worked, primarily because of the partnership of every area of the campus in the planning process. Elsewhere, Detweiler (1997) tells us that the strategic planning process at Hartwick College in New York was successful because a significant number of board members, faculty, administrators, staff, and students all affirmed their values for education (which included a strong commitment to technology) and went on to build their strategic plan based on those shared values. A smaller college, Hartwick nonetheless saw the importance of campuswide cooperation in developing and implementing its plan.

Using Force to Implement the Strategic Plan

In most situations related to colleges and universities, the use of force to create and implement a strategic plan is a very bad idea. Just as college and university campuses are creatures of collegiality and shared governance, there is usually no good reason for the governing board or the president or chancellor to mandate change on a college or university campus and then resort to measures of enforcement. Further, given the probability of state support and state reorganization capabilities, it is much less likely that force would be acceptable in a state college or university (though not out of the question), and more likely to be accepted in private colleges and universities, where resource bases can be much more tenuous and less likely to attract outside support.

Issues related to public relations, program excellence, maintenance of faculty and staff quality and morale, and legal concerns also bring into question the wisdom of attempting to use force. In most situations, therefore, the other methods we describe in this chapter should be the first options when campus leaders and strategic planners consider the most appropriate methods implementing the strategic plan. There are, however, exceptions.

The most obvious exception is a situation of crisis. When a college or university finds itself in a life-threatening situation, force may be the only way of making significant changes that will save the campus from going under. Steeples (1988) gives us an excellent example of such a situation as he describes the perils and ultimate resurgence of Westminster College of Salt Lake City. Founded in 1874, the college had a history of poor planning, poor governance, chaotic external events (including a student enrollment of zero during World War I and near bankruptcy during the Great Depression), but had managed to hold on. However, in the 1970s and 1980s things got bad again and the campus twice had to face closure decisions. Under a new president and a strong board, the college decided to do strategic planning and see what it might do to salvage the situation. The plan called for major retrenchment and refocusing, including the dismissal of tenured faculty, closure of programs, and the renaming of the college. In a surprise move, the board abolished tenure and put all faculty members on one-year contracts. It is not surprising that there were many negative outcomes from the decisions called for in the plan, including censure by the American Association of University Professors and a demand from the Northwest Association's Commission on Colleges that the college show cause why its accreditation should not be revoked. In anticipation of these and other challenges, the board, president, and planners had done their legal homework and made their changes within legal parameters. This did little to curb the poor public image produced by the changes, but it helped the institution survive. By the end of the 1980s, stability had returned to the campus, enrollments started to climb once again, and the long history of running financial deficits was over as the college began to run budget surpluses. The campus began to look forward to a much brighter future than had seemed realistic only a few years before.

Two crucial points are apparent from Steeples' example. First, the bad situation had to be pretty extreme and life-threatening for the board and administrators to toss out collegiality and shared governance in going forward with a strategic planning exercise. Second, there is no substitute for doing all the homework necessary prior to going into this type of planning mode. Of course, however, this is exactly why strategic planning works in circumstances such as those faced by Westminster College. It calls for an extensive inventorying of both the internal and external realities of a campus, then builds the plan based on those realities. Many realities—academic, programming, public relations, financial, legal, and human—are part of the inventory. The strategic planning process will not be successful, regardless of the amount of force the board and top administrators use, without the homework of coming to terms with all of them.

Luckily, very few campuses face the type of dire situation Westminster College faced, and therefore do not need to go to the extremes that Westminster did in charting a new direction. In a crisis situation, force may be the only alternative—though it should always be the last alternative. The bottom line here is that it is more important for the institution to survive than it is for specific programs or individuals to stay with the institution. Without this type of understanding, it is entirely possible that the strategic plan will get sidetracked, the situation will continue to deteriorate, and ultimately the institution will fail and everyone will lose.

Using Goals and Key Performance Indicators to Achieve Strategic Change

Another method of implementing change is through goals and key performance indicators (KPIs). This method is based on a series of achievement goals that quantify all the issues the strategic plan has addressed (Rowley, 1997). It requires everyone who is responsible for implementing the strategic plan to sign off on the plan and to commit to reaching the goals the plan has identified.

This is clearly a simpler process for quantifiable areas than nonquantifiable ones. For example, one strategic goal relating to controlling the quality of students entering the college or university might look at performance on the SAT exam and call for a ten-year upward movement of ten points for all admitted learners. Each year, the plan might benchmark a one-point improvement. In this example, the actual enrollment statistics can easily be measured and reported. (Please note, the strategic plan is not so simplistic that it only outlines goals and benchmarks. An effective plan must also state how university recruiters will change their recruiting practices to ensure that quality goes up while quantity does not go down.)

Quality issues, especially those related to academics, are much more difficult to relate to KPIs but not impossible. Normally, surrogate measures will serve as proxies for quality events. For example, if the strategic plan calls for more effective teaching (a phenomenon that requires a variety of measures), the plan might contain one measure for performance on exit exams. American Assembly of Collegiate Schools of Business (AACSB) schools of business can administer a standardized exit exam that measures each learner's performance on business and economics knowledge and provides the school with individual, school, and national comparisons. This example is a surrogate, but it also represents a fairly well recognized measuring method. To use it in the KPI process, a college or university might state that its goal is to have test results for its school of business as a whole average in the ninetieth percentile of all AACSB business student results.

For this method of implementation to be effective, it is important that all areas of the campus participate, find ways of measuring performance, and commit to carrying out the plan to achieve strategic objectives. At West Texas State University, for example, division heads developed a series of "key result areas" that helped division members track their goals and progress in that campus's successful strategic planning exercise (Roach, 1988). At Penn State University at Hazleton, the long-range planning committee closely monitors a variety of "strategic indicators" on an ongoing basis that measure university performance in enrollment management, academic programming, and academic results, as well as site and capital goal attainment (Penn State University at Hazleton [PSUH], 2000).

The long tradition of the academy believing that reputation is the best measure of quality outcomes doesn't square well with current trends toward accountability. Colleges and universities are already looking for ways of measuring quality performance, and this is a trend that should continue for some time, thus making the KPI approach to implementation more and more realistic.

Working with the Human Resource Management Structure to Achieve Strategic Change

Second only, perhaps, to the budget, a college or university's human resource base also has a tremendous impact in deciding how and whether a campus strategic plan will be implemented. As mentioned earlier, if administrators, faculty, and staff decide that they are not going to support the strategic plan, it will be extremely difficult for the institution to implement it. But if people across the campus get behind and support the plan, there should be little concern that the plan will be successfully implemented.

It is the first of these possibilities, however—administrators, faculty, and staff deciding not to support the strategic plan—that is the major reason that strategic planning fails in colleges and universities. In many ways, this is both predictable and understandable. Organizational behavior theory notes that there are three types of change and predictable reaction to it (Barnard, 1938):

- People support change that they themselves propose.
- People support change that others propose, as long as they know they will benefit from the change.
- People resist all other types of change.

One of the major problems with most strategic planning is that people throughout the organization fear the strategic planning process because the results of the plan are essentially unknown. (Will I lose my job over this? Will I lose funding over this? Will my workload increase? Will I be forced to do things I don't want to do?)

As we suggested earlier, it is crucial that campuswide leadership be behind the strategic planning and that communication about the plan be highly interactive. Most fear of change comes from a lack of information. This basic fact, along with a possible tradition of bad experiences related to top-down change, makes resistance to change completely understandable. Yet these are the areas that colleges and universities need to work on to facilitate strategy implementation.

Sometimes the strategic plan will call for reductions of administrators, staff, and even faculty members. Of course, no one wants to lose his or her job, and people who are going to be terminated will naturally resist that change. When such terminations are appropriate, however, how the campus handles these events will not only reflect the strategic plan in action, but will also be a signal to the rest of the campus how much humanity the plan is able to demonstrate. For example, the University of Southern Colorado made some major decisions about its direction within a broadly recognized strategic plan (Shirley, 1988). That plan called for the reduction or elimination of some programs, staff, and faculty in preparation for strengthening other programs and potential centers of excellence. Southern Colorado went about the reduction in faculty and staff positions by notifying people more than two years in advance and accompanied this notification with provision of some out-placement and relocation services (AASCU, 1993). These considerate actions helped the strategic planning process move forward by keeping people across the campus informed and by handling the human resources of the campus with respect and care.

Communication is always a choice. People choose what to communicate and how to communicate it. But some methods of communicating are clearly better than others. It is regrettable that a great deal of important campus information is trivialized by publishing it in a campuswide e-mail or weekly newsletter. Given all the other e-mails that are sent daily and the plethora of unwanted mail, it is easy for these methods of communicating to get lost or simply tossed as they come in.

It is far better for campus leaders to work out their own differences on the planning process first and then, as a united team, begin personal communication with campus constituents in groups and in one-to-one conversations. This method is time-consuming, which is the primary reason that many campus leaders don't do it, but it is also a much more effective way of getting the message out and receiving grassroot responses to feed back into the decision-making system. It is our view that campuses must take the time and effort to make sure that all campus leadership is "on the same page" with strategic planning, and then take the time and effort to communicate effectively with the balance of the campus—otherwise, their planning processes are doomed to failure. If, however, in the first activities related to strategic planning, top campus leaders commit to forming a full-campus leadership team and also commit to a full and open communications process, the resulting strategic plans will have a much greater chance of succeeding.

Using the Reward System to Achieve Strategic Change

Related to the human resource approach we just described, it is important to recognize that people will respond better to the planning process if they believe it will benefit them. This essentially sets up the second type of change we identified above (people will support change that others propose if they believe it will benefit them). We feel that too many college and university strategic plans set out major overall goals for how the whole institution will benefit but leave a nasty implication that in order for the institution to benefit, individuals and entire programs may be eliminated, reduced, reengineered, or consolidated. This sets up the third type of change we identified above (people will resist change of which they do not know the outcomes). This is really too bad, because college and university campuses have tremendous rewards they can bestow on participants of the strategic plan who help successfully implement it.

Certainly in an era of stretched resources, not all rewards need to be monetary (though some can and should be). Release time, program development and recognition, personal recognition, improved relationships, a sense of community, and a sense of accomplishment are all nonrevenue-related rewards that provide individuals with a positive outcome for their efforts. Clemson University was able to tie strategic benchmark activities of faculty performance in its strategic plan directly to the reward system, and this helped Clemson successfully implement its strategic plan (Bennett, 1994). At the State University of New York at Geneseo, campus leaders were able to move its strategic plan along by creating a $100,000 capital venture fund (with home office support) to improve its research activities (AASCU, 1993).

As for monetary rewards, many colleges and universities are looking at methods for determining and rewarding merit. There is no single model of determining what constitutes merit on a college or university campus, as there is no particular model for how merit monies should be allocated. For campuses that are serious about implementing their strategic plans and recognizing the importance of their human core, tying merit to strategic objective accomplishment appears to be an extremely positive way of rewarding individuals as well as accomplishing strategic objectives and goals.

Using Faculty and Staff Development to Achieve Strategic Change

Organizations can achieve structural change in one of three ways:

- Identify individuals and departments that no longer fit within its strategic direction and can let those people go.
- Identify programs with which it needs to be involved and hire qualified individuals to create and carry those programs forward.

- Retrain existing human resources to meet the organization's emergent needs.

Depending upon circumstances, these are the choices organizational leaders have.

That's the theory at least. In colleges and universities, it's not that simple. For example, tenure assures that certain people and certain programs have longevity, regardless of how disciplines or markets change. Firing a tenured professor (for something other than cause) or closing down a program that is staffed by tenured professors usually results in lawsuits. For example, the University of Northern Colorado closed down two schools and let dozens of tenured professors go in 1982 in a general reduction of force that was made necessary by a decline in enrollments accompanied by a decline in the demand for graduates from those two programs. Lawsuits abounded for the next twelve years, and the university spent millions of dollars in settlement and legal costs. Further, the general morale of the campus, including censure by the National Association of University Professors, did tremendous damage to the campus.

Could the reduction in force have been avoided or handled differently? In hindsight, yes. The university had seen trouble coming for some time but did not engage in a longer-term downsizing and attrition strategy to close the programs and eliminate positions over time. With time, the university could have out-placed faculty who were no longer needed or could have retrained some of the faculty to allow them to move to other departments. Without this strategic orientation, the university was starting to face a crisis when it decided on the actions it did. In the end result, it is difficult to find any one or any program that benefited.

This example demonstrates more of the potential positive benefits of effective strategic planning and implementation. As the campus shifts its academic programs over time, it has time to look at its human resources and ask how applicable their personnel's skills will be over the next few years. When the college or university can determine that programs and services are going to change, that is when to engage in staff and faculty development. By retraining and realigning the human resources of the campus as trends become clear, leaders and planners can retain valuable people and keep them current.

Isn't staff and faculty development expensive? Yes. It is also very important to understand that terminations are expensive as well, perhaps more so than retraining. In the University of Northern Colorado example above, the costs were literally millions of dollars, and the costs to the university's prestige were incalculable. When one understands that even in a routine termination, there is severance pay, substitute coverage costs, downtime costs, replacement recruiting costs, start-up costs, and training costs, investing in training doesn't seem to be such an expensive proposition.

It is interesting to note that many campuses will include training costs in budgets and assign them low priority. When terminations occur, there is no choice to the campus—it must pay the costs of change. Strategic decision makers, therefore, need to better understand and address training in a more strategic manner so as to benefit both the college or university and the human resources of the campus.

Another interesting example of how a campus should use faculty and staff development to achieve change is at the University of the Highlands and Islands (UHI) in Inverness, Scotland. Less than ten years old as of this writing, the university is a consolidation of thirteen small colleges in the northern half of Scotland. Many of these colleges have long histories; some are relatively new. All were small with focused programs, and so it was difficult for them to compete with other major universities in Great Britain, including Edinburgh University, Cambridge, Oxford, and with colleges and universities in the United States. This created a "youth-drain," because students who left northern Scotland for education elsewhere seldom returned. With the continuing growth of Scottish patriotism, creating a larger, more complete university made sense to the Scottish community, and hence the University of the Highlands and Islands was born.

Beyond the challenge of creating one university out of thirteen dispersed campuses, UHI also decided to challenge traditional teaching methods and truly implement a new philosophy of teaching in which the learner is paramount in the educational process. This decision represents two major challenges and potentially an implementation nightmare. The two biggest challenges were to somehow unite the campuses into a single entity and to reorient the faculty from traditional research and teaching methods into a new learner-oriented philosophy. UHI turned to strategic planning to solve their problems.

UHI solved their delivery issues with distance learning and technology. Using interactive television, radio, CDs, video tapes, the mail, and the Internet, UHI was able to create a system that provided any student attending classes on one of the thirteen remote campuses or thirty-nine learning centers around Scotland with the knowledge base that comes from the full combination of the thirteen original campuses into one. The faculty orientation proved to be a much more daunting problem, as one might imagine. As one of the founders of UHI has suggested: "The objective is to get the instructor to give up being the 'sage on the stage' to being the 'guide on the side'" (G. Hills, personal communication, March 1998). The answer was to devote a significant portion of the budget to faculty and staff development. The university allocated as much as 10 percent of its budget to faculty and staff development, and as the consolidation was moving forward, the new learning philosophy was implemented right along with it. UHI is clearly a novel experiment in learning, but one that is sensitive to the move from the Industrial Age to the Information Age and that is strategically attempting to build an academic setting that serves its learners and communities in a new and effective way. Although UHI has its critics in Scotland and England, it progresses toward its goals. We believe it is a model that other colleges and universities around the world should examine seriously.

The Role of Culture in Achieving Strategic Change

A good basic definition of culture is the pattern of behaviors that members exhibit in conducting the central operations of the organization. This pattern of behaviors describes the attitudes, motivations, and predispositions that people throughout an organization tend to conform to when they do their work. Also, this pattern is general. One can observe this pattern through watching the day-to-day activities of everyone within the boundaries of the organization. People seem to work according to a particular code. They seem to do things in a common way and at a common speed. They are comfortable with their surroundings and operational methods. Furthermore, they don't like to change their day-to-day patterns. This is the heart and soul of culture.

In the academy, if one looks at how people conduct their activities, these cultural patterns become immediately apparent. Here people also feel they have a right to behave as they believe to be best. Various campus constituents believe that they have built their college or university over time and that the institution stands as testament to the "rightness" of their efforts and of those who have gone before. Being a part of a particular college or university campus is like being part of a brotherhood, a sacred position that deserves to be protected at all costs. This is very strong culture and a hard one to change.

In the strategic planning process, it is easy to view the types of strategic changes the plan proposes as affronts to the revered culture of the campus. If campus leaders and planners do nothing to address this concern, the full weight of the powerful culture can become a formidable block to change. Swenk (1999), for example, found that the problems faced at Western University were partially the failure of implementers to recognize and adapt to the cultural differences between faculty and administrator decision-making styles. If those who are trying to implement change can do so within the culture of the college or university, the chance of their success goes up appreciably.

So how do campus leaders and strategic planners do this? First, they must recognize that culture exists. For the newcomer or the outsider, culture is much more apparent because these people have come from other cultures and notice the contrasts. However, identifying culture may be a challenge for long-time campus leaders because the culture is so pervasive, common, and comfortable, and that without trying to identify it specifically, it can be completely overlooked. In our experience, campus leaders often feel that their own personal leadership abilities are far more important in the implementation process than the culture. This is usually a mistake, because the strength of culture often overpowers the change tactics of leadership.

Second, campus leaders and planners must understand that the culture is strong. Once they understand that the culture exists, then they need to understand just how strong it is. For example, an emergent cultural aspect at the University of Northern Colorado (after the firing of tenured faculty) was a faculty (good) versus administration (bad) environment. The president, who presided over the firings, remained president for another nine years and did nothing to try to heal the wounds, and therefore the culture not only survived but strengthened. When the board of trustees brought a new president on board to help move the campus into the next millennium, he was immediately met by resistance from faculty leaders, particularly when he proposed developing a strategic plan. (The reduction in force from 1981 had been done under the guise of a "Campus Plan for the Future.") Try as he would, the new president was never able to form a coalition with the faculty and the parts of the strategic plan that the campus did implement were generally nonacademic.

Third, campus leaders and strategic planners must realize that the culture can be as much of an ally as a foe. Given that there are many facets to an organization's culture, there are many parts of that culture that leaders and planners can use to build support for their strategic plan. At the University of Northern Colorado, the bad relationship between faculty and administration made moving forward on a strategic academic plan extremely difficult, yet the relationships between faculty and department chairs was fairly positive. If the university had been able to develop a broad level of support among department chairs, it is highly likely that it would have been more successful in implementing its plan. If campus leaders and planners examine the culture to see how it works, they can find places where they can forge a positive alliance and are likely to be more successful.

Fourth, campus leaders and strategic planners must build change from inside the culture. Once they create alliances within the culture, they can use those alliances to implement the plan. If the campus leaders and planners at the University of Northern Colorado had been able to forge a strong alliance with the university's department chairs (one-on-one, as well as in groups), the administration could have worked directly with the chairs (as full-partner decision makers) to look at the existent academic programs and then recommend areas that needed to change: areas that the university needed to enhance and even areas that they might need to downsize or eliminate. The chairs had generally a good relationship with the faculty (who have ownership of the academics of the campus), and it is reasonable to assume that a multitiered, ongoing conversation in which everyone felt involved would have led to the development of a long-term academic strategic plan that would have benefited everyone.

And fifth, campus leaders and strategic planners must use culture as a way of establishing the change more permanently into the fabric of campus life. This is one of the great reasons working with the culture is such an effective tool: once it is culturally acceptable for employees to embrace new methods of doing things, the support for seeing these new methods through is appreciable. When the norms of the culture include the acceptance of a strategic academic plan that will better prepare the campus and the individual professors for the future in a positive way, the plan goes forward with essentially no resistance.

Choosing the Right Implementation Strategy

Each of the implementation strategies we have presented in this chapter represents action-driven activities that can be successful in helping a college or university implement its strategic plan. Even on the surface, this information is knowledge of which many college and university campus leaders and strategic planners are unaware—at least from a strategic perspective. On a deeper level, these methods of implementation imply a commitment of the campus leaders and strategic planners to move seriously ahead with the implementation efforts. On some campuses, some leaders and planners have been willing to go through the exercise but have not fully committed to the actual activities of implementing the changes that the strategic plan has called for. They really never did support the premise of planning or strategic change.

For campus leaders and strategic planners who are committed to the need for strategic change, the options suggested in this chapter (as well as in the next) require total commitment. These choices work, but only when the proper groundwork has been established and the homework has been completed. With these in place, choosing the option that is most appropriate to a focal college or university becomes an exercise in common sense. The result should be a successful strategic planning exercise.

Chapter Eight

Why Gradual Change Is Most Effective

In the previous chapter, we identified eleven strategies for implementing change on college and university campuses. We went on to describe eight of these strategies as immediate-action oriented. The last three strategies are different from the first eight in that they are much longer term and speak to structural and leadership issues that cannot be transformed overnight. In this chapter, we discuss these last three strategies. We then present a more theoretical discussion of the general nature of change and the challenges of implementation to help the reader gain a full sense of not only the methods but also the nature of implementation itself.

Longer-Term Implementation Strategies

Change and strategy implementation, like long-term investment in the stock market, isn't just a matter of timing, though timing certainly plays a part in the change process. In some instances, time is of the essence, and identifying change that can make an immediate impact is critical to the survivability of the college or university. In the last chapter, we talked about forcing change, and also concluded that the only time when force is recommended is when there is a crisis situation and there is no time to waste before making changes that will save a campus community.

In this chapter, we look at implementation options that institutions have the luxury of accomplishing over time. Regarding these, campus leaders and strategic planners can delve more deeply into the basic structural tenets of a college or university's purpose and direction to determine what should change and how it should be changed.

In addition to timing, change and strategy implementation is also a matter of effectiveness. In our example of Westminster College in the last chapter, we identified many negative outcomes that resulted in the traumatic changes that were necessary to save the campus. Many of these negative outcomes are still in place at Westminster and may never go away completely. This is one of the negative outcomes of having to implement change rapidly, thus placing a cloud over programs, administrators, staff, and faculty in the process. To avoid many of these negative outcomes, change that campus leaders and strategic planners put into place over time tends to be much less disruptive, longer-lasting, and therefore much more effective.

Manipulating Tradition to Achieve Strategic Change

Tradition is part of a college or university's culture and by its very nature has a long-term effect. It is also a serious consideration campus leaders and planners need to take into account in designing and implementing the strategic plan. Tradition speaks to what the college or university has become. Tradition is historic and honored. It engenders reverence, awe, and inspiration. Just hearing colleges' names brings images to mind of past glories (or in some cases tragedies); people ascribe certain values or splendor to them; and many even think of certain of them as supreme models. When one talks about the traditions of Oxford, Cambridge, Harvard, Stanford, Berkeley, Boulder, Ann Arbor, or Kent State, there is a certain permanence of reputation that immediately enters the conversation. And not just these, but every campus—large and small, public and private—has traditions that create the same types of emotions and responses. Every campus has its traditions, and these traditions have a role in the strategic planning process in basically three areas.

First, traditions may be linked to mission. Although in their earlier book, Rowley, Lujan, and Dolence (1997) showed little regard for statements of mission, they agreed with many writers in the field that identifying mission is a crucial part of the planning process. For example, if a particular campus has a tradition of being one of the top research institutions in the country but does not have a tradition of offering high-quality applied business programs, campus leaders and strategic planners need to ask, Why are we spending resources on the school of business when we have other centers of excellence that need our support? In this case, the campus might work with another campus that has a high-quality business program to consolidate their two programs, phase out its own business program but form a strategic alliance with the other campus to maintain the business school connection, or restructure its business program so that each campus complements but does not duplicate offerings (and use resources to help develop excellence in those few areas).

Second, tradition appeals to alumni, donors, potential students, the community, on-campus students, faculty, and staff. In defining the strategic plan, campus leaders and planners need to assure these groups that their favorable attitudes toward the college or university are not in jeopardy. As we have argued elsewhere in this book, these are important constituents whose support is highly important to the strategic planning process. The strategic plan must address and demonstrate to these stakeholders how tradition can be strengthened and perhaps improved.

Third, positive traditions have always been built upon dynamic programs and historic events. They are fluid. There is probably nothing more devastating to a positive tradition than the lack of on-going positive campus development. Just as the statement, "It's not what you've done for me, but what you've done for me lately," suggests, no campus can rest on its laurels. For this reason, connecting the strategic planning process to enhancement of positive traditions is a powerful way of supporting the implementation process.

The Role of Change Champions in Achieving Strategic Change

Rowley, Lujan, and Dolence (1997) noted that college and university professors have developed the overwhelming majority of new offerings available in Internet learning. The point they make is that whereas some campus leaders and planners might view campus faculty as stodgy and unsupportive, a significant percentage of faculty is actually making the changes their campuses are trying to cope with in the strategic planning process. Furthermore, these faculty members are potentially significant allies in the change process. Campus leaders and planners need to identify them and bring them into the planning process.

For example, if a campus wants to start offering courses on the Internet, and it finds that three or four faculty members have already placed course materials or entire courses onto the Internet, it needs to bring these people into the process to help discuss and plan out how the institution should move forward on this issue (regardless of whether or not the college or university wants to include the courses of these particular professors in its initial offerings). These are people who will be enthusiastic about Internet course instruction and will be excellent resources in recruiting, training, and helping other professors set up the specific course structure the campus wishes to support.

This is one example of a *change champion* in the academic ranks of a college or university. There are also examples from every other part of the campus that support the presence and potential benefits of finding such people and bringing them into the strategic planning process. By including them in the process, providing support for their ideas, and building parts of the appropriate strategic plan with these individuals, leaders and planners find that change champions go back into their own activities excited and even anxious to help bring about the change. They work with their colleagues, try to solve problems, and take advantage of this new opportunity. Through these efforts they help implement the plan.

Brown (1988) relates how the University of North Carolina at Asheville created a university planning council, a board of highly influential faculty and administrators, who worked cooperatively with the chancellor to develop a successful strategic plan. This plan achieved many of its goals in transforming a relatively new community college into a four-year institution with programs of excellence and created a comparative advantage in its service area. This type of cooperative effort is clearly one way of developing change champions.

Cyert (1988) tells us that often the campus president or chancellor must be this change champion as well. As president of Carnegie Mellon University, Cyert spent many years working with

deans, department chairs, and faculty to create changes in programs that create more focus, vision, and excellence. Cyert knew
what needed to happen and also knew that developing campuswide support would require a sustained effort. He was willing
to stay the course, develop strong board support, develop strong
academic support, and finally move ahead with strengthening
Carnegie Mellon. Another example of top leadership as crucial to
changing the direction of an institution is that of Keuka College
in New York. Keuka was near collapse when a new president came
on board and patiently guided the college over a ten-year period
to a successful outcome (Bonvillian and Murphy, 1996). Again, by
staying the course and following the guidelines of an austere strategic plan, Keuka was able to attain its highest student enrollment
ever and successfully completed an ambitious capital campaign.

Building on Successful Systems to Achieve Strategic Change

Keller (1983) observed that it is always difficult to institute a strategic planning system on a campus that is generally enjoying success.
Perhaps there is real truth in the old adage, "If it works, don't fix
it." We agree with this tenet of planning. However, many campuses
do face problems and have systems that don't work. For them,
strategic planning is still an important tool for relieving problems
and achieving success. Probably all such colleges have parts of their
campus that do work; perhaps some parts are even excellent. The
subsystems that work are already a part of the campus and its culture; consequently, they provide an internal source of information
that can be particularly useful to the remainder of the campus as
it strives to develop and understand its appropriate direction and
purpose.

Certainly there are also examples of successful systems outside
the campus that can provide useful information for campus leaders and strategic planners as they seek to create a more holistic and
positive strategic direction for the campus. Although we have
argued against looking at the business model too much in developing a focal campus strategic plan, there is clearly nothing wrong
with looking at other successful college and university experiences
in trying to develop a schema of planning options that could work.

Throughout this chapter, we provide examples of campuses where the strategic planning experience has been both positive and negative to help provide campus leaders and planners with insight into what has worked and has not worked elsewhere. There are other sources available, including recently published case studies and Internet sources. Campuses can look within themselves as well as beyond their campus walls to find essential elements of success.

How to plan is another issue in developing an effective model. One of the caveats of successful implementation is to implement the strategic plan incrementally (described more fully in the next section). By carefully selecting areas of the plan that will be easier and more straightforward to implement, leaders and planners can achieve success in the early stages of the implementation process. With this initial success, it is then easier to move to the next area in the plan and implement it with added support and confidence.

Incremental implementation also allows leaders and planners to build trust with some of the more skeptical campus constituents. By choosing carefully the first areas for change and by demonstrating success, campus leaders should be able to point out to the campus that nothing deleterious has occurred. The change was implemented, and nothing bad happened. Trust-building can continue to develop after the second change, the third change, and so on.

Of course, this system of implementation also depends upon the inherent honesty of the process. If campus leaders and planners hope to lull the campus into some sort of a compliant state, only to "drop a bomb" somewhere down the road, all the potential for resistance will reemerge. Or what is worse, trust will be significantly damaged and the hope of moving the strategic plan forward may well be dead. If there are parts of the plan that will adversely impact one or more groups, it is important to

- Talk about the possibilities up front
- Include the affected people early on to try to build as favorable an outcome as possible (with the affected people having some say in those outcomes)
- Seek to minimize any negative outcomes as much as possible
- Keep the entire campus informed as the process moves forward

For example, if it is clear that campus resources will not support low-demand programs, leaders and planners need to identify those programs early on and inform those involved that they are being scrutinized. Then leaders and planners should have a broad discussion with those people about the available options. Obviously, the more time everyone has to discuss the matter, the better. In developing options, campus leaders and planners (as well as the people affected) should seek alternatives that cause the least amount of disruption, are kindest to the people whom the change will impact negatively, and provide an example to the rest of the campus that demonstrates the necessity of the action and the positive human approach taken by the campus. Finally, during and after the planning and implementation process, leaders must keep the entire campus informed and be willing to engage in open discussion.

The result will be the down-sizing, consolidation, or elimination of the program. Although this is not a happy outcome, it will at least be an outcome that is understood. Open communication and trust should be able to hold up during and after the process. The campus will also see that events happened in the best way they could. What is so crucial in this example or in positive-change events is that campus leaders and strategic planners never depart from an honest approach toward developing and implementing the strategic plan, not even momentarily. Trust is a very fragile commodity, and once those in authority abuse trust, it is nearly impossible ever to get it back.

Although there is some overlap among the eleven methods of effective implementation we have outlined here and in Chapter Seven (tradition and culture, for example), these eleven approaches suggest different orientations, time frames, and constituencies that might characterize one strategic planning setting versus another. So which one should any given campus choose? The hard answer here is that it is really an issue of understanding the circumstances within which implementation will occur. There is no way out of doing the homework to understand what the campus predisposition is and then looking at the eleven options as a set of choices. In the best of circumstances, one particular piece of the plan will require one particular method of implementation. However, it is possible with other parts of the plan that campus leaders and planners will need to use more than one method. For example, in looking at devising and implementing a strategic academic plan, particularly one that involves reprioritization or downsizing, leaders and planners might want to use cultural approaches, the human resource management approach, as well as the budgetary approach to create and implement the plan. In any event, leaders and planners must have full knowledge of their campuses, the needs for change, and the methods of implementing those changes in order to have the proper data sets from which to draw their change scenarios.

Prioritizing Strategic Change Areas

One of the keys to successful strategic change is understanding that one cannot change everything at once. Given the time and effort that goes into developing a good strategic plan, it is very tempting to believe that everything *can* change at once. From another perspective, no one in the planning process wants to be left out of enjoying the potential benefits of the change, and those who have gotten excited about the positive prospects of change will not want to wait.

As we have explained throughout, though, change, and especially strategic change, affects a great number of people, programs, and operations. This range of influence makes the change event a complex phenomenon. Further, as change takes hold in one area of the campus, there may be unexpected consequences that impact the focal area or other areas of the campus. These outcomes may cause campus leaders and strategic planners to alter parts of the plan or the implementation before moving ahead. This would be far more difficult if all areas of the campus were in the throes of change already. So an incremental approach is a far more effective implementation process.

Linking Strategic Planning and Strategic Implementation

Having identified the eleven different strategic implementation strategies, we believe it useful to step back a bit and look at the entire process to help the reader see the general concepts involved in developing and implementing a successful strategy. Numerous scholarly books and textbooks have defined strategic planning, or strategy formulation, as a set of decisions that are designed to create a competitive advantage in order to achieve an organization's goals and objectives (Pearce and Robinson, 2000; Porter, 1985). In Part One, we have treated strategy formulation as the process of deciding what is the best, if certainly not an improved position of the college in the Information Age given the college's resources, philosophy, competitive approach, and competitive strategy. Likewise, *strategy formulation* refers to both the decision-making processes and outcomes that colleges and universities employ to align or fit their mission with their position in the marketplace (the environment), given the limited resources and capabilities of their internal systems (Lawrence and Lorsch, 1969; Chandler, 1962). Galbraith and Kazanjian (1986) have referred to strategy formulation as a matching process; one matches an organization's competitive strategies to the industry structure and to the core skills and internal structure of the organization.

Given the preceding definition of strategy formulation, we define *strategy implementation* as actions taken by a college or university to put their positioning plans into action by either changing their mission, changing their environment, or changing their resources, capabilities, and internal operations. The key term in the definition of strategy implementation is *change;* can the college or university *make the necessary changes* in order to move the college into a better market position? Yin, Heald, and Vogel (1977) suggest that strategy implementation is dependent upon two factors: the inherent validity or strength of the plan developed to position the college or university (Do our decisions make sense in light of the available information?), and the ability to produce the changes the plan requires (Can we change ourselves or our market as required by the plan?).

Successful and Unsuccessful Implementation Plans

Under our definition of strategy implementation there are two types of successful implementation plans and two types of unsuccessful implementation plans, as suggested in Table 8.1.

Table 8.1. Successful and Unsuccessful Implementation Plans.

	Required Changes Made	*Required Changes Not Made*
Valid Plan	Type 1 success	Type 1 failure
Invalid Plan	Type 2 failure	Type 2 success

Source: Adapted from Yin, Heald, and Vogel (1977).

Type 1 Success and Failure

Success type 1 and failure type 1 are straightforward. The college or university develops a valid positioning plan and either can or cannot make the necessary changes within the organization or in the marketplace because they have or have not established processes for enacting change. If changes are made, they result in the better positioning of the college and a more sustainable competitive advantage. If the changes are not made, the college's competitive position will at best remain stable or perhaps deteriorate over time.

As an example, Marist College, a small college in Poughkeepsie, New York, realized that with Vassar in their vicinity, they could not simply be a traditional liberal arts college. Also, State University of New York (SUNY)-New Paltz, a state college, was only thirty minutes away, which had the effect of negating price competition. After looking at its alternatives, Marist adopted a differentiation strategy that focused on targeting academically above-average residential students from upper-middle-class families in New Jersey, Connecticut, Massachusetts, and Long Island, New York by providing professionally oriented programs. To do this, they needed to improve their competitive position by heavily investing in what their students wanted most—nicer buildings and grounds. Marist proceeded to devote their resources to new classroom buildings, up-scaled dormitories that overlook the Hudson River, and a Jeffersonian-style student center. These changes, coupled with an aggressive marketing campaign, has increased their enrollment and made them a very competitive small college in their service area.

Type 2 Successes and Failures

Type 2 successes and failures are of a different ilk. A type 2 failure refers to a college or university having the change processes in place so as to institute an invalid plan; that is, the institution is able to change either the market or its internal operation according to its plan but the results of those changes were not the desired or intended results. In many cases type 2 failures have very detrimental effects on the college's market position and can reduce its competitive advantage and increase its risk.

For example, Adelphi University in the mid-1990s dramatically increased their academic standards to try to become a more differentiated private university in what may have been classified by Adelphi as a fairly homogeneous competitive environment. Classified as a Doctoral One University, Adelphi University's tuition ranked among the highest charged by institutions of their class, which includes room and board. Furthermore, Adelphi University returned an unusually small fraction of their tuition revenues to students in the form of institutional scholarships, thus countering a fairly common trend among the more expensive schools (MEMEX Press, 1997). Furthermore, in exchange for the comparatively high tuition, students at Adelphi gained access to a faculty that earned marks for scholarly reputation averaging in the bottom 25 percent. The 1995 peer review of the scholarly quality of faculty conducted by the National Research Council rated faculty in mathematics and psychology as having scholarly reputation rankings in the bottom 13 percent (National Research Council, 1995).

The misalignment between the mission of Adelphi and the quality of its faculty had at least a short-term negative impact. In 1995–1996, the number of full-time undergraduates enrolled was considerably smaller than the norm for institutions of its class. Enrollment equaled 2,281 (national average = 7,312), a decrease of 5.5 percent from the previous year's enrollment. This rate of change in undergraduate enrollment was unusual given that the national average increased 0.8 percent (*Integrated Postsecondary Education Data System*, 2000).

We are not arguing that Adelphi's plan to increase its academic standards to increase its differentiation was necessarily wrong. But we are suggesting that this new mission in combination with minimally discounted high tuition and the relatively low scholarly rank-ing of the faculty seemed to lack face validity as a differentiation strategy. What value-added benefits, besides the changed standards, was the college offering potential students from *their* perspective to warrant such a high tuition?

Going back to our typology of universities, Adelphi seemed to try to move closer toward an R-1 university type, upper left-hand corner of the typology model (Figure 3.2), by increasing their provider orientation. However, they had little in the way of addi-tional resources to add to their operation to support the move toward the research model. (In 1994–1995, revenues from tuition and fees were 84 percent of total revenues as compared with 53 percent, which was the norm for schools in Adelphi's class. Endow-ments, which were nearly $10 million, were lower than the average $55 million for comparable schools and received a mere 1 percent yield [the norm was 5 percent] [Integrated Postsecondary Educa-tion Data System, U.S. Dept. of Education, http://nces.ed.gov/ ipeds /index.html]). Hence, they had what we would term an invalid plan. Without increased resources to buttress faculty schol-arship or hire new faculty, decreased enrollments were predictable given the mismatch between their desired repositioning and the actual position they obtained by implementing their strategic plan.

Type 2 successes are rather intriguing in that "success" occurs when the organization develops an invalid plan and fails to imple-ment it. We are sure that many colleges and universities may have type 2 successes, but these are not the types of successes that these institutions are bound to report, or that are reported in many publications, since these institutions would be admitting to a dou-ble failure. The real question with a type 2 success is, how did the organization manage not to implement the invalid plan? This question brings us back to the heart of implementation: What are the conditions under which change will or will not be imple-mented?

Levels of Analysis and the Change Process

Organizations are a composite of interlocking or loosely connected social and technological subsystems of individuals who interact with one another for a particular purpose or function (Weick, 1979).

For an organization to implement a strategic plan and produce a change in the position of the organization in the market, changes have to occur within these subsystems. The concept of level of analysis deals with the notion that as one widens the focus of one's analysis from the individual (micro level) to the subsystems (macro level) to the organization as a whole (ecological level), different factors come into play when discussing change processes and strategy implementation (Scott, 1981; Sherman, 1991). The following sections address concepts and methods of change at various organizational levels.

Change and Strategic Implementation at the Micro Level

Change and strategy implementation at the microlevel views the individual as the unit of analysis and focuses upon efforts with specific employees. For instance, Barnard (1938), Mosher (1982), or Thompson (1967), when examining a type 1 failure or a type 2 success, might argue that the managerial staff, the middle-level professionals in the organization, acted as buffers to the technical core, or the line worker, by deliberately not following orders that they believed would not benefit the organization or themselves. The plan called for changes to be made outside these employees' "zones of acceptance" and "zones of indifference," thus resulting in a rejection of the authoritarian nature of the plan by the employees. According to Ouchi (1981), this control mechanism acts as an informal check-and-balance system whereby employees who perceive radical or negative changes suggested by top administration countermand or disregard those orders.

Alternative explanations for the individual employee not implementing the plan may have simpler, less psychologically based explanations. According to Barnard (1938), two other reasons may exist:

- The employees may not understand the proposed changes in the plan and therefore are incapable of acting upon the changes.
- The employees understand the changes but are incapable of carrying them out because they lack the knowledge, skills, or the resources to do so.

Consequently, for a plan to be implemented and produce the desired changes at the *microlevel,* employees must understand the changes desired, possess the resources and skills necessary to make the changes, and feel that the changes will benefit all involved, including themselves. Implementation at the microlevel deals with the psychological and job performance aspects of change for the individual as dictated by the plan.

This is not dissimilar to Lewin's (1951a, 1951b) three elements of force field analysis that we discussed in Chapter Six as well as Lewin's three-stage model of change (unfreezing, moving, refreezing). First, one determines the motivation and skills readiness of the employees to change, given the requirements of the plan. This involves developing the employee's realization of a need for change and providing a safety net for employees who are not ready and may feel uneasy about the proposed changes (Schein, 1987). The *moving* process involves the sharing of the plan and evidence to show that the recommended changes are both desirable and possible. Managers allow employees to question the plan, gather information, undergo training where required, modify their tasks in a way that accommodates plan requirements and personal goals, and offer appropriate rewards for instituting change. The last step involves a sort of fit testing. Have the changes made by the employee to implement the plan been performed? How comfortable are the employees and the organization with that level of performance?

Numerous techniques can be used to bring about change at the individual level. These include life and career planning activities, coaching and counseling, sensitivity training, education and skills development, work redesign, and behavioral modeling (French and Bell, 1995).

Change and Strategic Implementation at the Macro Level

One can further segment macro level changes into two levels of analysis: dealing with team and interteam dynamics, and dealing with structured organizational subsystems (that is, structure, culture, mission, and so forth). Katzenbach and Smith (1993) define a *work team* as "a small number of people with complementary skills who are committed to a common purpose, set of performance goals, and approach for which they hold themselves mutually accountable." For a team, such as an academic or administrative department or committee, to be effective, French and Bell (1995), as well as Peters and Waterman (1982), have stated that the team must have

- Clearly defined purposes, goals, tasks, and action plans
- Clearly defined roles and work assignments
- Shared leadership with a broad spectrum of working styles and task skills
- A cohesive, informal, relaxed, and comfortable relationship
- Excellent listening skills, open communication, and civil disagreements
- Self-assessment mechanisms and awareness of developments outside the team
- A change agent or individuals who champion the change

While one might consider team cohesiveness a strong attribute and a necessary condition for implementing change, teams are quite susceptible to the phenomenon known as groupthink, as discussed by Janis (1972). *Groupthink* refers to situations in which teams act as though they are superior, exclusive, and invulnerable. The team shuts off divergent opinion through social and political pressure and ignores information and requests from outsiders. Groupthink can become a major impediment to strategy implementation if the team decides that a plan imposed by administration is not in the best interest of the team or its individual members. Team cohesiveness should not be discounted in the implementation process.

For example, shifting a college or university toward a more consumer-driven orientation may require eliminating or altering the structure of academic departments and delivery of instruction so as to better meet the needs of students. Although this plan may be in the best interest of the institution and the individual members, the plan threatens the existence of teams whose members might react negatively. Rather than imposing the plan on the academic department, the administration would be better served by taking the risk of including faculty members in the formulation process, and then letting these faculty members, now as insiders, bring the changes to their fellow team members.

The first question for implementing strategic plans at the team level is, do these teams have the attributes of an effective team? If they are not effective, team-building techniques such as process consultation, role analysis, quality circles, and self-managed teams should be employed, as we present at length in Chapter Nine. The second question is, does the group become an impediment to change? Techniques such as appreciation and concerns exercises, empowerment, visioning, and survey feedback may be employed to overcome groupthink and facilitate the change process.

Interteam changes refer to the rearrangement of reporting relations between various academic and administrative units. Brown (1983) suggests that in many cases, structural conflict due to task interdependence requires the interfacing of administrative and academic units with different cultures, missions, and values. For example, the Division of Professional Studies at Southampton College of Long Island University was asked to manage the business programs at the Brentwood campus that had been formerly managed by the C. W. Post campus, along with the rest of academic programs at Brentwood. Although the academic programs and responsibilities were shifted to Southampton College, administrative responsibility remained with administrators at the Brentwood campus. This created new dependencies for both units and required the development of new management systems.

Implementing strategic plans at the interteam level is dependent upon the ability of the various organizational units to work well with one another. Brown (1983) also notes that it is the level of conflict between these groups that will determine whether the outcomes of these interactions are productive. Too much conflict will result in poor decision making and deterioration of future relations, whereas too little conflict will result in either no decisions being made (or made by default) or decisions made on little information. Appropriate levels of conflict lead to bargaining and problem solving. Chapter Nine deals with issues related to interteam relations and how to create productive conflict through intergroup activities, process consultation, and third-party peacemaking.

Change at the Subsystem Level

We define organizational subsystems as a set of tightly or loosely connected components that constitute the inner workings of the organization. These components include the organization's hierarchical structure, strategy, task-technology and reward systems, shared values and culture, skills and distinctive competencies, leadership style, and staff (human resources), as illustrated in Figure 8.1 (Peters and Waterman, 1982).

Some of these subsystems are tightly connected, others are loosely coupled. Tightly connected subsystems reinforce the organization's operation and maintain a dynamic equilibrium; loosely connected subsystems produce organizational dissonance and disconnects. For instance, a college that possesses a research-oriented reward system but hires faculty predominately with teaching backgrounds and interests will find that their nontenured faculty will either increase their research skills in response to the reward system (tighten linkage), try to change the reward system (again tighten linkage), or leave the institution (linkage remains loose). The point is that subsystems are coupled in such a fashion that a cause-and-effect chain evolves based upon the relative connectivity of the system (Kotter, 1978; Weick, 1979).

The cause-and-effect phenomenon is critical in understanding strategy implementation and change at the subsystem level in the short run. For example, going back to the example of a college hiring teaching-oriented instructors, let us assume for the moment that this was a change in hiring policy based upon the desire to shift the strategic position of the college toward a consumer orientation.

The college operationalized its strategy by hiring teachers rather than researchers, yet the impact of the change was unsuccessful because other subsystems intervened in the change process. The initial change resulted in a misalignment of the staff subsystem with the reward system and skills of the faculty. Faculty responded by seeking equilibrium by either aligning their skills with the reward system, trying to change the reward system to align with their own skills, or leaving the institution, thereby maintaining the imbalance.

Figure 8.1. The Organization and Its Subsystems.

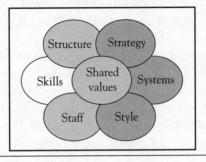

Strategy implementation in the short run (three to six months) must take into account cause-and-effect outcomes of any proposed subsystem change. Subsystem changes must be examined systemically; one cannot change one part of the college's subsystem without analyzing the impact on other subsystems. Kotter's (1978) analyses suggest the following questions:

1. What is the relative alignment of the current subsystems?
2. What are the proposed subsystem changes?
3. What is our understanding of the short-run cause and effect of those changes and its impact on the other subsystems?
4. When will the cause-and-effect chain reach equilibrium? What are the overall results?

The effectiveness of a college or university's operation is dependent upon the relative fit between the subsystems and the core of the campus's shared values and culture. For example, if a college's shared values, culture, and tradition support the traditional R-1 university model

- Academic reward *systems* should focus predominately on publications and research grants.
- Research *skills* of the faculty and support staff would be well supported by institutional resources.
- The core of the *staff* would be prestigious researchers, research graduate assistants, and academic administrators with a strong penchant for grant writing and administration.

- The *structure* would include not only traditional academic departments but also a plethora of research institutes whose main purpose would be to obtain and manage research grants, research projects, and publishing.
- The *strategy* should be differentiation because the institution would attract predominately graduate students and would be less concerned with traditional undergraduate education.
- The *leadership style* would nurture the independence of the content of academic programs and research but strongly control the cost of administering these programs.

Alignment of college subsystems is important for understanding the moderate-run (perhaps six months to approximately three years) dynamics of a college or university. It is a mistake to expect that all college's subsystems would be perfectly aligned and that perfectly aligned systems would remain so. Internal misalignments are normally caused by either changes in the external environment (political, social, economic, technological, and competitive position) that impact subsystems or internal changes meant to implement strategy or realign subsystems.

Most misalignments will realign themselves through the path of least resistance. Again going back to our example of a college trying to shift their consumer orientation, it may be easier for the new teaching faculty to increase their research skills or leave the institution than it would be to change the reward system, especially if the faculty is unionized. Deliberate realignments require planning, resources, time, and energy on the part of the administration, as we discussed throughout the book. Campus leaders and strategic planners should ask the following questions suggested by Kotter (1978) concerning subsystem realignment:

1. Are any combination of subsystems misaligned?
2. What type of change(s) might have caused the misalignment(s)?
3. What might be the path of least resistance for correcting the misalignment(s)?
4. What actions can and will the college take to realign the subsystems?

5. How long will it take for the misalignments to correct themselves?

Strategy implementation and change in the long run (three years or more) is impacted by those subsystems that act as the driving force for the organization and the adaptability of each of the subsystems. A *driving force* is defined as the subsystem or subsystems that steer the college or university; in many cases the driving force may be the core values of the institution. Driving forces are not necessarily constant and may shift from subsystem to subsystem.

For example, Marist College has had a long ecumenical tradition that reflected the ideals of the founder of the Marist Brothers, St. Marcellin Champagnat. With the naming of Dr. Dennis J. Murray in 1979 to the presidency of Marist College, Marist shifted its emphasis away from educating priests to becoming a more traditional liberal arts institution by embracing advanced technology through a joint venture with IBM and embarking on a major construction campaign to modernize the campus. Over 40 percent of the students now attending Marist major in communications and business administration; psychology, with slightly over 10 percent of student enrollment, is the only liberal arts major offered.

So what happened at Marist? Leadership style became the driving force for the college overcoming or augmenting the shared values and culture of the organization. The other subsystems followed suit: staff were hired with a stronger interest in the use of technology, both for research and instruction, the reward system shifted to reinforce the use of technology and applied research and instruction, faculty and staff were given state-of-the-art computers and development support, and the college promoted their IBM connection (differentiation) and constant investment in facilities.

The second factor determining the ability to implement strategy in the long run is the comparative adaptability of each of the subsystems. Change cannot occur if key subsystems cannot be altered to accommodate those changes. Going back to our example of the college who wished to become more consumer-oriented, assuming that the reward system was set by a collective bargaining agreement (unionization), there may be little hope of changing

the reward system, at least in the short term. The college administration should look at changing alternative subsystems with greater
flexibility (such as hiring faculty with a balance of teaching and
research) or changing their strategy based upon their inability to
change other subsystems.

In considering the long-run dynamics of their implementation
plan, college administrators might ask the following questions suggested by Kotter (1978):

1. What subsystem(s), if any, provide the driving force(s) for the
   college?
2. Why is this subsystem (or subsystems) the driving force(s)?
3. In what direction is (or are) the driving force(s) moving the
   college?
4. What impact would this (or these) driving force(s) have on the
   other subsystems if these subsystems were to become realigned?
5. How adaptable are each of the subsystems?
6. Is the college investing resources in the more static subsystems
   to make them more flexible?

Change and Strategic Implementation at the Ecological Level

Strategic implementation may require what we would term an
organizational makeover, a total change in the way the college
interacts with its environment based upon pressures from organizational stakeholders illustrated in Figure 8.2.

These stakeholders push and pull the college in different
directions (Lewin, 1951a, 1951b) and may have interests that run
counter not only to each other but perhaps even to the mission of
the institution. Regardless of the stakeholders' interests, stakeholders control certain resources that the college requires to operate properly; therefore, a dependency exists between the college
and these interest groups, as suggested by Pfeffer and Salancik
(1978). Part of the strategy formulation process accounts for these
stakeholders through the internal and external assessment
processes (strengths, weaknesses, opportunities, and threats
[SWOT] analysis). This may include taking actions to alter the college's dependencies by creating greater interdependencies
between the college and its key stakeholders. For example, colleges

Figure 8.2. The Organization and Its External Stakeholders.

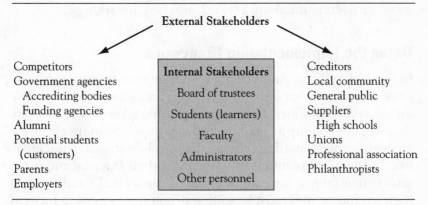

might absorb or form joint ventures with competitors or create strategic alliances and network organizations through devices such as articulation agreements.

Strategic implementation at the ecological level requires inclusion of the affected internal and external stakeholders in the implementation process; that is, it requires transorganizational development (French and Bell, 1995). Transorganizational development usually involves development of the roles, structures, and mechanisms needed to coordinate the efforts of multiple organizations and the various players who represent those organizations' interests.

Ecological changes also refer to strategic implementation plans that impact all the subsystems described in the prior section and are universal in nature. For example, the administration of a small private college that is a reactor-differentiator decides that it wants to start a strategic planning process. Since its strategy has been unintentional and emergent (not deliberate), it will need to educate the entire college, what French and Bell (1995, p. 209) would call "getting the whole system in the room." These comprehensive changes also include massive changes in the college's culture, or shared values, since the culture is the core of the organization. Systemwide changes include employing techniques such as total quality management, management by objectives, key performance indicators, cognitive and causal mapping, employee empowerment, cross-functional work teams, and benchmarking.

Doing the Implementation Homework

In this and in the previous chapter, we have tried to develop a complete picture of what implementation is and what it involves. The information contained here should provide a basis of knowledge that will help campus leaders and strategic planners choose a strategic implementation scheme that can be successful and effective. Leaders and planners must examine their external and internal environments, have a full grasp on the actual conditions of their campuses, and must be willing to commit to moving forward once they have identified a strategic plan they believe will work. Much of the success they will experience is based on their ability to create the databases that will answer their questions and direct their future activities.

In the next several chapters, we look at some of the issues that surround the implementation process in more detail. It would be wonderful if all strategic plans could be implemented smoothly and immediately, but unfortunately that is all too often not the case. Hence, in the next few chapters we try to help campus leaders and strategic planners handle some of the problems they may encounter so they can implement their plans successfully.

Chapter Nine

The Human Factor in Strategic Change

In the last two chapters, we examined the eleven methods that campus leaders can use to effectively implement strategic change. In this chapter we look at the specific challenges that confront many colleges and universities that face widespread hostility, resistance, dissatisfaction, and perhaps even outright rebellion when campus leaders and strategic planners attempt to make substantive strategic changes. These are behavioral issues and can occur on two levels, the individual level and the organizational level.

At the individual level, resistance becomes an issue of making decisions around a single person, so solutions will be dependent upon supervisory activities between the organization and that one person. Given the uniqueness of the millions of possible situations that can occur within organizations, we will not attempt to deal with the individual level of resistance here. Group resistance, however, demonstrates more common themes and patterns, and there is a respected body of literature that addresses these types of issues. We note especially that a great deal of wisdom can be found in the literature and practice of organizational development (OD). OD helps organizational leaders better understand the root cause of problems and provides a series of proven and recognized tactics that any organization facing serious internal difficulties can use successfully to solve such problems.

OD is not just a tool for business managers. OD can be extremely useful to campus leaders and strategic planners in helping them develop strategies for working with various groups that are involved in or affected by the strategic change process, but who resist those changes. The discussion of OD includes an examination of tactics such as empowerment, team building, creating cross-functional work teams, and developing organizationwide cognitive mapping. These methods can help campus leaders more effectively manage the change process by successfully overcoming resistance and providing an environment in which everyone is valued, has a say, and helps contribute to the success of the organization.

Why Organizational Development?

Few people would dispute the importance of the human core of any organization. Though some often overlook the human element in seeking to produce optimal organizational outcomes, that's always a mistake. Top managers and other organizational leaders certainly have an important role in envisioning what the organization should be, the direction it should pursue, and what it should produce, but it is the human core that actually gets the work done.

It is easy to assume that, just because people are getting paid, they will do what the organization expects them to do. This is the classical labor ethic: "A fair day's wages for a fair day's labor." But the reality is quite different. Work does not always get done properly and in a timely manner—but not because people don't try to do their assigned work as best they can or because individuals or work groups try to take advantage of their employers. It's not even that people use organizations to achieve personal ends. We are inclined to give employees and their managers the benefit of the doubt and assume that they really want to do a good job. Then what seems to be the problem? The answer lies in the *Human Side of Enterprise* (McGregor, 1960).

Humanness means that individuals are unique combinations of talents, aspirations, desires, beliefs, histories, and faults. It also means that people change over time: sometimes for the better, sometimes for the worse. Perhaps what is most important, it means that when people come to the place where they do their work, they bring their humanness with them. This fact of humanness is the single best explanation for why individuals and groups (the next step up in understanding behavior in organizations) act the way they do. It is also the best explanation for understanding why some individuals and groups will sometimes counter or resist the actions of the organization, for rational as well as irrational reasons.

Practitioners in OD recognize the humanness of individuals and groups in organizations and also recognize the importance of that organization being able to achieve its strategic goals. They recognize that often resistance to change comes from legitimate concerns, beliefs, or circumstances. Much of this type of resistance can result from misinformation, no information, or purposefully jaded information. Knowing the causes of this type of resistance is also the beginning of creating solutions that will correct communications and serve to build consensus. Practitioners in OD recognize that resistance may come from other forces within an organization's human core, such as power seeking, political activities, conflicting goals of organizational stakeholders, distrust, fear of change, and even seemingly irrational destructive motivations.

Golembiewski (1977) stated that OD has become one of the most successful bodies of thought to bridge the gap between traditional organizational theory and human resource management. By creating processes and techniques specifically aimed at facilitating change, OD creates an applied social psychology paradigm to business settings (Harvey and Brown, 1992). Further, Peter Senge (1990) described the importance of creating a learning component within every organization, which is another characteristic of OD. He described the need for all the members of an organization to become continuous learners and to help create an overall competency of how to better compete in the external environment. By learning how to learn, employees can successfully grow internal resources to benefit both the organization and the individual.

A Very Brief History

What we have come to understand about working successfully with the human component of the organization today comes from a historical development that was fraught with contradictions and controversy. The beginning of the discussion can perhaps be traced to Frederick W. Taylor, who acknowledged that in the great mental revolution required for managing in the twentieth century, first-class workers require proper training and job design (1911, p. 1388). Taylor believed that when employers and workers agreed to work with each other they entered into a contract. This contract served the interests of both parties based on predictable, manageable, and designable work-related methods, but it also guaranteed the success of the owners of the concern. Throughout the evolution of management thought, theories of management-labor relations have echoed this message (Wren, 1979).

The difficulties, however, are probably best characterized by the works of Douglas McGregor (1960). Summarizing the research from 1930 to 1960, McGregor concluded that "management should have as a goal the development of unique capacities and potentialities of each individual rather than common objectives for all participants" (p. 187). One of the clear advantages of an OD perspective is that it goes beyond developing an individual's potential. Bennis (1969, p. 2) noted that OD is "a complex educational strategy intended to change the beliefs, attitudes, values, and structure of organizations so that they can better adapt . . . to the dizzying rate of change." Other authors observed that the need to develop adaptability and change processes in individuals and the organization was driven by growing, dynamic external environmental forces (Lawrence and Lorsch, 1969; Marguiles and Wallace, 1973).

Characteristics of Organizational Development

OD has several fundamental characteristics. Marguiles and Raia (1978) have outlined them for us:

- It is based upon the systems approach to management. It assumes that various relationships exist between a variety of interdependent subsystems that interact with the external environment and the organization, thus creating dynamic homeostasis (Scott, 1981).
- OD employs a scientific methodology, an action-research model, to increase organizational effectiveness; data and information drive development.

- OD aims to increase organizational performance—not with "touchy-feely" exercises to make employees feel good but with serious techniques to increase quality and productivity.
- OD has humanistic underpinnings in that it emphasizes increased opportunity and the maximum use of human potential; people must be given a chance to excel by being educated as to the need to change.
- Given humanistic values and the need to share data, OD requires collaboration and the involvement of all levels of the institution; everyone must be heard and given the opportunity to participate in the change process.
- OD is planned change; since the system is constantly changing, OD alters the system's dynamics to achieve organizational goals.
- OD intervenes at any organizational level to produce the desired change; it encompasses a myriad of techniques that deal with individual, dyad-triad, intragroup, intergroup, subsystem, organizational, and interorganizational dynamics.

In summary, OD is one of the primary means of creating a more adaptive organization and getting the organization ready for change by employing a systematic approach of data gathering, analysis, and intervention.

Strategy Implementation and Organizational Development

We have identified strategy implementation as actions an organization takes to put their positioning plans into action by either changing their mission, changing their environment, or changing their resources, capabilities, and internal operations. One would then naturally think that a natural bridge exists between OD and strategy implementation. However, the field of strategic management has yet to acknowledge the significant role that OD plays in strategic implementation. A quick review of recent texts and journal articles in strategic management would lead one to believe that the fields are quite dissimilar. Sherman (1999) noted this divergence and observed that the learning process described in OD was not different from the field of strategic management's concept of developing distinctive competencies. He concluded that "strategy implementation provides a conceptual framework for enacting a strategic plan while OD provides the 'nuts and bolts' methodology of organizational change needed in order to operationalize the implementation at a 'personal' level" (p. 37).

Organizational Development, Ethics, and Competitive Advantage in Colleges and Universities

We believe, like the authors in the field of OD, that developing human resources is the right thing to do and the moral obligation of a college or university. What is more important, we believe that developing human resources is the most productive investment that an educational institution can make because *it fosters institutional performance (doing things right) and creates a competitive advantage.*

It is paradoxical that some educational institutions that want to increase their performance have very lofty ideals about human dignity and the value of the individual, yet have not embraced those ideals in their management practices. No matter how heavily these institutions invest in their infrastructure, program development, marketing, or public relations, they will find that they must focus on their human core and increase the people skills associated with providing a sound education regardless of other competitive advantages. To survive in this new competitive environment, however, these institutions will eventually stumble onto the moral high road because it is the only road that will create a sustainable competitive advantage that cannot be bought or duplicated. Human skills are the most difficult to refine and are organization-specific.

To give an example, one of us has heard continual student complaints about a tenured faculty member's degrading treatment of students in the classroom. This individual has been known to abuse students verbally with an incessant flow of sarcasm and name-calling. These student complaints have been funneled to the faculty member's unit manager and the academic dean for several semesters, yet neither the unit manager nor the dean took any action because they felt that it would have no impact on the faculty member. The administration only intervened when the academic dean discovered that the unit head was recommending to the complainants that they take an equivalent course at the local community college.

What Organizational Development Does: The Process

OD embraces Kurt Lewin's (1951a, 1951b) model of change, which we described in Chapter Six, and provides a continuous planning model for institutional change (Huse and Cummings, 1985). The OD model has been defined in several ways (see chapter four of Nutt, 1992, for a literature review on the methods of planned change); however, we can boil the model down to a simple four-step process that generally can be described as the DIET approach.

In the first step, D stands for diagnosis. Top administrators have recognized that problems exist, as indicated by some of their traditional key performance indicators such as enrollment, cash flow, and institutional rating by external sources. These problems are considered effects or symptoms of more deeply rooted problems; therefore, the institution needs to collect valid and reliable information about the organization in order to develop a true picture of its current status. There are numerous information gathering techniques, such as interviews, questionnaires, observations, and secondary data analysis, that may be employed as well as allied analytical techniques (see Nadler, 1977, p. 119). Most important is that, after the information is analyzed and the real problems are identified, this material needs to be presented to the members of the organization in a feedback session in order to help employees understand the data and identified problems, transfer psychological ownership of the data and the problems from the information gatherers to the employees, and energize the employees to use the data to develop action plans (Burke, 1982).

The second step, I, is intervention, and involves the matching of the problems to specific intervention techniques based upon the level of analysis in which the problem occurs and the target group of the intervention. (See French and Bell, 1995, p. 165, Figure 8.1, for further detail.) The intervention technique(s) selected must respond to a felt need of the targeted population, involve the targeted population in the planning and implementation of the intervention, and lead to acceptance of the change by the organization's culture. Argyris (1970) believes that an effective intervention must be based upon valid and useful information, that the targeted group have free choice in terms of the type of intervention employed, and that the targeted population has commitment and takes responsibility for the intervention. (For a discussion of the different intervention techniques, see French and Bell, 1995.)

Evaluation, E, is the third step, which involves asking two sets of questions:

- Were the desired changes realized? In other words, did the outcome of the OD intervention meet our desired, predicted, or expected goals?
- Was the OD intervention properly implemented? Was there a flaw in the process that would have impacted the outcome of the intervention?

Huse and Cummings (1985) note that although evaluation may seem to occur only after the OD intervention (a feedback control mechanism), feedback should also occur while OD techniques are in process in order to adjust for implementation problems.

An OD evaluation requires having a set of goals and objectives for both the OD process and its outcomes prior to the intervention. An assessment would then begin with a comparison of the actual results of the OD intervention with the expected results and a determination as to the causes of any variances found. A diagnosis (step one) would then be instituted, thus creating a feedback loop that would continue until the outcomes and the process meet organizational objectives.

The last step, termination, T, connotes an end to the change process, although this is certainly not the case. Termination refers to the institutionalization by the organization of the OD process and the departure of external parties who assisted in that process (Schein, 1969). At this point the organizational members have learned how to learn and have developed the competency to continue the OD process. (See Argyris, 1983, on double-loop learning.)

Who Is Responsible for Organizational Development

If OD is a systematic method for inducing change, then arguably anyone who champions change (Peters and Waterman, 1982) in a methodical manner could be classified as a change agent. However, this could not be farther from the truth. Successful change agents are generalists in their organizational perspective and specialists in the process of organizational diagnosis and intervention. Furthermore, they foster change by acting as integrators between the top management and targeted populations and between functional areas. Effective change agents are perceived as disinterested or neutral parties to the change process and have little to no power position among those impacted by the change; that is, they occupy marginal roles to the targeted groups. Credibility is another factor. Change agents must be deemed experts in their fields and have a positive history with the organization (Beer, 1980).

External Change Agents

Many organizations realize that very few of their in-house personnel have the expertise and the credibility to serve effectively as change agents. External change agents, OD consultants, serve a very useful purpose in that they provide a worldview, serve as sounding boards and counselors, provide conceptual stimulation, new ideas, and images, tend to be charismatic, and usually energize the change process (McLean, Sims, Mangham, and Tuffield, 1982).

Organizations that use external change agents have the task of educating the change agent as to the organizational processes, functions, and interdependencies (single-loop learning). It is through this education that the external change agent starts the diagnostic process. The danger is that the external consultant will get sucked into organizational politics and in the long run lose objectivity.

Internal Change Agents

Internal change agents are usually based in personnel offices, training departments, or management service departments (although they may be an assistant or an assistant to a major officer of the organization). They bring with them a wealth of knowledge about the organization and awareness of members' biases. They also have a tactical awareness in that they garner information about organizational coalitions and serve as intelligence-gatherers for top management. Internal change agents can cultivate new ideas and new attitudes by disseminating the most useful information to the proper parties. They also serve as trainers by developing and running management training and development programs (McLean, Sims, Mangham, and Tuffield, 1982).

Many organizational members, unfortunately, see internal consultants as tainted commodities. Internal change agents may be the most honest and sincere people, yet they all have organizational bosses they report to. Those involved with the intervention usually assume that the change agent's boss will eventually learn confidential information; therefore, they keep these change agents at arm's length.

The Team Approach

Numerous authors in the field have noted that the most successful method for inducing change has been to develop a change agent team of both internal and external change agents. This combination allows for the objectivity and expertise required for the development of employee trust in terms of data analysis and confidentiality and lays the groundwork for institutionalizing the OD process by having in-house personnel learn OD methodology. Furthermore, the internal change agents provide not only a linkage to the organization for the external agents, but they also serve as the first teachers of external agents about the processes and culture of the organization.

Why Organizational Development Is Appropriate in Colleges and Universities

Fullan and Miles (1983) observed that OD has been practiced in primary and secondary schools since 1963. Almost one-half of the over one thousand schools they surveyed at that time were practicing some form of OD. Results from their survey indicated that schools that continued OD programs for at least eighteen months obtained positive results. Colleges and universities are not unlike their primary and secondary school counterparts in that there has been an increased demand by their organizational stakeholders for improved accountability, quality, and operating efficiencies. Many postsecondary institutions had positively responded to their survey by 1992, and revealed that over two hundred colleges had instituted OD and quality management programs (Lewis and Smith, 1994).

Rather than jumping on the OD bandwagon for the mere sake of following the crowd, colleges and universities must understand that if they want their strategic plans to be successfully implemented, they must prepare their organizations for the upcoming changes. Colleges and universities that plan to undergo strategic shifts require the building of trust, political support, training, and procedural changes *prior to* (if not concurrently with) the actual start of the strategic planning process. OD programs are appropriate in colleges and universities because these programs reinforce the commitment of the board of trustees and the chancellor or president to quality management, organizational excellence, and human development. These programs signal to all the institution's stakeholders—particularly the faculty, staff, and students—the determination of the leadership of the institution to institute meaningful change in an inclusive manner.

From a more philosophical perspective, the values underlying OD parallel the values underlying most academic institutions. French and Bell (1995, p. 77) have suggested that these values include "empowering employees to act, creating openness in communication, facilitating ownership of process and outcome, promoting a culture of collaboration, and promoting inquiry and continuous learning." OD embodies the principles of most academic institutions and provides the processes and techniques that any academic institution can adopt to assist their employees in educating students to realize their full potential and make a positive contribution to the world (Southampton College, 1999).

How Organizational Development Might Work in a Campus Setting

McGill (1977) takes a very pragmatic approach to OD, an approach that seems very appropriate for a college setting. He describes a seven-phase process.

Phase One: Convergence of Interest

This phase requires the gathering of interested individuals by a top-level organization official, perhaps the chancellor or president, provost, or one of the vice presidents or vice chancellors, who is convinced that there is a need to gather information about the organization and take action based upon these findings. (This person assumes the role of internal change agent.) It is important to understand, however, that the individuals who are assembled may have very different interests and agendas, but they all recognize the need to work together in order to meet their separate objectives.

Whether this group should be formalized is an interesting question, one that is influenced by differences of campus culture and customs. Regardless of whether the committee is formalized, the formation of the committee needs to account for existing structural and social processes that have been historically empowered with the planning function. For example, administrators at Southampton College unilaterally formed a strategic planning committee that lacked both academic and administrative unit representation and seemed to overlap an existing standing committee's mission. Certain faculty and staff who were not represented on the committee were deeply offended by the process and felt disenfranchised. Although college administrators tried to clarify the role of the group as a steering committee, irreparable damage had already been done that marred the work and reputation of the committee.

In creating a strategic planning committee in colleges and universities, the group must be fashioned as openly and informally as possible for two very distinct reasons. First, membership of this group should be based purely upon willingness to contribute to the OD process. This should not be just another committee meeting that people go to because they have been assigned by their unit, but a meeting where contributors perceive that their own self-interest and the interests of the institution can be served. Informality will allow less committed members to quickly drop while new members may quickly join. Openness will help assure equal access and involvement of any interested parties.

Second, if the group fails to launch an OD effort, the malfunction will have less of a negative impact (although it certainly would have one) than it might have had with a formalized committee, especially on its individual members. Since the group was informal in nature, it had no real charge or mission and perhaps concluded that no action was warranted. Certainly the rumor mill might twist the reasons for the group's demise, but no one in particular, except perhaps the person who tried to form the meeting in the first place, would be heavily penalized for its inaction.

Phase Two: Establishing a Charter

This phase usually entails locating a consultant with expertise in the field (an external change agent) to assist the group with the OD process as well as formalizing the organizational development team. Team members should include volunteers from the original group as well as volunteers who have the authority to initiate change or the obligation to respond to it. Once membership is established, the team defines team goals that are related to the OD effort and that are feasible and justifiable. The last step in the process is formalizing the contract with the consultant based upon the established goals of the OD team.

Phase Three: Formalizing

Here, the OD team secures legitimization and sponsorship for its efforts from influential individuals and groups—and also meets resistance. These groups and individuals include those whose approval endorse, formally and politically, the group's actions (such as chair of the faculty senate, president of the union, and key board members); those who control the resources necessary to move the project forward (chief financial officer and comptroller, among others); those who remain neutral to the program (perhaps senior tenured faculty, or first-line administrative supervisors); and those who actively oppose the program. (We delve into these issues in more detail in the next chapter.) The primary purpose of this phase is achieved by broadening the circle of people involved in the OD effort to both internal and external stakeholders while more clearly defining the charter of the OD effort in the context of received feedback. The team is seeking permission from the organization to proceed while acknowledging the rights of all of its stakeholders to have a voice in the process.

Phase Four: Problem Identification

This phase needs to be systematic in nature and must include the concerns of the widest possible group of stakeholders. It must also be directed to significant problems, and the data gathered must be analyzed with the goal of producing further action. The team should not get bogged down in the science of research methodology and analysis. (Should we establish control groups? Should we accept a correlation coefficient with a significance level of .05 or .10?) Instead, the team should look for indications as to the attitudes, behaviors, and situations that contribute to defining problems.

The OD team is usually assisted in its task through an office of institutional research, whose jobs include providing the team access to secondary data sources (both internal and external), assisting with the development and implementation of any data gathering exercises (such as polling, questionnaires, focus groups, and individual interviews), encoding and processing of the data, and perhaps even providing assistance in interpreting the data and writing the preliminary report. This report is then shared with the college community in an open forum where the results are discussed, including implications for future action.

After the OD team has elicited feedback from the community on the results of their data analysis, the team, with the assistance of the consultant, creates a list of the problems and develops a general plan of action in light of the previously developed goals, the next phase of the OD process. This plan of action describes the OD intervention process, how the change will occur, the actual intervention techniques that will be used to bring about the desired results, and the evaluation methodology to determine whether those results were achieved. Part of this plan should include a description of the action hypotheses (McGill, 1977, p. 128), the *how* and *why* the plan should work. *Given problem A, we intend to use intervention technique C in order to bring about result F.* The need to spell out the logic behind the plan is critical to the success of the implementation of the OD effort. Employees will not follow a plan that they cannot understand (Barnard, 1938).

Phase Five: Reporting

Sharing, not telling or selling, is the next and undoubtedly the most decisive phase of the OD operation. It is at this point that the OD team comes back to the college community to seek their final input before the plan is put into action. The team must be prepared to describe the logic behind the plan, deal with obstructionists in a polite but firm manner, and modify the plan to accommodate viable suggestions and requests. Again, the team must go out of its way to include all the stakeholders in this process to avoid the perception of underhandedness or exclusion.

Phases Six and Seven: Acting and Evaluating

The final two phases, the action step and evaluation, test the action hypotheses as the change agents conduct the various interventions. This allows immediate feedback to the OD team and the college or university community on the success of the interventions, as well as modification to the content and process of the interventions. Team members should distribute progress reports and hold open meetings to get reactions from the participants in the OD process and the impacted stakeholder groups. Once the intervention has been completed, the team should conduct a final evaluation of the OD process in an open forum with the college community. The team should then create a final report to be distributed throughout the institution and should include balanced commentary from the open meeting.

The final evaluation should address the question of whether the institution achieved its goals by solving its identified problems and should ascertain additional actions required to meet any unmet goals. Furthermore, since the OD process is a fairly arduous one, the institution should also decide whether the previous effort created real value for the institution and whether a continued OD effort would be warranted or desired.

Goals of Organizational Development on a College or University Campus

Colleges are prime candidates for OD, given their shared governance model. This management approach often leads to blurry power relationships and to different groups possessing dissimilar goals and objectives. Groups with disparate goals need to work together to achieve the best results. The roles of each group must be clearly defined, and communication between groups becomes essential (Davis and Lawrence, 1977). In many schools, there is also competition for limited resources, thus exacerbating the situation.

Further, many factors involved in academic performance, student retention, and other outcomes are also hard to determine in a clear cause-and-effect manner, thus making it hard for planners to map actions to results and know what is truly effective. This situation is aggravated by the fact that many colleges are also faced with the need to cut costs dramatically while increasing academic support and investing in technology. In some cases, the students or their families are faced with lower incomes and cannot pay tuition increases; in others, colleges must work harder to recruit students; and in still other cases, schools or colleges are facing budget cutbacks or large expenses for maintenance and construction. In all these situations, new opportunities for saving time and money must be found without hurting service.

Regardless of an institution's particular problems, certain goals are common to most OD efforts. These goals focus on the development of the human core of the organization by increasing the technical, human relations, and conceptual skills of the employees while also increasing group cohesiveness and organizational subsystem integration (Katz, 1974; Jewell and Reitz, 1981; Kotter, 1978). The overlying goal of OD for the college or university is to increase the long-term health and performance of organizational systems by tightening the loosely coupled systems with the organization (Weick, 1979).

Team Building

The term *teams* has been the buzzword of the 1990s and has carried tremendous weight into the twenty-first century. The nature of managerial work has become so embedded in the committee or team motif that it is extremely difficult to envision a work setting that does not combine individuals' talents, resources, and knowledge (Mintzberg, 1973). Even telecommuters are involved in chat rooms, circulated e-mails, video conferences, and conference calls and cannot hide from being members of work groups.

Although team building may appear to be the latest fad in management, it has its early roots in the Hawthorne studies (Roethlisberger, 1941). Later works by Douglas McGregor (1960) and Rensis Likert (1967) enunciated the purpose of management as creating unity of purpose within each group and then coordinating the work of interdependent work groups. Afterward, Galbraith (1973) denoted teams as the appropriate unit of analysis for determining the causes and cures of task uncertainty and organizational information overload, and Janis (1972) cautioned managers as to the problems associated with group dynamics that he referred to as *groupthink*. Teams have been regarded as almost mystical in the last decade because of their potential for creative synergy versus their possibility for self-destruction.

The key to building a successful team lies in developing a highly cohesive group with high morale and excellent technical skills whose goals are aligned with the needs of the organization (Tubbs, 1984). Team development should begin with an intense need by work team members to improve the group's interactions and sentiments so as to enhance task performance (Dyer, 1977). As is true for OD in general, a team leader or manager begins team building by identifying what the members of the team believe to be the problems regarding the team's performance. This process usually produces a list of symptoms or indicators of problems, such as lateness, turnover, and low productivity, that the team believes should be addressed. Before attacking the problem head-on, the team develops a list of their strengths and weaknesses and tries to correlate their weaknesses to the perceived problems and use their strengths to develop possible solutions. The focus of these sessions is on the strengths of the team and their ability and desire to work together to solve organizational problems.

There are many specific OD intervention techniques employed in team development; their particular use is based upon the perceived needs of the team. For example, role-playing, role-negotiating, and role analysis techniques are employed to clarify members' role expectations and the obligations of team performance to improve team effectiveness. This might be used when a new faculty member from an R-1 institution is employed by a small college and is not adjusting well to the academic department's needs for student advisement, college committee work, and community service. Fellow faculty members might role-play their interaction with students and demonstrate the approach and attitudes they use when dealing with students. The new faculty member might then go through a series of planned role-plays with faculty, and possibly students as well, to practice observed behaviors. Other techniques such as goal-setting (establishing specific expected outcomes from performance), team management by objectives (MBO) (establishing plans for action and expected outcomes from those actions), and quality circles (formalized group meetings that discuss how the group can improve performance) focus on the team's ability to formulate and achieve goals. Process consultation, third party peace making, and visioning concentrate on the development of procedures for solving problems, dealing with conflict, and creating a shared image of the team.

Empowerment

Empowerment is one of the pinnacle virtues of OD and is embodied in the fundamental philosophy of any OD technique. Empowered employees are motivated employees. They excel at their job and profession. The *power* aspect of the term *empowerment* refers to the ability of an individual to get things done.

Power can become problematic. Lack of power, or alienation, occurs when employees feel a loss of control over their own lives and a tremendous dependency on an individual or institution. Abuse of power, what McClelland (1961) referred to as *personal power*, occurs when an individual uses his or her power base for private gain. Powerless and abused employees feel victimized and either try to destroy the organization or become indifferent and withdrawn. Either reaction is counterproductive and reduces the organization's effectiveness. This feeling of powerlessness is often the cause of what many managers perceive as irrational resistance to change.

Empowerment is an enabling and ennobling process whereby employees learn how to overcome their feelings of powerlessness, gain power, and invest their power in others. Empowerment interventions focus on the personal characteristics of employees (their task-relevant knowledge, personal attraction, effort, and behavioral fit with the institution's values) and their position characteristics (access to information, impact on work flow, discretion in position, job visibility, and job alignment with institutional priorities). (See Whetten and Cameron, 1993, and Cameron, 1994, for further details.)

Empowering employees makes them feel that they are important and significant to the organization, that their work is both challenging and exciting, that they are part of the team and the academic community, and that learning and job competency really matter. To empower employees, Yukl (1990) has suggested that administrators express confidence in the employees' ability to get the job done, foster employee initiative and responsibility, reward and encourage employees in personal and visible ways, involve employees in the assignment of work, build on success, and provide a collaborative work environment.

Whetten and Cameron (1993) describe the empowerment intervention as including a skill pre-assessment survey, a series of readings on power and influence, a skill analysis case, skill practice exercises, skill application activities, and skill evaluation. French and Bell (1995) start the empowerment intervention by requesting that participants describe their personal best leadership situation. They have the employees reflect on the feelings and behaviors that accompanied these situations and ask the employees and their administrators what both can do to create similar conditions. Regardless of methodology, increasing employee participation in the operation of the institution will increase organizational performance and employee job satisfaction.

Creating Cross-Functional Work Teams

Whereas empowerment and team building predominately concentrate on process issues (how people work), the cross-functional team is an intervention technique that focuses upon the key functions, problems, and core systems of the organization. The concept of cross-functional teams is based upon the notion that the institution operates with fundamental systems and procedures that cut across the traditional administrative-academic hierarchical boundaries yet require expertise and input from both operations. At Oregon State University, for example, researchers identified ten cross-functional issues, including recruiting and marketing, the undergraduate evaluation process, and graduate admissions, that required academic and administrative cooperation (Coate, 1992). Typical cross-functional teams deal with recruitment and admissions, academic advising, strategic planning, and outcomes assessment. Many campus committees that involve administrators and faculty could be construed as cross-functional teams. At Oregon State University, not only do cross-functional teams receive team building, interdependency, and responsibility-charting exercises, they also receive technical training and education to increase their knowledge and decision-making, planning, goal-setting, and problem-solving skills. Team members become expert in the process and, at least in theory, could be substituted as part of the service delivery process (Evans and Dean, 2000).

In another example, the academic dean and the associate provost of enrollment services at Southampton College took a very hard look at its academic advisement process for freshmen and decided to form a committee of college administrators and faculty to deal with the issue. The first few meetings were not spent discussing the problems with the advisement process, but sharing the expertise of each of the members and their good and bad experiences with academic advising. Administrators and senior faculty members then conducted a joint workshop to make sure that the committee members were knowledgeable about the process and content of advising. It was only then that the team started to set goals for dealing with the freshman advising issues and to identify shared and individual problems.

Self-managed work teams (SMWT) take cross-functional work teams one step further: They replace, rather than supplement, the traditional first-level supervisor. These teams act as compartmentalized units (Galbraith, 1973) in that they form independent structures around certain organization processes or functions. They are then empowered to manage their own budgets, operations, scheduling, goal-setting, assessment, and evaluation. In a college or university setting, certain academic or administrative programs may require interunit expertise but operate independently. For example, universities may enter the virtual and distance learning markets by establishing an independent branch of the campus. This independent unit will have its own curriculum, budget, faculty, and staff drawn from the traditional structure.

Doing Campuswide Cognitive Mapping

Cognition describes the mental models, or belief systems, that people use to interpret, frame, simplify, and make sense of otherwise complex problems. Writers refer to these mental models variously as cognitive maps, scripts, schema, and frames of reference. Mental models are built from past experiences and are internally represented concepts and relationships among concepts that an individual can then use to interpret new events.

This ability to interpret is important because decision makers have a limited capacity for processing information. When dealing with complex problems such as strategy and change, they can rarely process all the information that would be relevant. These mental models help decision makers select information and decide what actions are appropriate (Weick, 1979). Individuals' cognitions may thus shape organizational decisions, although the extent to which this will occur will depend on the social context and on their ability to influence decisions in their organization. There is growing evidence that the success or failure of change programs crucially depend on cognitions of key people in adapting organizations because these cognitions shape choices about the design solutions (Weick, 1990; Swan and Clark, 1992).

Cognitive maps contain two basic elements, concepts and causal beliefs. *Concepts* are variables that define some aspect or characteristic of the system under analysis; *causal beliefs* describe the relationships that link concepts within maps. When a cognitive map is drawn, concept variables are usually represented by points and the causal relationships by arrows connecting the cause variable to the effect variable. Causal relationships may be assigned a direction and value. Values indicate the strength of the relationship and are sometimes used to quantify the maps. Plus signs are used to indicate a positive association between variables (an increase or decrease in x causes an increase or decrease in y) and a minus sign a negative association (an increase or decrease in x causes a decrease or increase in y). A completed map provides a graphic representation of the structure of the system under analysis that includes the variables within the domain as well as the relationships between them that influence system processes and outcomes (Russell, 1999).

An example of cognitive mapping may be best demonstrated by going back to the ABC University case first described in Chapter Five and elaborated upon in Chapter Six. If you recall, the board reacted to the decline in enrollments by hiring new presidents to try to turn around the university and get it back in the black. They specifically asked each president to introduce cost-cutting measures to reduce overall costs and the cost of delivering course instruction, increase nontuition revenues (endowments, grants, alumni giving), and develop instructional programs or methods that would expand the student base (increase enrollment) and allow the university to reach out to new students. If we were to construct a cognitive map of the board we would include the variables *decline in enrollment, negative surplus* (assumed from the need to get back in the black), *cost cutting, increase noninstructional revenues,* and *expand student base.* We might then develop a flowchart of their relationships, as pictured in Figure 9.1.

One can interpret this map as follows: The decline in enrollment has *caused* a negative surplus (positive correlation), and cost-cutting measures and increases in noninstructional revenues will *reduce* the negative surplus (negative correlation). Further, expanding the student base will *reduce* the decline in enrollments (negative correlation), and thereby *reduce* the negative surplus (negative correlation).

If the board at ABC had developed and then shared this map, perhaps they might have been better able to identify some problems with the logic of their strategic plan. No one would disagree that cost-cutting measures and the increase of noninstructional revenues will decrease the negative surplus; however, in order to increase noninstructional revenues, either in the form of grants or endowments, new expenses may have to be incurred for grant writing, research, and donor solicitations. Also, cost-cutting measures may have a negative impact on ABC's ability to expand their student base both in terms of the funds available for student recruitment and the impact that cost-cutting will have on the quality of the services provided by the university. And finally, without looking at the instructional cost structure and classroom capacity, there may in fact be a fallacy that increased enrollments may reduce the negative surplus.

Cognitive mapping as an OD intervention technique has strategic and developmental value. From a strategic standpoint, cognitive maps first allow planners and administrators to determine from their stakeholders which variables and causal beliefs about those variables are critical to the implementation of the repositioning of the institution and what are the perceived barriers to change. Once the variables and casual relationships are deter-

Figure 9.1. Cognitive Map of ABC University Board of Trustees.

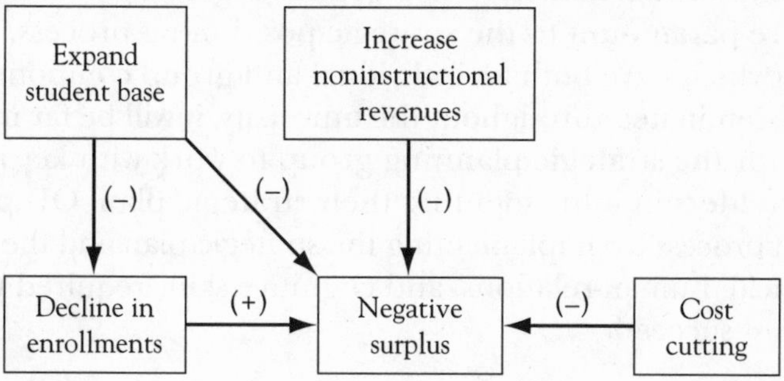

mined, maps are created and planners can test out their logic and ascertain the viability of their plans.

From a developmental perspective, mapping allows members of the institution to share their worldview of the internal and external environment. Furthermore, these maps set the foundation for discussions about the institution and provide a forum for understanding and agreement as to how the world appears to be from varying stakeholders' perspectives. One can gain tremendous value through this sharing process. Individuals receive acknowledgment for their perceptions. They accept that different people see the institution differently, but what is more important, they can visualize the commonality among the various groups and individuals.

Using Organizational Development to Implement Strategy in Colleges and Universities

Campus leaders and strategic planners can, and should, employ many of the OD techniques we've described in setting the stage for successfully implementing the college or university's strategic plan. As the preceding examples using cognitive mapping demonstrate, these tools allow administrators and planners to harness the creativity and expertise of their stakeholders (employees, students, alumni, feeder institutions) and obtain commitment from these stakeholders, thus ensuring a more fluid implementation process.

Several of the OD techniques we have not described focus on problem-solving, decision-making, planning, and goal-setting skills that are paramount to the strategic positioning process. If these skills (which have both an individual and group component) are not disseminated throughout the university, it will be far more difficult for the strategic planning group to work with key internal stakeholders in implementing their strategic plan. OD provides both a process for implementing the strategic plan and the specific technical, human-relations, and cognitive skills required to make the plan succeed.

Readying an Entire Campus for Change

College administrators and strategic planners must realize that before change can take place on any campus, the college community must be prepared for change. What we mean by *being prepared* is that employees need to come to understand the changes desired, possess the resources and skills necessary to make the changes, and feel that the changes will benefit all involved, including themselves.

OD suggests a particular methodology for preparing employees for change. First, one determines the motivation and skills readiness of the employees to change, given the requirements of the plan. This involves developing a need for change within the employee and providing a safety net for employees who are not ready and may feel uneasy about the proposed changes. The need for change should be couched in the most positive language possible, include a vision of the institution after the change, reference the institution's core values and key cultural icons, and denote the process in which employees will actively participate in that change.

For example, going back once again to the ABC University case, imagine if the new president starts the change process with a discussion on the economic crisis facing ABC University. Perhaps in the first few moments of her keynote speech, she mentions the demands of the board of trustees to increase revenues and reduce costs, and hints that both faculty and staff might receive pay cuts or even be discharged if the situation does not turn around. The president then goes on to lay out the entire change process, both the content and the context, and notes that faculty members have been assigned to committees to implement the strategic plan. The president has just sealed the doom of her administration.

There may be facts that college or university faculty and staff certainly need and deserve to know, yet it is fairly obvious that doom-and-gloom speeches neither motivate nor inspire people to work toward change. To make their faculty and staff ready for change, college administrators must first establish a change culture. This culture starts as a seedling in the form of a stirring message for change, a message that rouses the faculty and staff to work together to achieve a common purpose and mission. This message should be spread by as many leaders on the campus as possible—not only by the president or chancellor but also by the head of the faculty senate, the chief operating officer of the campus, union leaders, and other informal campus leaders. As members of the OD team, these campus leaders need to be fully involved in the development of the change process and be empowered to speak not only for their constituency but also for the administration.

Third, employees must feel that although change is needed and that their day-to-day habits might change, there is no ambiguity or uncertainty about the change process. Employees will be very skeptical of any request of administration to change the system if they feel that administration does not have a solid plan on *how* to change that system. College leaders need to include in their communications details of a highly structured process that demonstrates the administration's thoughtfulness and commitment to change.

Fourth, although the change process should come across as well thought out, the administration also needs to convey that the content of the change process (what they will change) is dependent upon the input and participation of the employees and is not a given. In reality, the administration is asking (not telling) their employees for permission to institute the change process and then demonstrating the need for total employee involvement in that process in order for the institution's mission to be fulfilled. The administration must go even further by creating structures that foster employee participation and informing employees about those structures.

Once a change culture has been adopted by the organization and the employees are psychologically prepared for change, the administration will then need to focus upon assessing the specific skills of employees as they pertain to the change process (Blanchard and Thacker, 1999). More specifically, if the institution is planning on repositioning itself in the marketplace, employees will require knowledge of strategic positioning to understand the content and process of repositioning as well as certain planning skills associated with strategic planning. Once the plan is formulated, additional skills may be required to implement the plan. (See Ulschak, 1983, for further details.)

Assuring Humane Change

Change is never easy, and unfortunately there are always casualties in the change process. Change must be instituted in the most compassionate manner possible in order to minimize the impact not only on those directly affected by the change but also on those who witness the impact of the change on others. Downsizing in businesses such as IBM and AT&T, for example, requires that not only do the "downsized" employees receive social, economic, and job search support, but also that the continuing employees receive support. As continuing employees see how well their ex-comrades have fared, they feel that the organization really did take an interest in individual welfare and feel better about the company and their own jobs (Robbins and De Cenzo, 1998).

There is an important lesson for colleges and universities in this regard. They need to learn the importance of performing a sort of change-triage to determine what impacts individuals and what individuals need to cope adequately with the change. This requires an assessment of the individuals' willingness to change and the role they will perform in the changed institution. For those who need to change to fit the institution's new vision and are unable to, the realities of the situation may dictate job reassignment, demotion, or dismissal. Administrators should discuss this situation carefully and courteously with affected individuals, with the perspective of minimizing the negative impact on them. The institution has to be both firm and fair in their decision, knowing that a harsh decision will have negative ramifications as it reverberates throughout employee ranks.

Employees who are unwilling to change should be given additional opportunities to understand the need for change and their important role in the change process. However, if their resistance continues, administrators must either marginalize their involvement in the change process (in the case of a tenured faculty member or a senior, unionized staff member) or terminate their employment. Still, we see termination as the last resort.

And finally, for those employees who are both willing and able to change, the institution must demonstrate their commitment to change by providing these employees with the social, economic, and technical support necessary to elicit the employees' maximum efforts. Studies have shown that employees who have high expectations of receiving desirable rewards for their efforts, who understand their role in their job, receive the proper training, and are fairly rewarded, will have excellent job performance and high job satisfaction (Hackman, Lawler, and Porter, 1983).

Marrying the Organizational Development Process to the Strategic Plan

As we described early on in the chapter, OD fosters institutional performance and creates a competitive advantage for the institution by creating a culture that supports change, empowers employees, and provides them with the tools needed to enact change. OD is a mechanism for psychologically and technically preparing the institution for strategic planning and provides the nuts-and-bolts methodology of the organizational change needed to implement that plan. This sandwich effect, before and after the planning process, reinforces the cyclical nature of planning and organizational development.

OD is a precursor to strategic management. Until the organization is ready for change, strategic planning is at best presumptuous and at worst foolish and time consuming. The skills developed by preparing the organization for change carry through the strategic management process and are critical to the successful implementation of the strategic repositioning of the institution, as suggested in Figure 9.2.

Referring again back to the ABC University case, because there had been no campuswide discussion of systemic problems and their implications, ABC University was not ready for any of the changes proposed by their presidents. Members of the greater organization were uninvolved, unreceptive, and technically unprepared for implementing the proposed strategies. Hence, change failed.

**Figure 9.2. The Integration of Organizational Development
and Strategic Planning.**

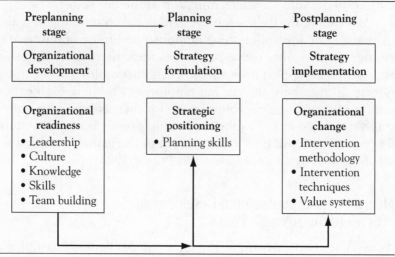

The New Academic Culture in the Information Society

The marriage of strategic management and OD creates a culture
that can sustain a competitive advantage in the brave new world of
the Information Society because institutions using this approach
have adopted lifelong learning not only as their credo for their
learners but also for themselves. Organizations that are attuned to
their marketplace and internal stakeholders will become learning
organizations because the knowledge, skills, and abilities needed
to succeed (no less survive) will constantly change as the information needs and the delivery systems of the learners change. Academic institutions, as organizations structured to teach others to
learn and create new knowledge, will themselves have to become
learners by participating in strategic and developmental techniques
aimed at better aligning themselves with the needs of the learners
(Ackoff, 1994).

Chapter Ten

Navigation and Negotiation Strategies for Change Leaders

Up to this point in the book, we have described the many forces that support or resist change that colleges and universities need to be aware of as they pursue a successful strategic planning experience. In the last chapter, we discussed the importance of developing and implementing an organizational development approach to dealing with general issues related to change and resistance to it. In this chapter, we identify several specific circumstances and particular groups that can be either extremely helpful or hurtful to the strategic planning process and describe strategies of dealing with them effectively.

As we identify these various internal and external groups, we do not wish to suggest that they are necessarily irrational stumbling blocks whose only desire is to make life impossible for the campus by derailing every initiative that comes along. On the contrary, every single one of these groups can be a positive force *for* change if campus leaders and strategic planners properly enlist their aid. At issue here is that every single one of these groups represents a parochial power base. Each group has its own objectives, motivations, concerns, and control of resources. As long as each group perceives that the strategic planning process is positively serving its interests, that group's help can be a powerful and positive force for effective change. Should one or more of the groups perceive that the strategic planning process will be deleterious to their interests, however, then those groups will naturally resist the efforts of campus leaders and strategic planners, and they will use their own resource bases to do so.

As we have said throughout this book, campus leaders and strategic planners have a choice as to how they work with these internal and external stakeholders. Further, it is important to keep in mind that sometimes many of these stakeholders have different objectives for the college or university. A heightened risk is then associated with the strategic planning process because it brings those differences to the surface. Risk is also increased through the planning process because it is impossible to maximally satisfy each group's expectations for the campus. Therefore, the choices that leaders and planners make can at best only "satisfice," a term coined by Simon (1976), instead of achieve optimal goals, as Larkley and Sproull (1984) suggested in the development of their Carnegie Model of organizational decision making.

"Satisficing" means that the plan that decision makers devise is based on the best information they can obtain, the best use of the decision-making processes they can put into place, and takes into account the amount of time that decision makers have to come up with the best decision they can. (The reality is that decision makers never have perfect information, or employ the best of decision-making methods, or have unlimited time.) The resulting decision is rarely ever the best possible one, although it is good enough from the decision makers' perspective to solve the problem.

Remembering that these decisions are made from management's standpoint, with the administration's values and expectations, stakeholders may view the impact of those decisions as having either a positive, negative, or neutral effect on them and therefore perhaps be less than optimal or even acceptable. It is both inevitable and unfortunate that those actions will be translated into "winning and losing." Decision makers consequently must take advantage of all the tools they have at their disposal to make the best decisions they can but not be overly concerned if those decisions don't satisfy everyone. As Larkley and Sproull (1984) tell us, this condition is normal and acceptable, since it is rational and reasonable given human limitations.

Assuming that campus leaders and planners do their best to take into account all of the issues and concerns of their several internal and external stakeholders, they should go ahead with the implementation of those decisions and deal with the consequences as they arise. If this assumption is incorrect, if the decision-making process is cut short, the problems with those who oppose the process will intensify, and campus leaders and strategic planners will be walking through mine fields.

The Internal Resisters to Change

In most cases, nowhere will the resistance to change be stronger than from inside the college or university campus itself. Here is where the people who will be most immediately affected by the proposed changes of the strategic planning process are located, and here is where the immediacy of the issues will be most pronounced. Here, too, the procedures of implementation will begin and be most profound (Pressman and Wildavsky, 1973). In the following sections, we look at each of these groups and describe a number of issues, including what resource base the group controls (explained in detail in Pfeffer, 1982, pp. 192–207), how the group can use their resources to either support or create problems for the strategic planning process, and the potential of either pleasing or displeasing the group and what that might mean for the strategic management process.

Governing Boards Who Resist Change

The college or university governing board is potentially the most powerful group on the campus. The relative success of strategic implementation starts with board support, particularly on most private college and university campuses (though on some of these, it may be the alumni or endowment providers who have the greatest amount of influence). Regardless of individual campus circumstances, all campuses have a governing board that wields tremendous influence over campus affairs. In this discussion, we assume the norm rather than the exceptions and describe boards that have full authority (Axelrod, 1994).

The governing board controls nearly all the resources available to the campus, including the properties, capital resources, and monetary resources that are in the name of the college or university. Individuals or groups select board members based on the incorporating documents of the campus, so there is some level of accountability here, but governing boards in the United States and beyond are generally given wide latitude in making decisions regarding the resources of the campus. (Most limitations are those normal to any organizational board, business or nonbusiness, in that board members are charged with protecting and strengthening the resource base of the institution under their care.)

The governing board is the single most important ally of any strategic planning process. For obvious reasons, the board has the single most powerful veto or nod of approval regarding the elements of a college or university strategic plan. For this reason, it is crucial for the board to be involved in the strategic planning process from the very beginning. Based on campus tradition and bylaw definitions, this participation may be more or less active or passive. Regardless, if a governing board is not willing to give its complete support to the strategic planning process, that process is certain to fail, period. However, if the governing board is completely convinced of the need for strategic planning and is further convinced that the plan that campus leaders and strategic planners bring forward is viable, their support will almost assure that the campus will be able to implement the process. Strategic planners and campus leaders must understand that their first and foremost task is to inform, educate, and persuade board members as to the necessity of strategic management of the university (Bozeman and Straussman, 1990).

It is certainly a mistake to assume that the president or chancellor and people close to the top administration are the only ones who have access to the board to make a case. Board members are, after all, human beings and have associations and friends on many parts of the campus, as well as throughout the community. As these constituents have concerns regarding the college or university, it is extremely common that they will contact a board member directly and exert whatever pressure they can to sway the board to see (and support) their particular viewpoints. So once again, making the strategic planning process an open one characterized by high levels of communication continues to be a hallmark of a successful process.

If one assumes that most board members are interested in what is best for the campus, the political process isn't necessarily an insurmountable threat. Most board members will listen to reasonable arguments and will ultimately come to support what they perceive to be in the best interest of the campus. If strategic planners do their homework and provide the board with honest and convincing evidence of the need for change and the ability of the tenets of their strategic plan to address change effectively, it should be a given that the board will wholeheartedly support the plan, thus making implementation much easier to accomplish.

Administrators Who Resist Change

When people in the outside world hear the term *administrator* applied to a college or university, they often think of a chancellor or president, and possibly vice chancellors or vice presidents. They do not realize that on the modern college or university campus, administrators can be found in all segments of campus life. In a business orientation, these campus people would be considered managers—upper-level, midlevel, and supervisory-level. On the college campus, however, the term *manager* is seldom used. This does not diminish the importance of the management duties and responsibilities that go on within a college or university setting. The only difference is that colleges and universities refer to the people who carry them out as administrators. To better understand where campus administrators fit into the scheme of overall campus life, think of college and university administrators in the three-tier hierarchical system that traditional business classifies its management personnel. See Figure 10.1 (Blau and Meyer, 1987).

The top administrators (president or chancellor and the vice presidents or vice chancellors) function in a fashion similar to their business counterparts. Some presidents and chancellors are even referred to as CEOs (chief executive officers). These are the most visible and most powerful of the campus's management team and make the executive decisions that affect the entire campus as well as the major divisions of the campus (including academic, student affairs, and campus administration). These individuals have operational control over resources—once again, a group of individuals who are essential for a successful strategic planning process. If, for example, the strategic planning initiative does not have the inclusion or support of the president or chancellor, as was true of the governing board we discussed, the process will not succeed.

Figure 10.1. University Hierarchy.

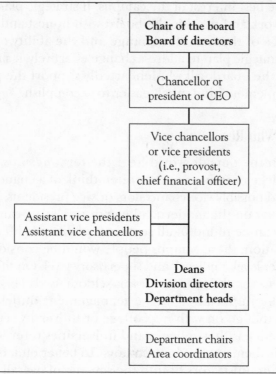

Chair of the board
Board of directors

Chancellor or
president or CEO

Vice chancellors
or vice presidents
(i.e., provost,
chief financial officer)

Assistant vice presidents
Assistant vice chancellors

Deans
Division directors
Department heads

Department chairs
Area coordinators

Without the support of the vice chancellors or vice presidents, the process will be extremely difficult, if not impossible.

Reporting to the vice chancellors or vice presidents are a series of other administrators with titles such as associate vice presidents (vice chancellors), assistant vice presidents (vice chancellors), perhaps even deans and department heads. This cadre of midlevel managers is primarily responsible for all of the program areas of the campus and operationalizes the plans and budgets set into place by the executive administrators and governing board of the college or university. Although the power base here is diminished from the executive level (through dispersion and reduced scope of decision-making power), these are still powerful people. For example, if a dean decides not to support a particular initiative, that dean might be able to create a strong enough political alliance with other deans or other department heads to obstruct progress (perhaps not kill it entirely, but seriously restrict positive activity).

There is also a level of administrators who report to deans or administrative department heads who oversee specific areas of operational responsibility. For example, on some campuses, academic department chairs report to an academic dean, while on other campuses, the responsibility of a departmental chair is more ceremonial than administrative and there is no real reporting relationship.

Depending upon the size of the campus, supervisory-level administrators form a large and influential group of administrative personnel (head of the book store, head of accounts payable, head janitor, head of food services for residence halls, to name but a few). Again, in terms of individual position power, these people do not have the level of power that the midlevel administrators have, let alone what one of the executive administrators have, but they are all in charge of the operation of their individual departments and can be helpful if they support the strategic planning initiative or hurtful if they decide to oppose the process.

Unlike faculty, and with the exception of department chairs, most college and university administrators act in a fashion similar to their business counterparts. They have no particular rights to their jobs (unlike faculty that may be tenured into their position) and can be rather easily fired or moved around at the discretion of the people they report to. As a result, most administrators will tend to do what will please their superiors, which means that when change comes along, most administrators look for guidance from top administrators and then go about implementing the changes that come.

Does this mean that they cannot block or impede changes they don't like? No, it does not. Individually, particular administrators may not be able to do anything to stop change scenarios; the potential for punitive action against them is far too great. In larger groups, however, they become a formidable foe and can stop the process in its tracks. Many college and university campuses may have unionlike professional organizations to which administrators belong. These organizations hold the potential of becoming powerful political bodies and as such could block changes they don't like. It's hard and perhaps a little insane to fire an organization's entire administrative staff.

Another way that administrators can affect the change process is by the attitudes and choices of priorities that administrators put on certain directives they are asked to carry out. Given the amount of power they might have, administrators might be able to put enough bureaucratic process around the directive to significantly delay it or possibly even kill it—and be able to say to others that they did not personally kill the initiative, the system did (Etzioni, 1964).

The ability to control implementation at the operational level—control of campus resources, the political system, and the organizational culture—is why the full complement of administrators have a significant impact on the strategic planning process. To help assure that the overall strategic plan will work, it is therefore prudent to work directly with the administrative core to help assure effective implementation (Mosher, 1982).

Staff Who Resist Change

On the surface, it might seem that staff people across the campus are the least problematic of the various groups who can affect change. One must recognize, however, that it is staff who actually get things done. Outside of the responsibilities of the faculty, members of the staff throughout the campus are ultimately the people who do the work that supports both the academics and the central operations of the campus. Staff ultimately have control of the resources that are allotted to perform tasks, and they have the ability to significantly determine exactly how those resources will be used (Bennis, 1966).

Like administrators, most staff members are limited in the amount of position power they might have. However, many staff members have acquired significant position power through their longevity on the job, and in many state and several private colleges and universities, staffers are organized and even unionized (either belonging directly to a union or part of a greater system, such as a state personnel system, that offers certain protections and controls). These extra protections allow staff members to accumulate greater position power and not be as subject to summary firings as are administrators. So although staff as individuals may not have enough position power to stop change, they might have enough to make implementation more difficult in the area they oversee. One must also remember that the sheer number of staff members on a campus makes staff the largest single group of people on campus (outside of students). This is a force to be recognized and reckoned with.

Faculty Who Resist Change

The faculty are the heart and soul of any college or university. Faculty members both create and disseminate knowledge, the primary mission of the campus. Faculty members have special rights, such as tenure and control over academic freedom, that make them an extremely powerful force on any campus. They are the line workers who deliver the service to the consumer, and they very well understand their importance in the university system. Along with the traditions of shared governance, faculty believe they have an extremely salient right to be involved in any and all matters that affect the nature, direction, and well-being of the college or university.

Perhaps subject only to the wishes of the governing board, faculty zealously protect their academic turf and often go into open battle with administrators whose ideas go counter to those held by the faculty. Thousands of presidents and chancellors have been fired because the faculty at their institutions wanted to get rid of them. Backed up by tenure and powerful faculty senates, faculty can very successfully block change. Although in some places the power base of the faculty is under attack as regulators question the value of tenure, and on some other campuses tenure does not exist, the power base of the faculty to oversee and control the academic program of the campus is hardly being questioned. In several states, college and university faculties are unionized to increase their power base. All together, this gives a college or university faculty tremendous power, power that they can easily centralize (Levy, Meltsner, and Wildavsky, 1974).

Of course, it is incorrect to assume that the faculty on any college or university are united or that they always act together. The huge differences one can find between different disciplines, pay structures, philosophical directions, and professional loyalties all play into the dynamics of a complex and diverse group. Politics is a normal part of life for faculty, and finding faculty members split among themselves on any number of issues is not at all the exception, it is much more often the rule. That is, except for certain vital issues.

Tenure, academic freedom, and control of resources are the types of issues that can unite a campus faculty. When a college or university faculty perceives that a strategic planning process will negatively affect their positions on these issues, the faculty will tend to unite—and chancellors and presidents will tend to get fired. No wonder so many campus top administrators are resistant to making changes that they fear will not please the faculty. This is clearly one reason that presidents and chancellors need to have 100 percent unwavering support from their governing boards when they propose changes that will negatively impact the faculty (such as reducing programs, altering tenure, shifting resources from one area of academic programming to another, or instituting a basic change in institutional philosophy, to name but a few).

As we have pointed out earlier, though, when one looks at the drivers of change in academic programming and pedagogical development, it is the faculty who are on the forefront of the revolution. This suggests that an institution's faculty are not necessarily obstructionist when it comes to the issue of change. Certainly, faculty are more likely to support changes that they themselves create or that they know up-front will benefit them (as a group). Just as faculty can be an imposing obstacle to change, they can just as easily be a daunting powerhouse for change. It's all a matter of how campus leaders and strategic planners have identified the need for change, how they have included the faculty into the data gathering and analysis process, and how they have worked with the faculty to implement the change effectively. (See Marguiles and Wallace, 1973, on change processes.)

Although we do not suggest that any group we are talking about in this chapter is one that leaders and planners can afford to ignore, certainly ignoring or downplaying the role of the faculty in the strategic change process is probably a fatal decision. Even in severe crisis situations, it is not a good idea to make major campus changes without including the faculty in the discussions. One of the worst outcomes of a crisis resolution process would be the loss of valuable faculty members that reduce the college or university's ability to adequately support programs of excellence or its competitive position.

In strategic planning, a program that many faculty tend to resent as being too business-oriented, campus leaders and strategic planners need to make sure that the communication process is open, honest, and two-way. As we suggested earlier, leaders and planners need to be able to convince a college faculty of the need for change and the need for the faculty to be involved in designing and implementing that change. Because they are recognized as experts, faculty members do not respond well to being talked down to, being told what to do, or being overlooked. Instead, leaders and planners need to build trust with faculty members, include them, communicate with them on an ongoing basis, and seriously consider faculty contributions and concerns in the decision-making process. This is a time-consuming and often frustrating process, but one that campus leaders and strategic planners cannot discount or avoid. In the planning-to-plan stage, therefore, the time and effort needed to adequately address faculty concerns and contributions needs to be a priority.

Programs or Structures That Resist Change

Several larger colleges and universities have particular academic programs or structures that make wholesale change particularly difficult. One obvious example is campuses that have medical programs. Given the gigantic costs of building these facilities, updating medical technologies, and educating medical students, any campus that has a quality school of medicine is going to dedicate a significant amount of its resource base to that program and will not make significant moves that will damage that program. This fact may make significant strategic changes extremely difficult to implement or may negate them altogether. Can a university with a good quality school of medicine decide that its optimal future lies in reengineering itself to become a comprehensive university instead of a research institution? Can a midsized urban college that is 60 percent an undergraduate college of business become a Research One institution? Can a college built to educate and train teachers drop their education program?

The answer is probably no, or at least not in the short run. Though the strategic planning process must be a function of applying internal resources to meet the needs of a college or university's most important stakeholders, this does not mean that the internal resource base is so flexible that major changes such as those we have just suggested are really feasible. Look again at the school of medicine example. What would it take to convert a research hospital to arts and science classrooms? What would one do with all the specialized lab space and equipment? How would one successfully attract students to an institution whose very nature and character has changed so dramatically? What would be the costs in money and reputation? Would it all be worth it?

Now if the environment had changed so dramatically that there was no need for the school of medicine and its programs had been in decline, one might answer yes, it is worth it, and go about the strategic planning process to create a whole new institution with a complete reengineering plan as the result. If the move to convert to a full comprehensive institution was the result of trends that certain campus leaders felt would simply provide a more exciting future for the college, however, the plan for change would make little sense.

The point here is that many campuses develop particular programs that tend to become dominant in the decision-making arena and in resource allocation. Developing strategic plans that negatively affect these programs, regardless of the importance or worthiness of those programs, throws up roadblocks that are very difficult to overcome. Although our school of medicine example here is purely hypothetical, the power of many college or university programs to influence strategic change positively or negatively is real. Ultimately the issue is whether the academic program is able to create and sustain both excellence and a competitive advantage. If the program can do both, one could seriously question the development of any strategic plan that would be harmful to it. If a program is unable to achieve or sustain excellence, however, the strategic question becomes one of how can the institution best use the resources elsewhere. Whenever a college or university can determine that one of its programs, even its hallmark program, is incapable of being excellent, that campus must make the hard decision about further support for that program. This can be a very contentious and potentially scarring debate, but in the long run, it is the health of the institution that is paramount to the health of any given program.

So what are we saying here? Is the existence of major programs a help or a hindrance to the strategic planning process? The answer lies in determining the actual value of the program to the campus. If the program is a program of excellence or has synergy with other campus programs, the strategic planning process needs to build around it, try to strengthen it, and use it as a steppingstone toward creating a better strategic competitive advantage in its service area. If the program is not a program of excellence and cannot easily become one, campus leaders and strategic planners need to work with the governing board to reallocate resources previously dedicated to the program and, over time, seriously reduce or possibly eliminate that program in favor of others that can do the campus a greater good.

For example, the business program at Southampton College has experienced nearly a 50 percent decline in enrollment since the late 1980s (this parallels other business programs around the country) and has moved from being the second largest program on campus to the fifth. College administrators, although questioning the viability of the program as resources have become very tight, have committed the college to continuing this program, since it still serves a portion of the student population based in the local community. Administrators asked members of the faculty in this program to develop several business models that would reduce operating costs, enhance the quality of the program, and simultaneously increase enrollment. Faculty members, however, rather than fighting the change, see the change as a possible opportunity to streamline the program, eliminate unpopular concentrations, and perform more outreach with local high schools and the community college.

Students Who Resist Change

Student activism is not a term attributable only to the 1960s and 1970s. Today's students (learners) are often more involved in campus decisions because they see themselves as the primary customer who is buying the services of the college or university. Rising tuition rates, the burden of large student loans, the concern for the quality of the education they are buying, and the ability of that education to secure meaningful and lucrative jobs after graduation are all reasons students have to be more involved in campus strategic decisions.

Students clearly have more power in private colleges and universities than they do in public institutions. Students have more power in public comprehensive and smaller colleges and universities than they do in the research colleges and universities. The marketing mechanism is the reason. In private colleges and universities, students foot a much larger tuition bill and therefore a greater percentage of the institution's overall operating budget. When they get what they believe they are entitled to, their activism is pretty benign. However, when they do not get what they believe they are entitled to, they either increase the level of their protest or they "let their feet do their speaking" for them as they (and their tuition) move on to other campuses (Hirschman, 1970). Today, many smaller private schools are in serious trouble for exactly these reasons. In not treating their students like the consumers, these particular private colleges and universities are failing and may even die unless they develop an effective strategic response.

In the public systems, students don't have quite as much say, since they generally pay somewhere between 30 percent and 45 percent of their educational costs (the states pick up the balance). They control a lesser resource base, so they have less of a say in overall campus matters. Today's students are nonetheless concerned with the quality and value of their education and are far more activist than their counterparts of the 1980s and early 1990s. Student councils exist on most campuses, and there are state associations of student councils that provide broader levels of communication and even political clout. In Colorado, for example, the Colorado Association of Students regularly lobbies the Colorado state legislature to keep a lid on tuition costs as well as student fees.

In the nonresearch institutions, students tend to have a bit more of an impact on campus decisions, including strategic decisions, because of the emphasis these institutions place on teaching. The student becomes the primary focus of the educational process. As many have suggested, including Rowley, Lujan, and Dolence (1997, 1998) and G. Hills (personal communication,

March, 1998), students may be also involved in the research agendas of the faculty (as is the case in many research institutions). This creates a tighter link between the student and the campus. As students have become more vocal, their voices have reached the ears of decision makers, and the decision makers have learned the importance of listening. In research colleges and universities, research is just as important as or more important than teaching. The students find they are relegated to a less powerful position. The institution frankly doesn't need the individual undergraduate student as much as the nonresearch institutions do (though it clearly depends upon graduate students), it needs grants and contracts that keep the research engines running. Decisions tend to be much more related to the needs of the research areas than to the teaching areas, so students tend to have less of an impact on the overall campus strategic decision-making processes.

The issues of involving students in strategic planning deal with the reality that any given student's participation and interest in the affairs of the college or university are short term (approximately four years), while the college or university must be concerned with the long term. Many campus leaders and strategic planners question the value of adding people to a process whose goals are clearly different from those of the campus. Even as alumni, graduated students and former students have different life expectations for themselves as does the college or university for itself. It may then appear that including students in a strategic planning exercise is at best public relations, not at all an important part of a successful strategic planning process.

In rejoinder to the above comments, who better understands the impact of the current college or university program base than the people who are partaking of it? Who has a better feel for what the institution needs to help them secure well-paying and satisfying jobs than those who are preparing for them? As the ultimate integrators of the knowledge they have been exposed to, who best knows whether or not students are getting the value out of their education they are supposed to? Finally, who better knows what needs to be fixed that will improve their education? These and many other realities make the student, as a consumer, a valuable contributor to the strategic planning process. It is also important to look at students not as representative of a short-term perspective, but as the current flow of a much longer-term stream—a stream of individuals who mirror society. Tapping into this stream and including its wisdom in the strategic planning process is an extremely valuable contribution and needs to be cultivated as such.

As student activism changes in the future, as it inevitably will, not including student voices in the campus strategic planning process could prove to be an even greater mistake. Although we are not predicting scenes reminiscent of the University of California Berkeley campus of the 1960s, or Kent State, or anything that approaches those levels of student protest, should students continue to become more and more organized, it may not just be the private colleges and universities that have students expressing their opinions by taking their tuition and placing it elsewhere. Public college and university students could well do the same thing. As we have suggested in Chapters Two and Three, they have a growing number of viable options from which to choose. Therefore, regardless of whether one takes the view of students as short-timers or as part of a long-term stream of consumers, college and university campus leaders and strategic planners are better off when they include student views in the strategic planning process. By treating students as partners in the development of the campus strategic plan, leaders and planners extend their planning capabilities and help assure greater levels of success in implementation.

Campus Leaders and Strategic Planners Who Resist Change

Throughout this discussion so far, we have implied that all campus leaders and those who are designated as strategic planners all support strategic planning. As many readers of this book know too well, however, not all campus leaders believe in the need for or value strategic change, sometimes including those people who are put into the position of strategic planner. This is clearly a problem, and for many campuses, this is the root of the problem of why they fail to develop an effective or successful strategic plan.

Although the problem of campus leaders and strategic planners who resist change is perplexing, the solution is straightforward. The top-level administrative team needs to be on the same page. They need to share a common vision of the campus. They need to act like a team and move forward together. There can be no in-fighting, no power struggles, and no secret agendas. Making this so is the responsibility of the college or university chancellor or president. In the ideal setting, the governing board has given the president or chancellor the right and power to create a top-level administrative team that will work together.

Not all governing boards, regrettably, give their top administrators those rights and powers, and many chancellors and presidents are severely handicapped in their abilities to create a unified team to administer a unified management program. If this is true from an operations viewpoint, it is equally true from a strategic planning viewpoint. Most second-time presidents and chancellors go into their second administration much differently from the way they went into their first. They usually want more of a say on who makes up the top management team, and they want greater levels of support from the board when they make their personnel decisions. With the board's support, they ask that all top administrators write their resignations and give them to the incoming chancellor or president, who will decide whether to accept them over the next few months. This particular tactic at least gives the president or chancellor the chance of creating that initial unified team.

But when we talk about campus leaders, we are not just talking about top administrators. We are also talking about academic leaders, lower-level administrative leaders, staff leaders, and student leaders. These much larger groups present a unity problem of much greater magnitude, but again there is an opportunity for the president or chancellor to unify a strategic direction through his own leadership ability. Building trust and confidence among this larger leadership group is (once again) time-consuming and often problematic. Nevertheless, if the campus is to go forward successfully on a strategic planning initiative, there really is little other choice. We absolutely believe that a successful strategic planning process is dependent upon a successful campus leadership team, and the key to that team is the chancellor or president (Finkelstein and Hambrick, 1996).

Finally, we suggest that the role of strategic planner is potentially a problem. It has become a source of amazement (and in some cases amusement) to note who colleges and universities tend to pick to take on the responsibility of strategic planner. In far too many cases, the person chosen has no knowledge of strategic planning other than that it is currently a popular term. These people don't know the difference between planning and strategic planning and suddenly find themselves in the middle of a process they do not understand and may not even like. Many will research, hire a consultant, or try out methodologies on their own. In many cases they will find nothing that helps prepare them for the intricacies and nuances of an effective strategic planning process. The result can be disastrous.

For instance, one of us was at an institution where the vice president for strategic planning interpreted the position to include an operational analysis of student-faculty ratios. This individual so micromanaged the course-scheduling process that decisions regarding individual enrollments literally needed to be approved at the university level on an individual basis. Although this improved the cost efficiency of the institution in terms of its marginal instructional costs, it also inadvertently shifted the strategic position of the university toward a more provider-driven orientation, away from its primary mission and target market. Drops in enrollment ensued, but the university has yet to discover this link between classroom management and strategic planning.

We believe that the position of a campus strategic planner is one that requires a full understanding not simply of strategic planning, but of strategic planning on college and university campuses. Whether the planner is an academic or administrative person is really not an issue. What is an issue is that this person possesses the knowledge of all that is involved in strategic planning in colleges and universities, can work effectively with campus leaders and campus constituents, and has a shared vision with the president or chancellor (as well as the governing board) to oversee the development of a plan that will work. Without these qualities, the process is in severe danger and the individual will most likely fail.

The External Resisters to Change

Although the biggest problems that any strategic planning initiative faces come from inside the campus, there are also external forces that can seriously affect the direction that the strategic plan will follow. In this section we look at some of the most important and potentially most disruptive of these stakeholders. As in the previous section, we examine the level of resources controlled by each of these groups, how these resources can be used positively or negatively relative to the campus, and what campus leaders and strategic planners can best do to work through the opportunities and threats these external forces pose.

The Regulatory Environment

Strategic management in a regulatory environment requires an accurate and usable understanding of the regulations and the institutions that enforce regulations. In most colleges and universities, this area of analysis is usually delegated to staff specialists or assistant vice presidents who may not be actively involved in the strategic planning process (Vietor, 1989). Since regulations limit choices and define the parameters of opportunities for an educational institution, knowledge of regulatory issues is critical for successful strategic planning.

Porter (1980) suggests that regulations affect the college or university's operation in three ways:

- They control the substance or content (through the imposition of operating standards and performance criteria).
- They influence work processes (also through operating and performance standards).
- They determine the operating domain (through entry and program restrictions).

There are essentially three external regulatory bodies that can affect the direction and content of a college or university strategic planning initiative. The first of these, state and governmental agencies, are more a concern to public colleges and universities than they might be to private campuses (though in terms of grants and contracts and issues such as corporate governance, there are areas where state and governmental agencies still play a significant role). Basically, these external regulatory agencies keep tabs on the well-being of public investments in the overall higher educational process and seek to create standards of conduct that will help assure that learners-consumers are treated fairly and receive value for their tuition investments.

State, County, and Governmental Agencies

In most state colleges and universities in the United States, and in public colleges and universities around the world, governmental agencies wield tremendous influence on higher education. There is a double-whammy in the United States because not only do state and county governments have a huge say in what public colleges, universities, and community colleges may or may not do, the federal government also controls most grants and contracts that institutions of higher education seek to fund their research and other campus activities.

In the case of state and county government and public colleges and community colleges, the state or county owns the campus. The state and county take primary responsibility to fund the campus and further, in many cases, the state and county make the primary decisions about the central mission of the campus. This gives states and counties the central authority and control of external resources over the campus. In terms of strategic planning, there may well be significant state regulatory limitations on just exactly what a particular college or university is able to do. For example, in Colorado, only the University of Colorado may have a school of medicine, only the Colorado State University may have a school of veterinary medicine, the University of Northern Colorado has been designated as the primary campus where teacher education occurs, and so on throughout the several state higher educational systems. If the University of Colorado wishes to take over the University of Northern Colorado's franchise on teacher education, or if the University of Northern Colorado wishes to open up a school of medicine, regardless of the wisdom or the need for these hypothetical moves, neither school may do so without the express consent of the Colorado legislature and signature of the governor. These are severe limitations (refer to the choices we described in Chapters Two and Three). State colleges and universities would have to engage in some fairly heavy political activity to move significantly from one mission to another.

The loss of strategic freedom (called imposed strategy—see Sherman, 1991) is offset by the significant state and county allocations that support well over half the college or university's budget. As one remembers that state colleges, universities, and community colleges are in place to serve what the states and counties have decided is in their best interests, this condition is understandable. Does this then mean that state colleges, universities, and community colleges cannot conduct an effective strategic planning process? No, it doesn't mean that at all. What it does mean is that each campus has a reduced sphere of strategic freedom, and can change that sphere only by engaging in significant political actions. The examples of the two Colorado universities we just gave suggest that the potential incursion onto each other's signature programs would be unlikely—but it would not be impossible. For example, if the rate of population increase continues to climb as significantly as some predict, there may be a need for a second school of medicine in the state, and the University of Northern Colorado might have as good a shot at getting it as any other campus. In this case, this particular strategic decision would rest on the need for another school of medicine and the willingness of the state legislature and the governor to support it. As always, the relative environment and the availability of resources continue to be the central dictators of significant strategic change.

Most federal control in public colleges and universities (as well as in many private schools) comes through auxiliary funding. The U.S. government does not decide whether a campus should exist (with the lone exception of Gallaudette University, the nationally sponsored university for the deaf and hearing impaired). The U.S. government does decide, however, how to spend the billions of dollars it has control of that is to be used for research, educational support, federal financial aid for students (a crucial resource component to both students and academic institutions), and national educational programs. For nearly all research colleges and universities in the United States, the U.S. government is a major (if not the major) source for research funding. Also, although the U.S. government does not generally concern itself with the other activities of a college or university campus outside the grant or contract area, its decisions about funding can significantly impact the strategic direction of a campus. For example, if the government decided not to fund research into a particular area any longer, and that area was a significant research area for a given college or university, that particular campus would need to make a significant strategic shift (Rivlin, 1971).

Around the world, the issue of governmental funding is coupled with governmental control. Countries such as Australia still depend rather significantly on the centralized educational directives that come out of Canberra to determine what programs and courses individual campuses across the country will provide. Until recently, even individual course content was reviewed in Canberra. The United Kingdom still has a centralized funding and control system in London, and Parliament determines the general budgets for higher education in the United Kingdom. Nearly all colleges and universities are public, including Oxford and Cambridge. Though Australia is moving toward a more decentralized system and the United Kingdom is also giving much more freedom to the campuses across the country, there are still limitations that can challenge strategic planning in these countries (as well as in most countries around the world), and individual campuses continue to look at ways of developing strategic options that will support them in the transition from Industrial Age education to Information Age education.

The Legal Environment

Although there are state statutes that say what a particular public college or university's primary mission may be, there are no laws in the United States or anywhere in the world that prohibit colleges or universities from taking advantage of strategic opportunities or protecting themselves from strategic threats, other than those that might violate civil or criminal law. Yet the legal system is the first place stakeholders and constituents may turn to when they disagree with what a college or university is doing (Barry and Whitcomb, 1987). Through the legal process, the court has the power to make pronouncements that can significantly alter the strategic direction of a college or university. In truth, it is almost inconceivable that any court would allow itself to become entangled in the political infighting that might go on during a strategic planning exercise, assuming that the exercise itself was legal, honest, and did not propose that any of its primary stakeholders be unfairly treated as a result of the planning process. Even then, there might have to be a fait accompli before a lawsuit might have any grounds for action.

The legal system is always present and has potentially extraordinary power to either bless or reverse (often with penalty) the decisions of a college or university, whether those decisions are related to strategic planning or not. As campus leaders and strategic planners begin the process and proceed through it, it is probably a fatal error to ignore the potential of legal intervention in the outcomes of the planning process—particularly true in crisis cases in which the college or university has engaged in strategic planning to reduce programs, reassign or fire faculty, or engage in any activity in which one or more close stakeholders stand to be hurt. This is not to suggest that campuses cannot or should not engage in strategic planning as the best means for addressing these types of crises. But the planning process needs to keep the potential of lawsuits in mind and make certain that its actions are lawful and that reductions or firings are fair and based upon solid reason (Freeman and Gilbert, 1988). This may not prevent the college or university from being sued, but it will help it win its case in court, should a court case become necessary.

Accreditation Bodies

The central purpose for accreditation bodies is to provide a stamp of approval that says that this college or university, or perhaps this program, meets certain criteria that reflect standards of quality and substance. Having demonstrated that the campus or program has met these standards, the accreditation then signals learners and other consumers of higher education that those products are of high quality and reflect what the campus says they are supposed to reflect. All of this is good, and in a growing world of more and more choices, accreditation is one of the few assurances learners and consumers have as they choose among colleges or universities where they will invest their time and money in pursuit of a high-quality educational experience.

In the strategic planning process, conversely, accreditation may have a significant downside. The reason for this is that accreditation processes tend to be cookie-cutter processes. There are a central set of standards and guidelines, a common timeframe during and between accreditation visits, a common method of conducting accreditation, and a common method of addressing problems, suggesting remedies, and finalizing the process. Although many accreditation agencies do try to be responsive to the individuality of various campuses, this tendency toward sameness of evaluation and expectation reduces the willingness of many campuses to engage in anything too experimental because it might make the accreditation people unhappy.

Certain accrediting bodies say that they really are not trying to make every campus and every program exactly like every other, and perhaps they believe this. The experience of going through accreditation, however, is normally a set of activities designed to find out what the accreditation people will want to look at, making sure those items or issues are in excellent shape, and then preparing a defense for all those areas where there is evidence that the accreditation team already has concerns. Sometimes the result is that colleges and universities (as well as accreditable programs) find that it is best to be like other successful campuses and not try to rock the boat when it comes to "hot buttons" on the accreditation team.

We present these concerns, not as absolute impediments that make strategic planning impossible, but as potential stumbling blocks in particularly aggressive and innovative strategic planning exercises. We find it interesting that in our experience, in more than one instance, accrediting teams have recommended that a particular campus engage in strategic planning to help solve its problems, so perhaps accreditation bodies are aware of the potential benefits of the process.

Our concerns vis-à-vis accrediting bodies lie in two areas: first, making sure that the accreditation team fully understands what the strategic direction of the campus is (as the result of a strategic planning process) and why, and second, making sure that wary academic and administration leaders do not see accreditation as a limitation to an aggressive and innovative plan. Given that the accreditation process is designed to be developmental in nature, and because receiving appropriate accreditations may be a matter of life and death to a campus or a particular program, the strategic planning process must be informative to those who accredit campuses and programs and must demonstrate that the college, university, or the program involved will be much better off, much higher in quality, and much more relevant to its community than it would have been without planning. This should help at least bend some of the cookie-cutter tendencies of most accreditation programs.

College and University Support Groups

By their very nature, college and university support groups want to be accommodating to the college or university. The authors are completely unaware of any groups that exist to create problems for particular colleges or universities. The nature of the support these groups give includes providing financial assistance, giving aid in recruiting students and perhaps even faculty and administrators, providing connections to the general community around the college or university, and in giving advice or service in some advisory capacity to help the campus achieve some desirable end. These support groups become difficult to the strategic process when they don't like what the college or university is doing or how it is doing it. They can withdraw their support, or worse, they can become vocal about their concerns and can damage a college or university's reputation or even its financial position. These can be very powerful groups.

Alumni

Some campuses use their alumni as a major group for potential support whereas others do not. Alumni appear to be a much greater concern to private campuses than to public colleges and universities. Part of the reason is economic, since tuition is anywhere from two to six times greater on a private college or university campus versus on a public campus. Students who attend the private institutions tend to come from more affluent backgrounds and will remain affluent upon graduation and in pursuit of their postgraduate lives. This makes these alumni particularly attractive to their alma maters, who must depend upon gifts and endowments to shore up their lack of public funding and the market limitations that impact tuition.

Another reason is that of loyalty. Private colleges and universities (by and large) go to special lengths to create higher senses of loyalty and connectedness between themselves and their learners long before they become alumni. Classes tend to be smaller. It is much easier to get to know professors, staff, and administrators. These same professors, staff, and administrators are more responsive to their learners and work harder to keep them happy and successful in achieving their degrees. As alumni, these former learners continue to feel loyalty and connectedness.

Among public colleges and universities, one can see a whole range of interest in alumni from practically none to very high interest similar to that in the most prestigious private institutions. Dependence upon gifts and endowments is a much lower priority for public colleges and universities than for private campuses.

Loyalty has fewer benefits for the public institutions. There may also be a tradition on the campus, a part of its culture perhaps, that alumni don't really matter.

The more enlightened campuses are more aggressive in keeping their alumni close to the life of the campus. Alumni represent a significant current and future resource base for colleges and universities, who universally face declining resource bases. What so many campuses overlook is the value to the institutions of college-educated individuals who acquire higher paying and more influential positions after graduation. It isn't just private college and university graduates who are more likely to be affluent. Public college and university graduates can be just as affluent or potentially even more so than their private school compatriots. This is a significant resource of which a public college or university needs to take more advantage.

Foundation Donors

Donors are another group of people who are naturally disposed to render positive support to colleges and universities. Donors to college and university foundations range from relatively impoverished individuals to highly affluent individuals and groups. The resource these people control is money, liquid resources that make things possible on college and university campuses that might not otherwise be possible. The money, however, usually comes with strings—that is, many gifts and endowments are to be used for only one purpose, and if the college or university does not use them for the stated purposes, the colleges or universities lose them. Once in a while gifts might be given unencumbered, but this is more the exception than the rule.

In the onset, donors must be happy with the performance of the college or university, or perhaps they see a need that their gifts can help alleviate, or they would never be donors. This can change abruptly, however, if the actions of the college or university do not meet the expectation of donors. At that moment, any streams of funding are cut off and, depending upon the provisions of the gift, the college or university might have to refund the initial gifts and endowments. Keeping donors happy is therefore vitally important.

For the most part, donors should be encouraged by a strategic planning process taking place. Since the majority of donors are successful business people, the more they see the college or university engaged in sound business practices, the more they like it. This is no guarantee, however, and should donors see that the strategic plan is heading in a direction that is counter to their interest in the campus, their positive support could evaporate instantly. For example, if a college were to decide that it could no longer support a music program, it is most likely that any donors or endowers to the music program will do one or more of the following: stop contributing, want their gifts or endowments returned, be unwilling to support the college or university in any other areas. Further, as influential business people, it is probable that they will share their displeasure with others, thus further confounding the campus's efforts to raise funds through gifts or endowments.

The Issues of Getting Everyone on the Same Page

As one can see from looking at the many different forces that are at play as a college or university conducts a strategic planning initiative, it is nearly impossible to keep everyone directly or indirectly completely satisfied all the time. Competing interests are at work here that make the task of campus leaders and strategic planners a challenge at best.

"You Can't Please All the People . . ."

College and university leaders and strategic planners would certainly understand the truth of a statement attributed to Abraham Lincoln: "You can please all of the people some of the time; you can please some of the people all of the time; but you can't please all the people all the time." Even in the most positive of strategic plans, where growth, innovation, and higher quality promise the improvement of the overall campus, there are bound to be one or more groups that will be able to find fault with the plan or the planning process. Of course, the more the process is related to crisis needs, the more groups will be in a position to be hurt. This is the nature of change, not just of strategic planning. It is natural and it is inevitable that in a crisis situation, someone might get hurt.

All this is to say that campus leaders and strategic planners cannot allow themselves to get caught up in fears of not being able to please everyone the campus strategic plan will affect, whether those people or groups are inside or outside the campus. The real key is to do as little harm as possible to any contingent, and then to be completely honest with those whom the plan may affect negatively. Early warning is a real benefit here, and the fewer (if any) surprises in the impact of implementing the plan, the greater the integrity of the process and the greater the chances for overall success.

The Costs of Alienation

One of our central points in this chapter has been to identify and evaluate many of the potential forces that can negatively impact strategic change. This is important knowledge for campus leaders and strategic planners and, if nothing else, a forewarning of some of the inevitable negative forces they will face as they move forward in both the planning and implementation stages. Understanding the potential costs associated with alienating one or more of these groups is part of a prudent planning process. For example, knowing that the direction of the planning process will lead to the elimination of one particular campus program will mean that those individuals and groups who have a stake in that program are going to become alienated.

This doesn't mean that just because the plan is going to have some negative fallout the plan should be scrapped or revised. What this means is that the overall good of the college or university is paramount to the good of an individual or a group. These realities are part of the hard choices that campus leaders and strategic planners must make in order to assure the effectiveness of the strategic planning process. By building in the costs that come from alienation, along with the other costs of the process, a truer picture of the actual impact of the implemented strategic plan will become much more lucid, and decision makers can make progress knowing much better how the process will turn out.

The Necessity of Securing and Retaining a Competitive Edge

That either initiating strategic planning or creating a competitive edge will be done with everyone in full agreement and accord is a ridiculous hope. It is fascinating, nevertheless, to look at individual college and university strategic planning initiatives and see the level of naiveté with which so many of these groups set forth along their particular paths. Very few planning groups think up-front about the stakeholders and how they are likely to respond to the planning process, particularly when it becomes clear that the planning process is going to affect them.

Campus leaders and strategic planners need to better understand the complexity involved in creating an effective strategic planning process and the need to do this up-front. They need to be realistic about the needs for change, the costs for change, and the likely outcomes of change. Too many of these planning groups have gotten fully involved only to be totally surprised when the naysayers and ghouls come out of the woodwork. At that point, embarrassment, anger, reproach, and even revenge begin to figure into the scenarios, and the entire planning process can be put at risk. In the planning-to-plan stage, understanding the potential for and the power of the naysayers should be a significant part of the discussions.

After all, what is at stake here is the ability of the college or university to build or maintain a competitive edge as it seeks to serve its particular constituencies effectively. Slipshod planning can only damage the ability of a campus to do this. Being uninformed about what could go wrong, as well as what should happen if everything goes right, is part of how to make the strategic planning and strategic implementation processes work and work well. By planning better and by implementing on an informed basis, the campus significantly increases its ability to be competitive and have a brighter long-term future.

Chapter Eleven

Preserving and Nurturing Changes That Are Made

In Chapters Six through Ten we have looked at several issues related to preparing for change and then going through the process of implementation. Colleges and universities are highly complex, so of course the process of change is complicated as well. The lack of understanding on the part of campus leaders and strategic planners regarding this level of complexity has led to many planning problems that have eventually led to failure of the planning process.

By this point in the book, the reader should understand that shortcuts don't work in creating and carrying out a successful change process. Everyone involved with strategic change on college and university campuses must give a significant amount of time and effort to the process. They must do their homework and be committed to the process. They must take on the harder and more time-consuming projects in order to assure that the process will succeed. When campus leaders and strategic planners do this, the plan will probably go forward much more successfully.

However, in developing the best plan and the best implementation process, leaders and planners may still not have a complete handle on the entire process. There is nothing to guarantee that once leaders and planners have implemented the program that it will stay implemented (Yin, Heald, and Vogel, 1977). There is a very solid possibility that people who really never liked the plan will try to undermine it once it is in place. Resisters by and large do not go away. Further, via the political system, some individuals find ways of attacking the weaknesses in both the plan and the implementation process and attempt to reverse the plans. Since planning and implementation are clearly human processes, it is impossible to build perfect plans or implement them perfectly, and hence there are always points of vulnerability (see Allison, 1971 on rational, organizational, and political decisions).

Campus leaders and strategic planners need not be surprised. In nature, there is always a tendency to reverse change and return to original conditions. For example, most rivers that flood return to the original channel, regardless of what road workers or construction projects have done to alter the natural flow of the river to accommodate human convenience or growth.

On college and university campuses, many people are so comfortable with the conditions and the associated routines that even if they are forced to change, many will pine for the old ways of doing things. Furthermore, given the chance, they will find ways of reversing that change (Levy, Meltsner, and Wildavsky, 1974). This is a normal and natural antecedent to any organizational change. One is reminded of the story of Moses bringing the Children of Israel out of Egypt toward the Promised Land. Despite conditions of slavery, starvation, and severe mistreatment, many of the Children of Israel actually wanted to go back after they have passed through the Red Sea. Of course they couldn't because the Red Sea had come together again, taking hundreds of Egyptian soldiers to a watery grave, but many wished to anyway and some formed coalitions to defeat the leadership of Moses. Set in a strategic context, Moses was lucky that he had a resource like the Red Sea because it was one of those rare elements associated with implementing change that could not be reversed. Most college presidents and chancellors do not have a Red Sea to depend on or God's help to cement their plans. They need to rely on other realities of cementing the plan into place, once it has been implemented, as well as methods of control that will help assure that the campus actualizes the benefits of the plan. This is what Lewin (1951a, 1951b) meant in describing the refreezing process, as we discussed in Chapter Eight.

In this chapter we describe several methods of controlling the strategic plan once a college or university has begun its implementation process. The promise of these methods is to provide campus leaders with tangible, operational instruments for determining how well the plan is actually working and for learning about areas that need more attention. We also look at ways of keeping the strategic planning process dynamic and in compliance with the changing world around colleges and universities. We conclude with a discussion of how colleges and universities might use total quality management (TQM) as a tool for engendering continuous improvement and keeping a connection with the ever-changing external and internal environments.

Understanding Change

Change needs to be seen and understood as a process, not an event (Bennis, 1969). In nature, things change all the time and there is never a time when something isn't in flux. In the development of a strategic plan, people often assume that a single or perhaps a series of events will transform an institution to a different state. People just don't see that this drive for change is an ongoing process and that change is both evolutionary and revolutionary (Greiner, 1972).

Certainly, campus leaders and strategic planners have enough difficulty gaining campuswide support for a single strategic planning process. To go to the campus and suggest that this is only the beginning (or worse, that there is no end in sight) is a bitter pill to swallow, perhaps too bitter for many people to accept. Nonetheless, the truth is that change is the rule and not the exception, and because the world is changing, our perceptions of its needs and wants must always be flexible (Drucker, 1995). We discussed in Chapter Nine the crucial need for honesty in relating what is going on in strategic planning. Another situation that calls for honesty is for campus leaders to explain to the campus that what they hope to achieve in developing an effective strategic plan is a better method of dealing with future change. Again, this is a hard thing to do, but it is so important that all campus constituencies understand that what is happening in strategic planning is the creation of a dynamic state, a state that is by nature different from the way things were up to this point (Kochan and Useem, 1992). The institution's leadership needs to help the rest of the campus become comfortable with the change.

Methods of Controlling and Cementing Change

As we've suggested, no strategic plan or implementation process is going to be perfect. There are challenges throughout the two processes, and campus leaders and strategic planners need to stay on top of them to assure that the plan succeeds. To answer these challenges, there are several things leaders and planners can do to make certain that the process stays on track. In this section, we will describe and discuss several of these methods.

Key Performance Indicators

We have already introduced the idea of using key performance indicators (KPIs) in the implementation process. Here we describe how campus leaders and planners can use KPIs to control and cement the change process. As Rowley, Lujan, and Dolence (1997) have pointed out, the use of KPIs is one of the strongest and most effective methods of controlling the strategic planning process that campus leaders and planners have. The simplicity of its design and its measurement feature make it an easy tool to understand, though as we suggested in Chapter Seven, it is not always an easy tool to design.

Once a college or university has implemented a particular portion of a plan (meaning that planners have completely thought out this particular portion of the plan and have determined how they can best measure performance), they can then introduce a KPI system to control its ongoing performance. Again, as we suggested in Chapter Seven, KPIs are related to goals. Here we need to reaffirm that we are talking about long-term goals and shorter-term objectives. So, for example, if we state that we want to increase minority enrollments from a beginning percentage of 8 percent to a more representative figure of 25 percent in ten years ("more representative" meaning that our service area has a 25 percent minority population rate), we have stated our goal. Now to get to our goal, we want to backtrack from the goal incrementally so that we know on a year-to-year basis what our progress should look like (develop short-term goals). In this example, then, we might say that our objective for the first year is an increase of 1.5 percent in the total number of minority students who register for classes over our beginning point (in other words, at the end of the first year, we should be able to see that we have a total minority enrollment as a percentage of total enrollment of 9.5 percent).

Now assuming that our plan has also spelled out for us how we hope to accomplish our goals and objectives or our tactical plans, we should be able to monitor results in a straightforward manner and can intervene if necessary. For example, at the end of the first year, we take our measurement and find that we have had partial success—we now have a total minority enrollment of 9 percent. (The method of measuring variance is described by Chadwick, 1991.) The first question will then be, what does this tell us? We show improvement, but not as much as we had expected when we set our goals and objectives. The answer to this question is that we need more information before we can draw a conclusion that something is wrong. This again underscores the reality that change is a process and not an event. As we look into what happened over the last year, we might find that although we appear to have a solid plan in place, it took longer to actually get parts of the plan moving than the planners had anticipated. For example, it was more difficult to attract qualified minority candidates than predicted. As a result, outcomes were slightly below expectation, but there is every indication that the methods prescribed in the plan are sound.

Overall conclusion? No need to panic at this point. If the people who are charged with the success of this particular part of the plan are reasonably certain that the process is working, we do nothing. At the end of the second year, we will take another measure and compare it to our objective and then make another determination as to whether the plan appears to be properly thought out.

In an alternative example, let us say that the measurement at the end of the first year was 7 percent. Not only is the campus moving in the wrong direction, there would also appear to be no positive impact of the plan on minority enrollments. Once again, before we draw conclusions, we would want to investigate what happened. If we find that the people who were given responsibility for implementing the plan did everything they were supposed to do and still the results showed adverse outcomes, we need to revisit that part of the plan and make some major changes in it. Again, if

lack of minority applicants was an issue, we might increase our promotional efforts and review their tuition packages. The same conclusion might be drawn if our results after the first year were 14
percent. Certainly this is a very positive and happy condition. However, since the plan called for something much less, there is obviously something wrong with the plan and campus leaders need to
get a much firmer handle on the dynamics that impact minority
enrollments.

Control of the implemented strategic plan also suggests that
no part of the plan can be considered sacred (Harrigan, 1985). As
in the example above, if, upon analysis, the initial campus leaders
and planners had misevaluated the actual environmental conditions and now see a different set of opportunities or constraints,
those leaders and planners should alter the plan, including changing goals and objectives. Once again, we understand that this creates additional credibility problems for campus leaders and
strategic planners. We are not only saying that the plan should be
based upon attainable and measurable criteria and that these measures should be used as a foundation for a KPI system, we are now
saying that once a campus has done all this work, it must be willing to toss parts of the plan out, change other parts, and restructure what it is doing as it progresses. Flexibility is the key to
managing changing times, and it is one of the key components of
organizational excellence in strategic management (Harrigan,
1985; Peters and Waterman, 1982).

One of us (D.J.R.) recalls a personal experience (also related
in Rowley, Lujan, and Dolence, 1997) of sitting in a university
strategic planning meeting and proposing that the committee
alter some of its strategic planning goals. This came after a year's
measurement process and reports that suggested that a couple of
enrollment goals were way too modest and a couple of other
financial goals were way too optimistic. Two of the academic
deans, who were also permanent members of the committee,
became extremely agitated and incensed by the suggestion. They
went on to suggest that this was a clear sign that strategic planning
would never work if people were constantly willing to alter goals.
Goals are goals, they emphasized, and once in place, they should
never be changed. This philosophy of what amounts to stagnating
goals espoused by several managers is why our discussion of

varying goals may be construed as quite controversial to some college administrators.

We have all been taught that goal-setting and goal achievement are noble activities. The idea that goals can be altered merely to reflect a more accurate picture of reality (changes in the marketplace) is reprehensible to some. These people regrettably miss the point of strategic planning and goal-setting. Strategic planning is about achieving better alignment with the environment, and strategic planners do not create goals in a steady state. As the environment changes, the college or university must also strategically change how it attempts to accomplish alignment. Goals and objectives that appear to be correct for one conditional set of the environment at one point in time may be incorrect at another. In the strategic implementation process, a college or university should never set itself up for defeat by establishing long-term goals that do not take into account or adjust for environmental change. Pearce and Robinson (2000) call this technique "premise control." As campus leaders and planners know more and more about how their environments are changing, they become better able to anticipate and quickly modify their planning premises over time.

In this discussion thus far, we have not discussed KPIs as a control tool for the academic side of the plan. We do not want to imply in any way, however, that academic leaders and faculty cannot use KPIs to control the successful implementation of the academic plan. Even though many faculty tend to look at an academic plan as an event more than a campuswide strategic plan, the academic base is always moving and faculty are the ones who are driving it. Identifying long-term academic goals and short-term objectives is still a very appealing way of cementing the academic plan. For example, if a college of business is American Assembly of Collegiate Schools of Business (AACSB) accredited and uses the Educational Testing Service (ETS) examinations (which are exit exams given to all business graduates), it gets feedback as to mean scores in several business and economic areas (Educational Testing Service, 1997). The scores also come with national comparisons. So if a particular school sees that its overall performance on the understanding of international business is significantly below national norms, and in the academic plan the school has set a strategic goal of raising ETS scores to 20 percent above national averages throughout, academics may follow the same type of measurement and decision-making scenario we described for the enrollment example above. KPIs can be applied to many other academic areas as well (Fields, 1993).

Environmental Monitoring

To continue the discussion of environmental interface that we began in the last section, campus leaders and strategic planners can never take the environment for granted. The environment determines the well-being of a college or university and can either reward or punish that institution for serving it well or serving it ill. Campus leaders and strategic planners consequently must always be vigilant to what is going on in the environment, thus engaging in what Pearce and Robinson (2000), among several others, refer to as environmental scanning.

In the postindustrial era, change in the environment is constant and it is increasing. The explosion of information and technology alone has created unprecedented changes in terms of its impact on human life and learning. There is simply no way the academy can remain unresponsive to these changes.

In any effective strategic planning team, at least one member should take responsibility for environmental scanning by analyzing the activities of stakeholders who can both positively and negatively affect the college or university. Often part of the strategic planner's basic job description can include this as a major activity of the job, particularly once the campus has implemented the plan. Though the macroenvironment is far too great for just one person to scan effectively, having at least one person permanently assigned to keep an eye on the environmental forces that are mostly likely to impact the institution is a minimum requirement of the control portion of the process. Having more people engage in environmental scanning is an even better idea. As changes in this more immediate set of environmental forces become apparent, this individual (or group) can alert the planning committee, and the committee can then determine how best to respond. For example, if a major donor is becoming unhappy, if governmental forces are becoming more critical of campus activities, or if a nearby college or university announces a new and competitive program, the scanner can feed this information to the committee immediately so that it can decide on its best course of action.

Further, as campus leaders and planners become more comfortable with the scanning process, they will find that their predictive skills will also improve, thus giving them even stronger control of the ongoing strategic management process. Over time, as the strategic planning process has solidified and formalized the key environmental indices, strategic planners usually delegate these functions to permanent staff departments, such as the office of institutional research.

Benchmarking

There is much going on throughout the world of higher education that can provide exceptional examples for college and university leaders and planners as to what they can do to improve their own campuses, as well as provide guidance as to how to get things done. Within the several niches described in Chapters Two and Three, there are campuses that do things well and campuses that do things poorly. Some campuses do things exceptionally well. It is this last group of campuses that hold some promise for other campuses that are going through their own strategic planning process. It is not that one campus can easily turn to the leadership of an outstanding college or university and be given major assistance in conducting change. Rather, these exceptional campuses (or perhaps exceptional programs) can serve as benchmarks to other campuses developing strategic plans and provide real-world examples of what can be done and how it can be done (the implementation and postimplementation phases of the process).

For example, if a small college in the Southwest wants to reengineer its music program to become one of the nation's top five music programs (as established by accreditation agencies or top academic professional organizations), it must first look at the current top five music programs around the country and determine what makes these particular programs outstanding. What is the makeup of the faculty? How and where were they educated? What is their research output? Where is their scholarship published or presented? How do these schools recruit students? Where do the students come from? How do faculty and students interact? What kinds of strategic alliances do these schools have and with whom? What is the portion of the institution's endowment that belongs to the music program? How has it grown? How is it used? What sort of support does the program enjoy from its alumni, from its community? Why do these schools enjoy the reputation that they do? Finally, do the answers to all of these questions adequately explain why the top five schools are considered the top five schools?

The answer to each of these questions will be a benchmark. Each of these benchmarks also identifies important goals and operational objectives that can suggest to the small Southwestern college what it needs to do to move toward its overall goal and identify several of the KPIs that help contribute to the quest. This is best accomplished by looking at a group of other colleges and universities, not just one. As in our example here, looking at five colleges and universities provides five sets of data, and one will quickly notice that the data vary from one campus to another. Each of the analyses will demonstrate inherent differences between campuses, just as much as they will demonstrate the commonalities. One campus may have a highly distinguished faculty, while another will have a reputation for producing high-quality graduates. One campus might have a huge endowment, while another might have a major investment in technology. Furthermore, diverse colleges may have dissimilar strategic positions in the marketplace, employ different strategies, or have varying strategic orientations to the marketplace.

It is therefore always a mistake to look simply at one campus and try to clone it. Rather, it is important to look at the pattern of excellence that the data suggest and then look at the focal campus to see where the possibilities lie. Once the college has matched the opportunities to the available resource base, the elements of the plan that mirror elements of the top five programs that the small college wishes to emulate provide the initial goal set and ongoing comparison group to help the small college achieve its goal of becoming one of the top five.

Assessment Controls

As we stated early on in this book, more and more external authorities and agencies are pushing for better assessment of college and university program outcomes as funding agencies look for better ways of allocating scarce resources. We have already suggested in Chapter Three that some colleges or universities might become totally assessment-based in their orientation and marketing efforts. Beyond those environmental realities and possibilities, assessment can also be an important tool for the strategic management process as the implemented plan moves on.

The assessment process is similar to the use of KPIs in that direct and indirect performance indicators are employed to measure student mastery of specialized knowledge, skills, attitudes, values, and norms at the programmatic level. Knowledge gained from the assessment is then compared to the institution's mission and functions to determine what programs (or parts thereof) require improvement (Commission on Higher Education, 1996).

Academic Outcomes

When one thinks of assessment, one normally thinks of measuring the performance of students upon their completion of an educational learning experience. Certainly we do not dispute the importance of this area of assessment. It just isn't all there is to assess.

A college or university is really interested in several academic outcomes: high quality graduates, first-rate faculty (as a work in progress), high-quality basic and laboratory research results, first-class applied research, and high-class and meaningful academic services to the community, state, nation, and world. Potentially, there are a lot of areas here that the campus needs to assess.

There are some standardized assessment tools that one can currently find in K–12 as well as higher education. Testing is the most common method. As we suggested in the business school ETS example above, these standardized tests are available and provide colleges and universities significant information about graduating student performance in business and economics subject areas. A variety of these tests already exist for other academic areas.

For adequately assessing faculty performance, the jury is still out. Every faculty member is reviewed yearly or periodically based on generally loose criteria related to teaching, research, and service. As we well know (both of us are currently academic chairs), measuring these areas is difficult at best. What does one measure? Are there national norms or standards? What constitutes good teaching? How does one evaluate meaningful research? And finally, what makes up quality service?

One realizes that there are no national norms or standards for teaching at the college level, that measurement is problematic, and that in many cases the end result of evaluation is a gut feeling. "Good teaching is like pornography—it's impossible to define it, but I know it when I see it," a departmental chair said at a recent administrative staff meeting in preparation for an annual faculty review. This statement mirrors (although not necessarily in context) what many other chairs or academic deans have conveyed to many nontenured faculty members looking for guidance in classroom instruction.

So what are we suggesting? Simply that each campus needs to understand what it wants from its faculty and must determine internal benchmarks for what it expects (Kerr, 1975). What is more important, the strategic academic plan needs to outline clearly what those benchmarks are and how one can achieve them. For example, if research and publication are important to the academic direction of a particular campus, the plan needs to spell out specifically what the campus considers excellent research (types of acceptable journals, number of publications per year, and number of juried presentations per year, as an example). For teaching, the plan needs to detail what should happen in the classroom (use of a variety of pedagogy, phase-down or phase-out of the lecture method, student performance on assessment exams, interaction with students to include joint research, and placement of students following graduation, as examples) (McKeachie, 1986). As for service, the plan needs to say what it considers appropriate college and community service (importance of committees faculty sit on, participation and leadership on those committees, amount and importance of external service, and impact of service on the college or university, for example). Deciding what manner of faculty a given campus wishes to cultivate and defining exactly what that faculty should accomplish will help cement the implementation of the academic plan, and will also tell individual faculty members what the institution expects from them and allow them to formulate their own planning to better conform to the needs of the college or university.

Fiscal Resource Outcomes

In the ongoing strategic management that follows the strategic planning and implementation segments of the overall process, fiscal assessment should be a constant part of the review process. Simply, each campus needs to know whether the resources it has expended on strategic initiatives are generating the anticipated results. Unlike businesses that will be anxious to generate and measure profits, public colleges and universities are treated primarily as cost centers (meaning that they expend resources rather than generate them), so much of the fiscal responsibility one would see on a public college or university campus is simply meeting their budgets and not exceeding expenditures beyond revenues.

Private institutions, however, although certainly not endeavoring to create huge surpluses, require surplus as an important source of financing (Anthony and Young, 1994). Private universities must update their infrastructure and purchase expensive and sophisticated equipment, but they do not have the luxury of obtaining government-driven financing. They also cannot finance these assets purely through debt, since debt service obligations cannot exceed annual cash flows.

Also, any organization, public or private, that employs a growth strategy will experience a time lag between the new expenses incurred due to new program development and the collection of new revenues raised from those endeavors. One can consider surpluses a healthy vehicle for sustaining institutional growth. Short-term debt is an alternative, but a costly one (Young, 1994).

Finally, some of the assets of the public and private institutions are restricted to a specific purpose of a specified time period. Endowment funds, although they may represent a large asset base for the institution, are not flexible and do not signify sources of capital beyond their specified purposes. It is quite possible for a private university with large endowments and a negative cash flow not to meet their financial obligations. (An interesting example is Upsala College, which can be found on the Internet at http://www.upsala.org/histouc2.html.)

There are some revenue-generating operations on a campus that can provide additional resources, especially for campuses that are engaged in distance learning and virtual learning on the Internet. For example, campus services such as the bookstore, student housing, and food services all have the potential of having better operating efficiencies that can help the campus generate some extra revenues through savings, or help the campus be economically more competitive with other colleges and universities in its service area. Many of these services have been subcontracted out to reduce operating costs and reduce payroll expenses. Contracts with subcontractors may be reconsidered in light of the need for additional sources of revenue. Therefore, it is important to have included these services in the strategic planning process and be able to assess their performance on at least an annual basis.

As we suggested earlier, distance learning and virtual learning through the Internet are potential moneymakers for the campus. Since there are generally no restrictions on how many students a particular college or university might serve through these media, the market available to the campus is gigantic. Also, since most of the programs and courses that the campus will make available through these additional media are duplications of courses and programs faculty have already developed, there is the potential for appreciable returns through economies of scale. Although undoubtedly these activities *must* be developed and operated with strict business principles (by including these areas within the strategic plan, setting specific objectives for their operation, and controlling them with KPIs), these activities can be very lucrative for the campus. In an era of stretched resources, these types of additional resource generators may be of significant value.

Philosophical Outcomes

The term *philosophical outcomes* may seem awkward—for aren't philosophies what most people look for up-front before anything is done? Perhaps, but here we are concerned with the philosophical dispositions at the end of a measurement period just as much as we are at the beginning.

As we described in Chapter Two, philosophies of focus are a choice for colleges and universities. For example, if a campus has been in flux, has found that it was more provider-driven than it ought to be, and through the strategic planning process has decided to become more consumer-driven to match more appropriately the position it hopes to achieve within the domain of higher education (as suggested in Figure 3.2), then just as it needs to assess its resource position and the progress it is making toward its goals, it also needs to assess its philosophies to see whether the philosophical movement it is looking for is becoming a reality.

Certainly, measuring and assessing philosophy is a far more difficult challenge than measuring and assessing resources. Through some of the same procedures the college or university can use to assess learning and the educational process, however, it should become apparent whether the campus is moving in the right direction. For example, one might look at a growing inclusion of learners in joint research projects with faculty, growing inclusion of outsiders in course planning and assessment, evidence of greater use of alumni follow-up data and specific changes that have resulted from that, or the actual decline in days spent lecturing versus days spent in experiential or group learning, to name only a few potential areas for analysis. These examples provide several ideas of activities that campus leaders and planners can actually measure.

Attitudes are more difficult to measure. Assessment of attitudinal change may be more subjective than objective. As one looks at the political activities across a campus, though, one can tell whether it is heating up or cooling down. One can also tell what direction it is taking. Since politics are natural on any campus, they will not go away, but they will change. Watching that change will tell leaders and planners whether the politics are becoming more tolerant of the strategic planning process, just as they can tell whether the politics have actually become an ally. When campus leaders and planners can determine that those politics are still negative, or perhaps even more negative at the end of an assessment period as opposed to what they were at the beginning, the assessment would be that there is still a great amount of work to do. Therefore, philosophies can be assessed, at least in general terms.

Keeping the Strategic Plan Dynamic and Cutting-Edge

Throughout this chapter, we have tried to emphasize that follow-up is absolutely essential if a campus is to continue to maintain the momentum it will have started when it implemented its strategic plan. Strategic implementation instills in people's operational psyche the understanding that what is really changing on a campus is how people do things, how they think about their own work as well as that of the overall campus, and how they interact with their learners or outside stakeholders. Part of a successful implementation process must be, as we discussed in the previous section, a philosophical change toward doing things differently in the future from how they were done in the past.

In moving toward a different kind of a campus there are several areas that campus leaders and strategic planners need to keep a handle on to keep the process strong and effective. These are areas that they must constantly monitor and assess in terms of what is happening and how it affects the campus.

Keeping Trust

Right at the top of this list is keeping a high level of trust between campus leaders and the rest of the campus—faculty, staff, and students. Trust is a delicate commodity. It is difficult and complicated to build and nearly impossible to rebuild. Zand (1981) reminds us that administrators and faculty express their feelings of trust through their ability to share information, allowance of others to influence their behavior, and need to control the change process. Employees who trust disclose pertinent facts and feelings, are receptive to influence, allow for interdependence, and impose minimal controls on others.

Keeping in mind that the strategic plan will probably develop change scenarios that are potentially threatening to people (or at least perceived to be threatening), there is bound to be not simply resistance to change, but a certain level of mistrust as well, which intensifies resistance (Zand, 1981). This is the primary reason the strategic planning process must be as open and inclusive as possible so that the people that the strategic plan will involve and affect will have the opportunity to voice their opinions and concerns about the implementation process. Campus leaders and strategic planners must keep the process open, be willing to listen to other members of the campus, and respond appropriately and in a timely fashion. At some point, the process should come to a resolution, whether by actions taken by the governing board, top-level mandates, or even campuswide referendums. At some point the planning must come to an end and the implementation stage must begin.

This is where the doubters and pessimists will sit back and wait for the plan to fail. This is also where some antagonists will try to find ways to make the plan fail; low-trust groups will self-destruct. Of course, the first time these groups will pounce will be when some implementation aspect of the plan or some outcome of implementation is not what campus leaders and planners told the campus it would be. They will hold this out as a demonstration of the validity of their mistrust, and they will then build on this to destroy the rest of the process.

This scenario is particularly likely if there has been a history of bad relations among faculty, staff, and the administration of the campus. In referring back to the situations we have described at the University of Northern Colorado, we recall that the 1981 reduction in force was an outcome of a campuswide planning exercise, and it became apparent that the reduction in force was the primary goal of the administration when they began that campuswide planning event. This goal, however, was not one of the objectives the administration had stated up-front, and it became apparent only in the later stages of the process. The faculty and staff felt betrayed, and rightfully so. This mistrust of planning carried over to the 1992–1995 planning process, and was used repeatedly by antagonists to try to stop the process. This is a clear example of the problems that arise when trust is lost between campus constituencies in campuswide activities.

What can campus leaders and planners do? As we have stated throughout, the process must be open and it must be honest. As campus leaders begin to implement the strategic plan (and again, we suggest this be done in an incremental manner, putting into place an easier portion of the plan first), they must be completely certain that they are up-front and sincere about everything that happens. They must follow the plan. They must monitor how the implementation is occurring. They must report both successes and problems to the campus, and be willing to take the heat for honest mistakes as well as be forthright about how they plan to correct them. Openness and frankness must continue to be the hallmarks of the implementation process.

The greatest danger to the planning and implementation processes is that these are human events. That means that they are less than perfect and mistakes will be made. The potential of hidden agendas and the reality of mistakes can raise the specter of justifiable distrust. To combat these two issues, there simply can be no hidden agendas and when mistakes are discovered, campus leaders and planners must be open, forthright, and absolutely honest. They need to take the blame, and then they need to tell the campus what they want to do about it. It is only through complete candor and truthfulness that the faith is kept. The doubters and antagonists have real problems dealing with honesty, and when they see that there is no dishonesty, they will probably go back into the shadows and wait for the next problem to surface.

Looking Forward to Future Change

The essence of the strategic planning process is that change is not a one-time event—it is a continuous phenomenon. As we have stated throughout, this is not a popular prospect to faculty, staff, students, or even to many administrators. The whole idea that people have gone through a change in how they do what they do, only to realize that they may have to change things again not too far down the road is, to say the least, disconcerting. The certainty is that the major changes we are making in society today are not permanent changes. Our society has moved from heavy dependence upon physical industry to a growing dependence on the flow of information and the technology that supports it. Information is, perhaps, becoming the most crucial institutional resource. While most people do not know what the next economic driver will be, entrepreneurial activities are constantly testing and searching for better ways of doing things. When better ways are found, the academy will need to change yet again to accommodate yet another societal and economic change. Change is inevitable but an institution's ability to adapt to change is not (Toffler, 1970).

The implication to the college or university is clear. *If you are enjoying this change, you are really going to love the next one (and the one after that, and the one after that, and. . . . .).* What is particularly disturbing is that the rate of change continues to accelerate (Peters, 1987). This means that the Information Age may be far shorter than the nearly three-hundred-year period the world experienced in the Industrial Age. Some scholars tell us (Drucker, 1985; Toffler, 1990) that the next major change event could occur in as little as twenty to twenty-five years. If colleges and universities are having difficulty making changes to accommodate the technological revolution of the Information Age, they will have extreme difficulty again in the next twenty years or so accommodating another age shift.

The lesson here is to build a campus paradigm that supports ongoing change. Certainly, this cannot occur if the campus stakeholders do not find ways of trusting each other or do not find ways of working together so the campus can move as one (instead of trying to herd cats, to repeat a popular metaphor). The best way of creating this type of culture and climate is to get through the first set of changes with as little disruption and disappointment as possible. This occurs when the process is open and honest, and when there is real care for the humanity of everyone involved. When people can come through the planning process and see that they have not been diminished but are actually better off than they were originally, they are far more likely to support going through another change process. Then, as they experience positive outcomes from that, they will be even less resistant to subsequent changes (Zand, 1981). Creating this sort of culture is an issue of management choice. Just as honesty, openness, fairness, and concern are all choices, deciding to build a culture of positive change responsiveness is also a choice. Understanding this up-front should help campus leaders and strategic planners design the strategic plan and implementation processes in such a way that they can build trust and change tolerance for the future.

The College or University as a Learning Organization

From the literature on organizational theory we understand that successful organizations are learning organizations. A learning organization is one that stores in its collective memory the cumulative experience of the organization and its members and what outcomes of events have been (Wick and Leon, 1993). In a sort of Pavlovian context, organizations learn from their experiences and mistakes and use that knowledge to reposition themselves for future, similar events. Organizational learning reflects a series of choices.

One of these possible choices is to ignore the past. In this choice, campus leaders and planners make a decision that what happened in the past is an isolated event and has no bearing on the present or future. While this may be partly true, unfortunately the past event is stored in the collective memory of the campus (Katz and Kahn, 1966). People remember what happened, even if they were not present when the event occurred. For example, one of us (H. S.) vividly remembers attending a faculty senate meeting where the faculty members were debating an issue concerning the purchase of a campus in the 1960s. Although none of the members of the senate were part of the institution at that time (or could have been), they were so indignant over the administration's actions that one would have supposed that the purchase had recently occurred. Stories, traditions, cultures, and behaviors all reflect what has gone before, and new people on campus soon learn about the history of the college or university and can become as deeply invested in the past event as though they had actually experienced it.

Another choice is to belittle the past. Here, campus leaders and planners acknowledge past events, but downplay their importance. Sure, they might say, mistakes were made in the past, but we would never make the same mistakes again. With a loud silence, the campus sits back to wait and see. Generally, it is a mistake to take the past for granted. Not only is institutional memory in play, but also the events of the past shape the future and more than likely contain valuable lessons for present-day planners. Attributing past events to poor leadership (that is now gone, perhaps), or to unexpected difficulties that no one could foresee (because no one was looking for them), or to lack of proper support (which will be even more difficult to co-opt this go round), may doom current protagonists to repeat past mistakes.

The third choice is to learn seriously from the past. When campus leaders and planners take the time to analyze what happened in a past event, and what is more important, determine why it happened, they give themselves the opportunity to avoid making the same mistakes again. For example, to revisit the University of Northern Colorado examples, if campus leaders and the strategic planners had been up-front with the campus, particularly its faculty, and stated what the plan would not do (no reduction in force, no program consolidation, no decline in benefits) they would have gone a long way toward demystifying the process, enhancing trust, and increasing the likelihood of the successful implementation of their plans.

Campus leaders and strategic planners must support the organizational learning process by being aware of the institution's history and by adding to it in their actions. The real benefit for the campus will be that the focal change process will be added to the collective memory as a good event (Stonich, 1982). This kind of history will make it even easier and smoother to move on to the next change event. By creating an awareness of what works and what doesn't work, not only do campus leaders and planners avoid the mistakes of the past, but they also set themselves up to be even more successful in terms of how things will actually work in the future.

The Role of Total Quality Management in Colleges and Universities

We conclude this chapter with a discussion of total quality management (TQM) as one of the components of the college or university's strategic planning objectives. We feel it is appropriate here because TQM represents a philosophy, a mindset, and a method of operationalizing strategic planning that will have many long-term benefits for the campus. While some may scoff at TQM as a management fad (similar to *Theory Z* [Ouchi, 1981] or *In Search of Excellence* [Peters and Waterman, 1982]), TQM has weathered that particular storm and continues to enjoy great respect from many sectors of the economy. Lewis and Smith (1994) note over two hundred universities employing TQM, most notably Harvard University.

The Goals of TQM

Proponents of TQM emphasize the fact that TQM is an input-output system that conceptually and procedurally is meant to integrate management, social, and technical organizational systems to maximize customer satisfaction. The goals of TQM are fairly straightforward and have been characterized by Lewis and Smith (1994) as the "Four Pillars of the House of Quality" (p. 91).

• The first pillar is customer service. Consumers will always get the product or service they purchase on time and at the highest level of quality possible, with quality defined from the consumer's perspective. The customer must be completely satisfied, the first time, every time. Since the customer determines whether quality has been achieved in its totality, and the customer only experiences the finished product or service, the organization must internalize customer-driven quality to guarantee that the management process meets quality standards (Dobyns and Crawford-Mason, 1991). (The underlying assumption is that only by having the management process meet quality standards can the organization's finished products or services meet similar standards.) Therefore, employees are also considered customers and they must also be completely satisfied.

• The second pillar is continuous improvement. The manager's job is to improve the management process continuously so that all the employees are focused on satisfying their particular customer groups' needs (Johnson, 1998). Clearly, then, it is the administrators, not the employees, who are responsible for developing and implementing systems changes to maximize customer satisfaction.

• The third pillar is processes and facts. Quality must be designed into the production and distribution of every product or service, not relegated to a separate quality control operation, to ensure satisfaction of internal customers (employees). The development and implementation of the processes of producing the products or services are the fundamental underpinnings of total quality management (Melan, 1993). Furthermore, customers require timely and accurate information in order to use products and services in an efficient manner and must also be satisfied as to the data that accompany those products and services.

• Respect for people is the fourth pillar in the TQM process. Quality of output (what the customer receives) is highly correlated to the quality of work life (one of the inputs) and every employee (also the customer) must function at full potential and be actively involved in the operation.

Translating the Goals of Total Quality Management into a Campus Setting

Lewis and Smith (1994) state that the first step in translating TQM goals into a campus setting is to define the internal and external customers of the institution and their relevant needs. Internal customers can be academic (students, faculty, programs, and departments) or administrative (students, employees, units, departments, and divisions) customers. Direct external customers include any group or individual who provides inputs or receives outputs from the university (such as high schools, students' employers); indirect external customers are organizations that affect or are affected by the university (such as community, accrediting bodies).

It may be very tempting to assume that one knows the needs of each customer group. Colleges and universities are cautioned not to assume they know what the customer wants but rather to list their own perceptions of customer needs and then check this list by actually gathering primary data; that is, directly ask the customer. For example, one of us (H. S.) once had a rather protracted discussion with a university administrator concerning the declining enrollments in the institution's MBA program. When H. S. asked what the competitive advantage of the MBA program was over their local competitors' programs, the administrator responded, "We're a university, our competitors are merely colleges." When H. S. questioned the administrator as to whether the customer saw going to a university rather than a college as an added value, it was clear that the administrator was employing impressions and not customer-based information. Later questioning of MBA students by H. S. revealed that university status played a minimal role in their choice of academic institution.

Once the needs of each customer group have been established, they can then be translated into KPIs (Dolence, Rowley, and Lujan, 1997). For instance, students may perceive the number of students in a class as at least a partial indicator of their satisfaction with their education. A discussion with student groups might reveal that they really don't mind classes with forty to fifty students but truly abhor the impersonal nature of lecture-hall style classes with over a hundred students. The administration would then need to move to the second step or pillar of TQM, continuous improvement, which involves planning, doing, checking, acting, and planning again.

Continuous improvement begins with *planning*—asking questions: What are the needs of the customers and what changes and results are needed? What are the potential roadblocks to change? What information is needed to complete the task? Going back to our prior example, further questioning might reveal that students really don't mind the lecture format but would also like to have smaller discussion groups in order to explore topics in more detail. The faculty members and the students then work together to develop a new class format that reduces the lecture time of the class but introduces once-a-week small group discussion sections led by graduate students.

Once the plan is developed it is pilot-tested on a small scale (called the *do* stage) to provide further information for broader implementation. (In the above example, one course is singled out to test this methodology.) *Checking* compares the results of the pilot test with expected outcomes, and *act* modifies the original plan, given data comparisons, and broadens the implementation of the plan. (In the above example, undergraduate students might want to be graded on their learning in their small groups, while the graduate students would be given the authority to assign homework that accounted for 20 percent of the students' total class grade.) Since the process is continuous, *planning* would again occur to see if the students required additional improvements.

The third pillar or step of TQM, managing the facts, requires the institution to develop the information infrastructure and the necessary relevant analytical tools so that customers can get the information they need when they need it. Many universities not only have Web pages that describe their programs and related courses, but also allow their students to register for classes, determine graduation requirements, pay bills, examine last semester's grades, surf key research databases and library holdings, and communicate with faculty and fellow students.

Universities must be prepared not only to invest in the hardware and software needed to provide their internal and external customers with fast and reliable data, they must also be prepared to train users (faculty, staff, students) on how to manipulate and interpret the data. Some customers may be computer-challenged or lack the analytical background or skills necessary to create and interpret statistical data. Learning organizations must devote time, energy, and resources to ensure that all of their key customers are competent in the use of the organizations' vital planning and development tools.

Respect for people, the fourth step in the TQM process, we have discussed in the section on trust. Without repeating the prior discussion on trust, we emphasize that empowered employees are committed to the goals and ideals of the institution and will be a value-added resource. They will be eager to implement change because they will believe it is in the best interest of their customer, themselves, and the institution.

Final Thoughts

Solidifying and tweaking change requires understanding change, controlling and cementing change, and keeping the strategic plan on the cutting edge and dynamic. We cannot underplay the human side (McGregor, 1960) of strategic implementation and change: the best-made plans of any college or university are doomed to fail regardless of the best intentions, if all those impacted by the change process are not actively participating in the development and implementation of those plans.

Freeman and Gilbert (1988) have noted that for many organizations, "the central truth of the strategy process model is that people are the problems" (p. 134) and that strategic solutions "deny the relevance of individual human actors, the values that cause their actions, and the inevitable conflicts among those actions" (p. 155). We would further assert that any college or university that devalues their human resources and treats their personnel as cogs in the machine will inexorably underperform their competitors.

Colleges and universities must confront their own culture in terms of the worth and trust they place on their human capital. This may mean taking a very hard and unpleasant look at their current value system and realizing that substantive strategic changes will be impossible before the faculty and staff members are afforded equal ownership in the change process.

Chapter Twelve

From Strategy to Change: A Summary Perspective

As you have read through this book, it is likely that you have sensed that this phenomenon known as strategic management is a highly complex process characterized by a highly fragile series of events. There seem to be so many imperatives, things that campus leaders and strategic planners must be aware of and over which they must be in control if the strategic planning process is to be successful. The process may appear so complex as to be overwhelming, something normal people really can't do.

This particular impression, however, need not be true. Clearly, many colleges and universities have engaged in a strategic management process only to become disappointed and disillusioned. On many campuses, the mere mention of strategic planning elicits a chorus of laughter, jeers, or expletives. Upon analysis, it isn't strategic management that is the culprit at all, rather, it is the process that the campus adopted in the name of strategic planning that was at fault.

In this book, there is a great amount of information that most college and university leaders and strategic planners simply do not have. As Rowley, Lujan, and Dolence warned in their first book (1997), the tendency of many campuses is to try to adapt the textbook, *business* strategic planning model, and most fail. This is because strategy formulation and implementation in colleges and universities is quite unique, just as what we do on the modern campus is unique compared with what happens elsewhere in the economy. The strategic planning process and the resulting strategic plan itself must thus be unique. By building on the ideas presented in this and other books dedicated to strategic planning in colleges and universities, campus leaders and strategic planners *can* and *do* create successful plans. It is hard work, but the rewards are very much worth the effort.

In this chapter, we tie together the two major themes of this book, the various choices open to the academy we developed in Part One and the several methods of implementing those strategies we developed in Part Two. Then we tie this material to some of the major themes that Rowley, Lujan, and Dolence (1998, 1997) presented in their two earlier books. Finally, we incorporate these ideas into a discussion of the continuing importance of developing and maintaining a sustainable competitive advantage. We describe some of the problems of not only creating but sustaining excellence, as suggested by Miles and Snow (1984), and also discuss how successful implementation is the key to an institution's overall success.

Tying Strategic Options to Strategic Implementation Strategies

In Chapters Two and Three, we introduced and discussed sixteen types or models of higher educational institutions. We presented these as strategic options. In Chapters Seven and Eight, we introduced and discussed eleven methods of implementation that can be effective in securing the college or university's strategic plan. In this chapter, we discuss how colleges and universities can operationalize and integrate the sixteen models with the eleven implementation options.

Choosing the Appropriate Option or Set of Options

The sixteen models of higher educational institutions represent macro-choices. They represent strategic directions a college or university might choose as part of its overall institutional design. Strategic planners need to determine which single model, or which combination of models, they might want to pursue in the future, and then build their plan based on that choice.

Making a choice as to the specific strategy (university model) an institution will follow is the single most important decision strategic planners will make. From that decision, all the rest of the strategic planning process will emerge. As Rowley, Lujan, and Dolence (1997) stated, the decision should rest primarily on the external and internal environmental analyses and the institution's relative fit with its mission. The institution must understand what the needs of its service sector are and then look at its distinctive capabilities to provide for those needs if the strategic management process is to be effective. This is the environmental imperative, and the planning process cannot ignore it (Grimm and Smith, 1997).

If the environmental analysis results in the conclusion that the college or university is pretty much on track as it is, and simply needs to tweak a couple of its programs and services, the strategic planning process should be built around the type of institution the college or university is (comprehensive, specialty, etc.). In situations where there is a relatively good fit between the institution and its environment, the focus of the institution's efforts should be internal—investing in and developing the resources and skills necessary to produce greater customer satisfaction from a TQM perspective (Blanchard and Thacker, 1999). Using the resource and philosophical guidelines from Figure 2.2, the institution would then steer the plan toward building and sustaining the types of resources it needs and identifying and instituting the types of programming philosophies that it ought to represent.

If the environmental analysis suggests that the college or university's mission is seriously mismatched with its environment (if use of Figure 2.2 suggests that the consumer needs different services and programs other than what the institution currently provides) or is in a high-risk market position, then the strategic plan needs to focus on either changing the mission to better fit the current market position, or changing the institution's market position to better fit its mission or to reduce risk.

When there is a misfit between the institution and its environment, the focus of the institution's efforts should be first external and then internal. The institution will first need to determine what external forces are causing the misalignment, and then what actions the institution can take (both within the marketplace and internally) to reduce the gap between the organization's mission and market position. Most important, the institution will need to determine whether it would be easier to alter its current mission or whether it would make more sense to move its market position.

A mission-shift to better fit the marketplace requires that the institution focus its attention internally. College and university strategic planners will need to develop a new vision of the institution, create a culture that will serve as the new core, and provide resources and a reward system that support the new mission. For example, several proprietary colleges in New York and New Jersey started as two-year institutions, focusing upon job-driven high school and adult students who could not, for whatever reason, obtain entrance into a public community college. As these institutions grew, they realized that the job market had a greater demand for students with four-year degrees. They have tried (some successfully) to obtain four-year degree programs. This shift in their mission, however, has not been an easy one. We have interviewed several faculty recently hired by these institutions and found that these academics (with a strong research orientation and a familiarity with the culture and operations of a not-for-profit organization) do not seem to fit well in a proprietary culture. No real accommodations have been made by these institutions to modify their reward and operational systems to better fit their new mission and only time will tell whether these faculty will be assimilated into the culture or leave these institutions.

If the institution chooses to shift its market position to better fit its mission or reduce risk associated with its market position, the institution needs to

- Determine the direction, or directions, it needs to pursue, and based on that resolve plan for the proper resource base
- Alter and then reinforce the campus's philosophical mindset

For example, assume a small Midwestern college (4,500 students) determined after doing its environmental analysis that there was a real risk associated with being a fairly typical liberal arts college and decided to move their market position toward becoming a

Research Two institution. The models in Chapter Two would tell planners at that college that they must first build a significant resource base and acquire a faculty who are oriented toward basic research. If the college had only a few master's degree programs and no doctoral programs, it would have to include expanding its current program base and create a much stronger graduate program. It would also need to develop a major grants and contracts division and find research professors who do work that can attract major grant monies.

Of course, this would not happen immediately. With an aggressive plan, however, the college might reach this objective in five to ten years. The strategic plan would need to focus on the specific needs of the college and map out how to acquire them. As every reader of this example will already know, this particular college has chosen a tall mountain to climb and there will be many roadblocks along the way. Just because the college wants to become an R-2 institution (and even though there is a demonstrated need for an R-2 institution), there are no guarantees that the college will be able to accomplish its goals. The campus leaders and strategic planners will have to devote significant time, resources, personal effort, and imagination to this effort. The entire campus (and keeping in mind that with the changing of the nature of the faculty and staff, some will not be around when the new R-2 campus is up and running) needs to get behind the shift in strategic position.

Other examples of choices might include the following (again, always based on the results of the strategic environmental analyses). A corporate university might decide to break away from its corporate parent and become a nonprofit specialty college. An R-1 university might decide to branch out into supporting a full virtual university. A comprehensive college might decide to develop a virtual presence, develop a full virtual index, and develop three or four additional campuses around the state that all act as independent specialty colleges. A virtual university might decide to build a campus (brick-and-mortar business) and add a comprehensive university branch to its offerings. The examples can go on and on. The point is that once the college or university has been able to determine how it can best match the opportunities in its service environment (as well as identify the various threats that also are there), it can choose from among its list of options and set a strategic direction that then forms the basis of the strategic management process.

Choosing the Appropriate Implementation Option or Set of Options

As the strategic planning process progresses, campus leaders can look to the eleven implementation options for choices of how to activate the plan. As we emphasized in earlier chapters, this needs to be done during the planning formulation stage, since planning and implementation are intertwined and mutually dependent. Certain strategies may dictate the appropriate implementation procedure, whereas other choices will not be quite so obvious. For example, a major program change may involve reengineering much of the campus. To be effective, the college or university will need to spend a fair amount of time and expense in training or retraining its human resource core. In another example, an increase in out-of-state recruiting will require budget changes to add resources to the recruiting activities of the admissions office and to reduce resources somewhere else on campus (which may involve additional implementation activities).

This is a situational problem. Since every campus is largely unique (even different campuses within systems tend to have their own unique problems and issues), each specific plan needs to include an evaluation of the general state of the campus and its readiness to accept change. This evaluation will help campus leaders and strategic planners better determine what type of implementation procedure will be appropriate. Again, based on the character of the campus, this process can be rather simple or quite complex. A good rule of thumb, however, is that the larger the proposed changes, the more complex the implementation will be.

To return to the example of the college that wanted to become an R-2 institution, the implementation procedure would be rather complex. (Given the radical nature of the changes the campus is planning, this should not be a surprise.) As a result of examining what is needed to reengineer the campus to an R-2 college, and with all the planning in place, campus leaders would most likely use the implementation processes of controlling the budget to support the change, working with the human resource core, developing a new culture, and keeping track of progress by monitoring the KPIs to put their plan into action. This will involve a lot of procedure and detail to keep track of the proposed changes. Nonetheless, if the true commitment of the college is to achieve R-2 status, and the plans to achieve it are reasonable and functional, the extra amount of detail watching seems to be a small price to pay for an effective and fluid transition.

Less ambitious strategic initiatives will require less complicated implementation schemes. For example, if a midsized comprehensive university determines that it should add a distance-learning component to its offerings, it would probably institute a modest resource allocation change (one that might not affect any other programs on the campus) and do human resource training for the faculty and staff that will be affected by the change. Yes, this is a good amount of work, but compared to the previous example, it is far less complicated, consumes far fewer resources, and is far less disruptive to the general life of the campus.

The caveats here, again, are taking into account the unique conditions of each college and university campus to support change, and the current level of institutional health that characterizes the campus. Regarding this second important consideration, some campuses are healthier than others. Those that have healthy resource bases and positive and strong cultural forces will be able to go through the change process much more easily than campuses that do not. A campus that is in serious trouble, perhaps with an eroding student base, little to no endowment, and lots of conflict between campus constituents, may have no choice but to change. They may find, however, that the change process is so threatening to faculty and staff that the strategic management process seems fraught with extreme difficulties. It is ironic that the institutions that are in the most serious trouble and require the greatest amount of change will have the most difficulty changing. Their past inflexibility has created a self-destructive pattern.

Choosing the most effective implementation method (or combination of implementation methods) in the midst of all these possible variables becomes a function of the internal environmental analysis. The analysis includes

- At the micro level, analyzing the competencies of employees, their readiness for change
- At the macro level, analyzing the effectiveness of team and interteam dynamics, and the alignment of the institution's organizational subsystems
- At the ecological level, analyzing the impact of internal and external stakeholders on the institution and its internal operations

Testing the Choices

To help make certain that the strategic choices are correct and that the implementation processes are appropriate, campus leaders and strategic planners should check on the progress of the plan on a regular basis. As we suggested earlier, taking an incremental approach—what David (1994) calls *milestone planning*—will help make the implementation process more palatable and more effective. Milestone planning includes defining the most important assumptions of the plan, the important events to be completed and the intermediary stages for those events, and the sequencing or critical path the events must follow. At the completion of each milestone, the institution should review its original assumptions and decide what changes are necessary to the plan. The earlier leaders and planners can determine that a problem exists, the earlier they will be able to intercede and correct the course of the plan, preferably before people are adversely affected by the changes. It is a lot easier to pause and make small corrections midcourse than it is to stop and change direction or make major corrections down the road.

As campus leaders and strategic planners test their choices, they should feel that they can make both small changes and major changes. It could well be that one or more sections of the strategic plan, or the steps the college or university had determined to follow to achieve a particular objective, is seriously flawed. If so, the flawed aspects must be changed. If this means that redeveloping those parts of the plan or the implementation steps leads to a major redirection for the strategic planning process, then that's what it means. Campus leaders and strategic planners cannot back off from being dedicated to the process, and they must not lose confidence in the power of the process. They need to remember that strategic planning is a human process, and as such, is prone to error. Again, making these types of determinations sooner rather than later is always preferable and more beneficial to the campus.

Living with the Outcomes

After the planning and the implementation of the strategy, the organization will have changed. The hope is that the results will be what the strategic planners had envisioned. It is much more likely, however, that the results will be at least slightly different from what was envisioned. One major reason for this difference is that the environment is in constant flux and the ability to keep up is difficult to achieve. Another reason is that the process is, as we have stated, a human process. Unlike machines, the people who actually put the process into effect will significantly influence the implementation process. Although this inclusion will probably make the process more acceptable to those who must live with the strategic change, it may also cause the final results to be less optimal for the organization.

All this to say that campus leaders need to be tolerant of how the implementation process moves toward fruition. Expectations of 100 percent compliance with the plan, 100 percent participation of designated implementers, and 100 percent desired results are probably not going to happen. But not only is this expected, it is also all right. In a human-sensitive society, leaders and planners must be willing to bend, just as they are asking other members of the campus community to bend in making the strategic plan a reality.

Preserving the Right to Be Wrong

Part of this bending on both sides of the change process also involves being able to say from time to time that someone or something is wrong. The implementation process should have a climate that encourages looking critically at the process but sympathetically toward the participants. For all the reasons we've talked about throughout this book, making strategic choices and deciding on strategic implementation procedures are both subject to error—human error. Rather than look for scapegoats to punish, those involved in the ongoing evaluation of the process need to be compassionate, understanding, and forgiving. In doing so, they empower people to be more objective and realistic about what is going on, including themselves. This climate of achievement can only be accomplished in an environment that encourages evaluation rather than one that punishes the human decision-making process when it fails.

This dynamic consensus may be hard to achieve because of the perceived differences among ranks on a college or university campus. Shared governance aside, there is a perceived pecking order on campuses, and it is far easier to find fault with those in authority than to admit to personal error (some campuses are clearly better at this than others). What we are talking about here is one of the elements that helps to make the strategic planning and implementation process more effective—one that helps develop a newer, more positive internal environment and that helps set up the campus for a longer-term, positive change mentality.

Developing the Strategic Management Process

The long-term prognosis for a successful strategic plan is progression into a strategic management process. Though this might sound like meaningless jargon, there are some very important differences between strategic planning and strategic management. Strategic planning is the determination of what should be done and how the college or university ought to do it. It is the process of determining the conditions of the external environment and then developing a planning tool that will help align the campus with the environment. Strategic planning tends to be a beginning, in that it is the decision-making process of an institution.

What comes after the beginning, what should be emerging while the implementation process is going forward, is a new way of thinking and a new way of doing things. Strategic management is different from the type of decision making that was traditional on the campus. It seeks to achieve a new culture and a new set of relationships among campus constituents. What is most important, it seeks to make all decision making strategic in nature. As people go about their daily routines and come to various decision points, the decisive question will always be, how does this decision impact the strategic direction of the campus? Furthermore, this mental framework will be pervasive throughout the campus. So as faculty design their research, interact with learners (as we would hope all faculty come to view the people we have so long referred to merely as students), and work with other faculty, staff, and administrators, they are conscious of how their actions impact the well-being of everyone involved with them and the strategic position of the university. Individual faculty members will do this within the context of helping the institution achieve a better alignment with its environment and a competitive advantage in the marketplace.

Strategic management is not just what we might expect of administrators. Rather, strategic management refers to everyone in the organization and how each person manages her or his own responsibilities. This new culture of thinking and acting is the ultimate objective of the strategic process. When accomplished, the campus is prepared to deal with any opportunity, challenge, or crisis that might come along, and it will have helped establish its long-term survivability in an increasingly competitive market.

Identifying the Key Success Factors

How does one know if the strategic planning process has been successful? Beyond what we suggested in the last section about the ability of the campus to move from strategic planning to strategic management, there are several other signs of success. In this section, we identify and discuss several of them.

Adequate Databases

One of the hallmarks of the strategic planning process is its propensity for gathering and analyzing data. The logic is that one cannot make an informed decision if one is not informed. The more a college or university can develop its internal and external knowledge bases, the better prepared it is to make decisions about its interface with stakeholder groups and crucial issues. It would be a serious mistake to assume that the gathering of this information is a one-time event. Again, in developing an ongoing strategic management philosophy, individuals across the campus take responsibility not only for maintaining the currency of the databases they use in making their decisions, they also engage in activities that discover emergent databases and analyze them for information that could be of significance to the health of the campus.

We realize this is an amazing statement to make about the world's colleges and universities. Some might say that one of the central objectives of colleges and universities is to generate and collect data. True, but the reality is that the data gathered by the academic side of the house on campus is not necessarily the knowledge administrators are looking for or that is needed for the strategic planning process. In our work on many college and university campuses over the past several years, we have found that many campuses do not have much of an idea as to what is going on around them, and in some cases, don't seem to understand what is going on within them. Some campuses have allowed highly parochial and segmented groups to develop; as a result, a professor in biology may have no idea what type of learners the registrar is admitting (sociodemographics as well as academic records) or what new technological advances are occurring in the field of medicine.

A strategic management approach would dictate that our biology professor would not simply be informed as to whom the registrar is admitting but that the professor would adjust some of his or her classroom activities accordingly. The same professor would become better informed of new medical technologies because they might impact his or her research opportunities. This is important to the professor because this might help the department better support its programs of excellence, which help establish the positive reputation of the institution. More important, the same professor might even work with the admissions staff in helping to determine the admissions criteria as well as assist in the recruitment of students. Strategic management creates a partnership between administration and faculty with one common goal—the survival and prosperity of the institution.

Seeking, having, organizing, and using a variety of databases constitute a major acquisition of power. This power allows the organization to be open and informed about all the areas that it is connected to internally and externally. It fits within the general mission of knowledge generation and dissemination, and it helps provide for a more solid decision-making core across the campus.

Forces for Change

Recognizing and working with the various forces for change that exist in and around a college or university is clearly one of the successes of the strategic management process. Although strategic planning may have been the first campuswide process to try to identify these forces and formulate plans to address them, knowing what these forces are and working with them becomes second nature in the ongoing strategic management process. In having developed this type of strategic mentality, it is easy then to identify emerging forces and to meet them head-on long before these forces for change have the ability to become disruptive.

Developing this type of strategic mentality is part of a re-legitimization process that many colleges and universities need to deal with in our postindustrial society. The level and intensity of some of the attacks on higher education that Rowley, Lujan, and Dolence (1997) described can be linked with a general sense of some colleges and universities that they were above having to change, that they were immune from outside criticism and attack, that they did not need to be accountable to anyone other than themselves. This is clearly no longer the case, and campuses that are aware of and deal effectively with the forces of change that can impact them generally are not the targets of some of these external stakeholder attacks.

As we described earlier in this book, these forces for change are increasing in number, in intensity, and in their speed of change. Campuses that are reactive to change will find it more difficult to cope, but campuses that have learned how to learn from the process of change will be able to insulate themselves from serious, perhaps even catastrophic, attack. This is a clear benefit of the successful strategic planning process leading to a long-term strategic management system.

Options for Change

Strategic planning could well be the first formal opportunity a college or university has taken advantage of to look at options and opportunities for change. Many colleges and universities may understand the importance of strategic planning but do not have a good handle on what their options are once they start on the planning event. When one looks at the thousands of planning documents that are available (in libraries or on the Internet), one is struck by the sameness of the plans and the lack of detail. Many seem like plans to plan. This lack of detail stems from a lack of understanding of what the options are, what they look like, and how they work. A successful strategic planning process, therefore, is one that has determined what the appropriate options for the campus are and which of those options work best for that particular campus.

Like the forces of change, the options for change will emerge over time. In Figure 2.2, we hedged our discussion by identifying one of these options as the sixteenth or the emergent model in the domain of higher education. Just as the virtual university was by no means a well-conceived concept or even a seriously imagined phenomenon twenty years ago, there are other such models of higher education on their way. That is a certainty. Campus leaders and strategic planners must therefore keep a vigilant eye open for the emergence of the next model; this should prove to be both an exciting as well as potentially rewarding experience.

There is still another side of this issue of options that is even more exciting. That is, someone will design and develop these models, and almost any college or university might be the one to do it. Suffice it to say, however, that reactive campuses will never develop the new models, but the strategically managed, proactive campuses have a real shot at it. Of course, we are not predicting just a single emergent model, but several new models and hybrids of older ones. Being aware of the possibilities, and either taking early advantage of new opportunities or taking the initiative to create these opportunities, is another clear benefit of the strategic planning process.

The Human Resource Base

There may be no industry in the present or future world that is as dependent upon its human component than is education. Though K–12 and higher education is buying more and more into the world of technology, technology is a means and not an end. The world of knowledge management is dependent upon the creativity of humans and the ability of humans to communicate and connect.

Technology is helping education reach new learners and making the transfer of knowledge easier and more effective (and even more fun), but it is dependent upon the human core for its programming and its application.

We have tried to make it clear throughout this book that the fear that the strategic planning process will somehow be deleterious to the human component of the college or university campus is unfounded. In the long run, it is the early use of the human resource base that helps make the plan succeed. The strategic plan should be a key operative in improving the human resource core, not a way of relegating it to a lesser status on the campus. This is true of faculty, staff, and administrators. Strategic planning is based on a belief in win-win situations, where people are empowered to do more because they are capable and desirous of doing more (McGregor, 1960). True, a college or university may find that it needs to address the mix of a beginning set of people within the resource base and engage in some level of reengineering to bring it up to the level of effectiveness that the campus needs, but this reengineering can be a humane activity, and the objective of the reengineering should be a positive boost to everyone involved. Again, this represents a win-win situation.

The human core is crucial to the well-being of a well-run, strategically oriented campus. An outcome of the strategic planning process is having a new culture of cooperation and creativity that will clearly benefit the campus.

The Resource Base

In Chapters Two and Three, we built the general model of the domain of higher education on two components: philosophy and resources. Clearly, to move toward Zone 3 (the least risky zone), colleges and universities need to develop a strong resource base. Although we include the human resource base in the overall classification of resources, in this section we talk about the other resources of the campus, the capital resources a campus has or is able to acquire. A successful strategic management process will improve the capital resource base of the campus.

Certainly, as one objective of the overall process, reorganizing, creating, or enlarging the campus's resource base helps make change more feasible and easier to accomplish. For example, if a campus had several billions dollars in its unrestricted endowment fund (a highly unlikely event, but for demonstration purposes we assume the possibility), there is very little restraining it from taking advantage of the most lucrative opportunities it might find in its external environment. This would be a wonderful world to be a part of, but it is highly unlikely for most campuses.

Nonetheless, improving a campus's capital resource base does provide that campus with more leverage and a greater ability to take better advantage of important opportunities. When one takes into account the growing concern over ever-rising tuition rates, it is clear that the best way to improve the capital resource may not mean raising tuition. This is a short-term tactic at best, and in the long term will push the institution into a less price-competitive position. (Several private colleges have used their competitors' price increases to their own advantage. St. Joseph's College of New York and Briarcliffe College charge approximately $8,500 per year and have allowed other local private universities to charge nearly double their rate.) The campus needs more solid capital resources to help assure its long-term health and survival. Endowments, grants, contracts, buildings, facilities, grounds, and gifts are all areas that a strong college or university strategic plan should include. Forging new positive relationships with alumni and community leaders (perhaps in the form of an ongoing learning relationship, or in providing other services that create, build, and sustain loyalty and mutual support) can result in major contributions to the capital resource base of the campus.

Choosing a Direction for Future Growth

Given that the strategic management process is a process and not an event, it is entirely appropriate to look continuously for future growth opportunities—even when the college or university is basking in the glow of a successfully accomplished strategic plan. Change is the name of the game, and institutions of higher education will always be affected by change or create it themselves (Bennis, 1966).

As a success factor, looking at opportunities for change following an initial strategic planning event should be a much more exciting opportunity than the potentially divisive event it might have been the first time around. This can only happen if the first event was a positive and honest one, if people feel they benefited from the change, and if a new culture has begun to flourish. If faculty, staff, administrators, and learners all feel positive about the changes that have occurred and are anxious to bring even more improvements to the campus, this is a clear sign of successful strategic planning.

Evidence of the Strategic Mentality

In the previous section, we talked about the importance of developing a strategic management mentality as part of the strategic management process. Here we recognize the importance of being able to identify that on the whole, people across the campus are making their decisions in a strategic manner. Of course, in the short term, this will not be possible to measure, but in the longer term, the evidence should become more plain.

In the short term, people may speak strategically to conform to the direction spelled out in the strategic planning document. In areas that the strategic plan has not yet addressed or affected, however, individual faculty members and staff may go back to their old ways of making decisions and carrying out their responsibilities. This potential recidivism is why the follow-up phase of the process is so vital, because once the plan has been implemented, the people who are affected by the plan need to be rewarded to think differently about what they do and how they do it. This was the objective of using human resource training and development implementation methods we described in Chapters Seven and Eight. However, this kind of change takes time. People have to practice these new behaviors, a topic in Chapter Nine. They have to get comfortable with it, and it has to become the preferred way of getting things done.

This lack of opportunity for experiencing the benefits of the process is why campus leaders and strategic planners will probably not see much evidence of strategic thinking in the short term. It is more realistic to begin to see such patterns of decision making emerge in the longer term as people learn the new behaviors and become comfortable with them. When it becomes more evident that people across the campus are making their decisions based on the hoped-for strategic mentality the plan has fostered, though, leaders and planners will see another success of the strategic management process.

Developing and Sustaining a Strategic Advantage

While competition continues to grow and diversify, the academy is transforming into a much more vibrant and multifaceted domain of activity. Though some elements remain familiar and comfortable, the movement from the Industrial Age to the Information Age has brought unprecedented changes that have initiated revolutionary change in the academy. This brave new world is one of opportunities and threats, but through it all, the academy is becoming stronger, more diverse, and more viable than ever.

It's too bad that this statement does not apply universally to individual college and university campuses. Various colleges and universities will experience change differently; for some, change will be an exciting reality, whereas for others it will be very hard to face. Gone are the days when the term *Ivory Tower* meant a world apart. Today, the Ivory Tower is very much a part of everything, yet many colleges and universities have difficulty interacting with, yet alone understanding, many parts of the rest of the world. Perhaps the worst realization has been that colleges and universities must now compete for students (learners), faculty, high-quality staff and administrators, and limited resources.

In this book we have advocated the importance of strategic management in colleges and universities by describing the specific strategic choices and methods of implementation that can help campuses become more effective competitors in the changing domain of higher education. By choosing wisely, campus leaders and strategic planners can create a significant competitive advantage for their institutions. This is the essence of the strategic planning process. The rewards are long-term prosperity and academic success.

Alignment with the External Environment

In their first book, Rowley, Lujan, and Dolence (1997) said that strategic planning is the aligning of the organization with its most crucial environments. In this book, we have identified a series of options that campus leaders and strategic planners can choose from to find the exact model or combination of models that best aligns the campus with the needs of its service community. The development of databases on external forces, the creation of structural responses to better respond to those forces, and the ability to implement the plan all signal a healthy relationship between the college or university and its environment.

Strategic planning isn't just about learning about the environment. It is also about partnering with the environment. Moving away from the image of a sacrosanct Ivory Tower where wizards of knowledge create information for others to learn to a realization that colleges and universities are a vital part of a much larger economic whole, today's campuses are not a world apart but are inextricably tied to the rest of the commercial and intellectual world. By recognizing and participating in this type of communal development, colleges and universities will continue to provide much of the important substance upon which the quality of life will continue to evolve. This is not only a noble goal, it is also a matter of survival and one of the major reasons every college and university should engage in strategic planning and develop a strategic management process.

Alignment with the Internal Environment

One of the other clear benefits of a successful process is the transformation of the internal culture and operations of the college or university campus. Imagine a world where campus politics is a positive phenomenon instead of the road to disaster, where faculty, staff, learners, and administrators are all working toward the same goals and objectives, where creativity is the central activity with which everyone on the campus is fully engaged, and where learning is not confined to four-year programs or degree pursuit but grows from lifelong interactive and creative series of events. This is the promise of the academy in the advent of the Information Age and beyond.

The creation and sustaining of a clear competitive advantage depends upon the quality of every college and university's human core. By creating conditions in which the spirit of success and accomplishment are the norm rather than the exception and in the spirit of the imaginings in the preceding paragraph, people can get excited about doing better, and about being better. Campuswide, these human drivers will create a competency and creative atmosphere that will drive the institution's competitive advantage.

Choosing Excellence

Competition for more and better learners, more and better faculty, staff, and administrative personnel is already fierce and will only grow more vicious as time goes by. The move toward creating excellence and away from duplication and campus sameness is well under way. Today, there are easily identified centers of excellence in many parts of the world. These centers of excellence have developed a clear strategic advantage over similar programs in the same areas that cannot (or do not) provide the same levels of quality (and may even charge more for their offerings) or simply haven't figured out how to do things well. As learners and resources migrate from poorer campuses to better campuses, the competitive mechanism kicks in. As the saying goes, the rich get richer and the poor get poorer.

The key is that to be excellent or not to be excellent is much more of a choice than predestination. Although the resource base is never large enough for every campus to seek to offer excellent programs in every discipline, the strategic choice of matching particular campus resources to particular service area needs suggests that it is all right not to be all things to all people—no campus is or can be. What is important is to choose the options that meet the needs of the community and capitalize on the excellence capabilities of the campus, thus creating strategic advantage and helping assure long-term success.

Effective Implementation, the Key to Success

We began this book and will end it by recognizing the central dilemma that faces so many college and university strategic planning events: it is much easier to plan for strategic change than it is to accomplish it. The stumbling blocks may be that campuses do not realize what their options are or they may not understand the choices they have in implementing them. But the fact remains that many strategic plans go all the arduous way through development and approval only to become filing material sitting on an administrator's or a faculty leader's shelf.

Implementation is hard and it can be risky for all the reasons we spelled out in this book. It is understandable that when it comes right down to it, many campus leaders and even some strategic planners are hesitant or simply afraid to implement the strategic plan for fear of heavy resistance or failure. Nonetheless, what is at stake is the well-being, perhaps the survival, of the college or university itself. In a world of growing competition and declining resources, without the willingness to conduct a thorough strategic planning process and the bravery to implement the results, the campus will flounder and find that its struggles will only increase. The competitive world is an unforgiving one, and strategic planning and strategy implementation are any college or university's best defense.

A Final Word

The world of higher education continues to be mixed. There are superb colleges and universities throughout the world that are innovative, creative, extremely exciting, and contributing to the development of the new millennium. There are other colleges and universities that seem to struggle, seem to miss their potential, and appear to be without direction. So many of these struggling colleges and universities are surprised at their conditions and feel that they have been denied their appropriate respect or status. Some don't know just how it happened, but they do know they are worse off than they were before and that future trends are not promising.

This book is intended to demonstrate that colleges and universities can make significant and conscious choices that will help place their legitimacy and well-being on solid ground. Through the years, the strategic planning process has weathered many storms as researchers and practitioners have developed and refined it. Through it all, it has become more and more clear that strategic planning is a viable method for identifying a clear mission, developing plans to achieve that mission, contending successfully in a highly competitive world, and ultimately thriving. Though strategic planning in the academy tends to present unique problems and circumstances, when a campus can properly develop and implement its plan, the process can work as well as it has been demonstrated to work in the private sector. In a period of incredible change, growth, and development, strategic management helps colleges and universities identify and achieve their potential. This is the ultimate success of the process.

Miles and Snow's List of Strategic Variables

In order to determine the college or university's approach to the marketplace, campus leaders must determine the institution's characteristics relative to the four strategic types the authors present in Chapter Four. Miles and Snow (1978) have constructed a list of variables that denote characteristics by strategic type and are listed below (excerpted from Miles and Snow, 1978).

Variables Discerning Strategic Orientation to the Marketplace by Strategic Type

Domain Establishment and Surveillance

Defender

- Program-market domain is narrow and stable
- Aggressively maintains prominence in domain
- Ignores developments outside of its domain

Prospector

- Domain is broad and in a continuous state of development
- Has the capacity to monitor a wide range of environmental conditions, trends, and events
- Creates change in its market

Analyzer

- Domain is a mixture of products and markets, some of which are stable, others changing
- Extensive marketing surveillance mechanisms
- Avid follower of change

Growth

Defender

- Penetrates deeper into current markets
- Occurs cautiously and incrementally

Prospector

- Primarily through location of new markets and development of new programs

Analyzer

- Through program and market development

Operational Problems and Solutions

Defender

- Updates technology to maintain efficiency, continuous improvement
- Establishes core processes (vertical integration) to achieve efficiency

Prospector

- Technology and resources are devoted to the development of new programs
- Technology and assets are rooted in people, not routines or mechanical operations

Analyzer

- "Dual" technological core with stable and flexible components welded together by an influential applied research group
- A moderate degree of technological efficiency

Dominant Coalition and Management Succession

Defender

- Financial and operational experts wield considerable power
- Coalition has longevity and has been promoted from functional areas

Prospector

- Power centers around marketing and new program development
- Coalition is large, more diverse, and transitory
- Promotion both from outside and within the organization

Analyzer

- Centers around the functions of marketing, applied research, and production

Planning

Defender

- Intensive, oriented toward problem solving, undertaken prior to taking action
- Planning leads to action, which is then evaluated

Prospector

- Broad, oriented toward problem finding, contingent upon feedback from experimental action

- Evaluation leads to action, which is then formed into a plan

Analyzer

- Both intensive and comprehensive
- Evaluation leads first to planning and then to action

Structure

Defender

- Functional organizational structure
- Extensive division of labor and high degree of task formalization

Prospector

- Product organizational structure
- Little division of labor and low degree of task formalization

Analyzer

- A matrix structure—functional and program divisions operate independently
- Functional divisions are highly formalized while product divisions have low task formalization

Control

Defender

- Centralized, using vertical information systems (Galbraith, 1973)

Prospector

- Results-oriented, horizontal feedback loops

Analyzer

- Manages fundamentally different control systems (centralized for functional units, decentralized for program units)

Coordination and Conflict Resolution

Defender

- Uncomplicated and inexpensive forms of coordination (i.e., standard procedures)
- Conflicts between units handled through normal chain of command

Prospector

- Complex and expensive forms of coordination (i.e., project coordinators)
- Conflict by units handled through project coordinators via confrontation

Analyzer

- Both simple and complex forms of coordination, which operate independently
- Conflict is predictable and handled through project coordinators who arbitrate between production personnel (instructors) and applied researchers (program developers)

Performance Appraisal and Maintenance

Defender

- Compares present performance with previous time periods

Prospector

- Compares past and present performance with similar organizations

Analyzer

* Twin appraisal system: stable units use efficiency measures, program units compare performance against projections

Notice that the reactor strategy was not included for two reasons: administration has failed to communicate a specific strategic approach, or reactor organizations have inconsistent and unstable patterns and therefore present a mix of characteristics of defenders, prospectors, and analyzers.

The preceding list should therefore be employed as a checklist to determine the overall strategic orientation of the college or university. Please observe that although no college or university will be a perfect fit with one particular strategic approach, there should be a predominance of characteristics that border defender-analyzer or prospector-analyzer. Institutions that find that they have a combination of defender-prospector characteristics (and perhaps some analyzer characteristics as well) should accept that they possess reactor traits.

Glossary of Terms

The genre of strategic planning and strategic management has tended to develop terms that may or may not be familiar to the reader. For that reason, we present a number of the terms, with definitions, that we use throughout the book. We borrow most of these definitions from Rowley, Lujan, and Dolence (1997), and add some of our own.

Aligning. Recognizing and exploiting knowledge about an institution's strengths, weaknesses, opportunities, and threats to achieve congruity between the institution and the environment. Alignment achieves a dynamic equilibrium of the ecosphere of an institution and its environment.

Environment. The political, social, economic, technological, and educational contexts within which the college or university resides. It is both internal and external to the organization.

Implementation. Assignment of specific tasks and duties to organizational members to reflect the direction the organization has chosen as a result of its strategic planning activities, and a program of assurance that guarantees that those who are responsible for performing those specific tasks and duties will do so faithfully, effectively, and expeditiously.

Strategic. Refers to the relationship between the institution and its environment.

Strategic choice. A choice from among a variety of alternatives that has organizationwide implications and a major guiding impact on all members of the organization.

Strategic decision making. Deciding upon the optimal choice or choices that best fit the needs of the institution's strategic plan or strategic management.

Strategic management. The assurance that the institution's attention and focus are applied to maintain an optimal alignment with the environment.

Strategic planning. A formal process designed to help an organization identify and maintain an optimal alignment with the most important elements of its environmental set.

Strategic thinking. Arraying options through a process of opening up institutional thinking to a range of alternatives and decisions that identify the best fit among the institution, its resources, and the environment.

Strategy. An agreed upon course of action and direction that changes the relationship, or maintains an alignment that helps to assure a more optimal relationship, between the institution and its environment.

References

Ackoff, R. L. *The Democratic Corporation: A Radical Prescription for Recreating Corporate America and Rediscovering Success.* New York: Oxford University Press, 1994.

Allison, G. T. *Essence of Decision: Explaining the Cuban Missile Crisis.* Boston: Little, Brown and Company, 1971.

American Association of State Colleges and Universities (AASCU). *Wise Choices for Tough Times: Innovative Resource Reallocation Strategies to Strengthen the University.* Washington, D.C.: American Association of State Colleges and Universities, 1993.

Anthony, R. N., and Young, D. W. *Management Control in Nonprofit Organizations* (5th ed.). Homewood, Ill.: Richard D. Irwin, 1994.

Argyris, C. *Intervention, Theory and Method.* Reading, Mass.: Addison-Wesley Publishing Company, 1970.

Argyris, C. *Reasoning, Learning and Action: Individual and Organizational.* San Francisco: Jossey-Bass, 1983.

Association of Governing Boards (AGB). *Priorities.* Winter, 1996, *6*, 10.

Atwell, R. H. "Foreword." In D. J. Rowley, H. D. Lujan, and M. G. Dolence, *Strategic Choices for the Academy: How Demand for Lifelong Learning Will Re-Create Higher Education.* San Francisco: Jossey-Bass, 1998.

Axelrod, N. R. "Board Leadership and Board Development." In Robert D. Herman and Associates, *The Jossey-Bass Handbook of Nonprofit Leadership and Management.* San Francisco: Jossey-Bass, 1994.

Barfield, J. T., Raiborn, C. A., and Kinney, M. R. *Cost Accounting: Traditions and Innovations* (3rd ed.). Cincinnati, Ohio: West Publishing Company, 1998.

Barnard, C. P. *The Functions of the Executive.* Cambridge, Mass.: Harvard University Press, 1938.

Barry, D. D., and Whitcomb, H. R. *The Legal Foundations of Public Administration.* St. Paul, Minn.: West Publishing Company, 1987.

Beer, M. *Organization Change and Development: A Systems View.* Glenview, Ill.: Scott, Foresman, 1980.

Bennett, A. W. "Expanded Outreach at Clemson University: A Case Study." Paper presented at the annual conference of the National

Association of State Universities and Land Grant Colleges, Minneapolis, Minn., June 9, 1994.

Bennis, W. G. *Beyond Bureaucracy: Essays on the Development and Evolution of Human Organization.* New York: McGraw-Hill, 1966.

Bennis, W. G. *Organization Development: Its Nature, Origins, and Prospects.* Reading, Mass.: Addison-Wesley, 1969.

Birnbaum, R. "The Latent Organizational Functions of the Academic Senate: Why Senates Do Not Work But Will Not Go Away." In R. Birnbaum (ed.), *Faculty in Governance: The Role of Senates and Joint Committees in Academic Decision Making.* New Directions for Higher Education, no. 75. San Francisco: Jossey-Bass, 1991.

Blanchard, P. N., and Thacker, J. W. *Effective Training: Systems, Strategies, and Practices.* Upper Saddle River, N.J.: Prentice-Hall, 1999.

Blau, P. M., and Meyer, M. W. *Bureaucracy in Modern Society* (3rd ed.). New York: Random House, 1987.

Blustain, H., Goldstein, P., and Lozier, G. "Assessing the New Competitive Landscape." In R. N. Katz and Associates (eds.), *Dancing with the Devil: Information Technology and the New Competition in Higher Education.* San Francisco: Jossey-Bass, 1999.

Bonvillian, G., and Murphy, R. *The Liberal Arts College Adapting to Change: The Survival of Small Schools.* New York: Garland, 1996.

Bozeman, B., and Straussman, J. D. *Public Management Strategies: Guidelines for Managerial Effectiveness.* San Francisco: Jossey-Bass, 1990.

Brown, D. G. "The University of North Carolina at Asheville." In D. W. Steeples (ed.), *Successful Strategic Planning: Case Studies.* New Directions for Higher Education, no. 64. San Francisco: Jossey-Bass, 1988.

Brown, L. D. *Managing Conflict at Organizational Interfaces.* Reading, Mass.: Addison-Wesley, 1983.

Bryson, J. M. *Strategic Planning for Public and Nonprofit Organizations.* San Francisco: Jossey-Bass, 1989.

Bryson, J. M. *Strategic Planning for Public and Nonprofit Organizations, Revised Edition.* San Francisco: Jossey-Bass, 1995.

Bryson, J. M., and Bromiley, P. "Critical Factors Affecting the Planning and Implementation of Major Projects." *Strategic Management Journal,* 1993, *14,* 319–337.

Burke, W. W. *Organization Development: Principles and Practices.* Boston: Little, Brown, 1982.

Cameron, K. S. "Strategies for Successful Downsizing." *Human Resource Management,* 1994, *33*(2), 189–211.

Carnevale, A. P. *America and the New Economy: How the New Competitive Standards Are Radically Changing American Workplaces.* San Francisco: Jossey-Bass, 1991.

Chadwick, L. *The Essence of Management Accounting.* (2nd ed.). New York: Prentice Hall, 1991.

Chandler, A. D. *Strategy and Structure.* Cambridge, Mass.: MIT Press, 1962.

Clark, B. R. "The Insulated Americans: Five Lessons From Abroad." In D. Dill and B. Sporn (eds.), *Emerging Patterns of Social Demand and University Reform.* Tarrytown, New York: IAU Press, Pergamon, 1995, 162–164, 374.

Cline, N. M., and Meringolo, S. M. "A Strategic Planning Imperative: The Penn State Experience." In J. F. Williams (ed.), *Strategic Planning in Higher Education.* Binghamton, N.Y.: Haworth Press, 1991, 201–221.

Coate, L. E. *Total Quality Management at Oregon State University.* Corvallis: Oregon State University, 1992.

Cohen, S. S., and Zysman, J. "Countertrade, Offsets, Barter and Buybacks." *California Management Review,* Winter, 1986, *31*(2), 41–56.

Colorado Free University (CFU). "The Quick Facts About Creating a CFU Class." [http://www.freeu.com], 2000.

Commission on Higher Education. *Framework for Outcomes Assessment* (2nd ed.). Philadelphia: Middle States Association of Colleges and Schools, Commission on Higher Education, 1996.

Comte, T. E., and White, R. J. "Northern Kentucky University." *Case Research Journal,* Fall 1999, *19*(4), 65–92.

Cyert, R. M. "Carnegie Mellon University." In D. W. Steeples (ed.), *Successful Strategic Planning: Case Studies.* New Directions for Higher Education, no. 64. San Francisco: Jossey-Bass, 1988.

David, B. J. *Milestone Planning for Successful Ventures.* Danvers, Mass.: Boyd and Fraser, 1994.

Davies, G. D. "Higher Education Systems as Cartels: The End Is Near." *Chronicle of Higher Education,* October 1997, *44*(6), A68.

Davis, S. M., and Lawrence, P. R. *Matrix.* Reading, Mass.: Addison-Wesley, 1977.

Detweiler, R. A. *Case Study: How a Commitment to Technology Advanced Our Strategic Plan.* AGB Occasional Paper, no. 32. Washington, D.C.: Association of Governing Boards of Universities and Colleges, 1997.

Dill, D. D., and Sporn, B. *Emerging Patterns of Social Demand and University Reform.* New York: Pergamon Press, 1995.

Dobyns, L., and Crawford-Mason, C. *Quality or Else: The Revolution in World Business.* Boston, Mass.: Houghton-Mifflin, 1991.

Dolence, M. G. "Virtual University Indexes." [http://www.mgdolence.com/tours/virtual1.htm]. Michael G. Dolence and Associates, 2000.

Dolence, M. G., and Norris, D. M. *Transforming Higher Education.* Ann Arbor, Mich.: Society for College and University Planning, 1995, 7.

Dolence, M. G., Rowley, D. J., and Lujan, H. D. *Working Toward Strategic Change: A Step-by-Step Guide to the Planning Process.* San Francisco: Jossey-Bass, 1997.

Dooris, M. J., and Lozier, G. G. "Adapting Formal Planning Approaches: The Pennsylvania State University." In F. A. Schmidtlein and T. H. Milton (eds.), *Adapting Strategic Planning to Campus Realities.* New Directions for Institutional Research, no. 67. San Francisco: Jossey-Bass, 1990.

Drucker, P. F. *Innovation and Entrepreneurship: Practice and Principles.* New York: Harper and Row, 1985.

Drucker, P. F. *Managing in a Time of Great Change.* New York: Truman Talley Books/Dutton, 1995.

Duderstadt, J. J. "Can Colleges and Universities Survive in the Information Age?" In R. N. Katz and Associates (eds.), *Dancing with the Devil: Information Technology and the New Competition in Higher Education.* San Francisco: Jossey-Bass, 1999.

Dyer, W. G. *Team Building: Issues and Alternatives.* Reading, Mass.: Addison-Wesley, 1977.

The Education Resources Institute (TERI). *Life After Forty.* Washington, D.C.: The Institute for Higher Education Policy, October 1996, *8,* 13–19.

Educational Testing Service. *Major Field Tests: Business II.* Princeton, N.J.: Higher Education Assessment, Educational Testing Service, 1997.

Etzioni, A. Modern Organizations. Englewood Cliffs, N.J.: Prentice-Hall, 1964.

Evans, J. R., and Dean, J. W. *Total Quality: Management, Organization, and Strategy* (2nd ed.). Cincinnati, Ohio: South-Western College Publishing, 2000.

Farmer, D. W. "Strategies for Change." In L. A. Sherr and D. J. Teeter (eds.), *Total Quality Management in Higher Education.* New Directions for Higher Education, no. 71. San Francisco: Jossey-Bass, 1990.

Farrington, G. C. "The New Technologies and the Future of Residential Undergraduate Education." In R. N. Katz and Associates (eds.), *Dancing with the Devil: Information Technology and the New Competition in Higher Education.* San Francisco: Jossey-Bass, 1999.

Fields, J. C. *Total Quality for Schools: A Suggestion for American Education.* Milwaukee, Wisc.: Quality Press, 1993.

Finkelstein, S., and Hambrick, D. C. *Strategic Leadership: Top Executives and Their Effects on Organizations.* St. Paul, Minn.: West, 1996.

Foote, E. T. II. "The University of Miami." In D. W. Steeples (ed.), *Successful Strategic Planning: Case Studies.* New Directions for Higher Education, no. 64. San Francisco: Jossey-Bass, 1988.

Freeman, R. E., and Gilbert, D. R. Jr. *Corporate Strategy and the Search for Ethics.* Englewood Cliffs, N.J.: Prentice-Hall, Inc., 1988.

French, W. L., and Bell, C. H. Jr. *Organizational Development: Behavioral Science Interventions for Organization Improvement* (5th ed.). Englewood Cliffs, N.J.: Prentice-Hall, 1995.

Fullan, M., and Miles, M. *The Cutting Edge: Current Theory and Practice in Organization Development.* La Jolla, Calif.: University Associates, 1983.

Galbraith, J. R. *Designing Complex Organizations.* Reading, Mass.: Addison-Wesley Publishing Company, 1973.

Galbraith, J. R. *Organization Design.* Reading, Mass.: Addison-Wesley, 1977.

Galbraith, J. R., and Kazanjian, R. K. *Strategy Implementation: Structure, Systems and Process* (2nd ed.). New York: West Publishing Company, 1986.

Gijselaers, W. H. "Connecting Problem-Based Practices with Educational Theory." In L. Wilkerson and W. H. Gijselaers (eds.), *Bringing Problem-Based Learning to Higher Education: Theory and Practice.* New Directions for Teaching and Learning, no. 68. San Francisco: Jossey-Bass, 1996.

Gilmour, J. E. Jr. "Participative Governance Bodies in Higher Education: Report of a National Study." In R. Birnbaum (ed.), *Faculty in Governance: The Role of Senates and Joint Committees in Academic Decision Making.* New Directions for Higher Education, no. 75. San Francisco: Jossey-Bass, 1991.

Golembiewski, R. T. *Public Administration as a Developing Discipline. Part 1: Perspectives on Past and Present.* New York: Marcel Dekker, 1977.

Greiner, L. E. "Evolution and Revolution as Organizations Grow." *Harvard Business Review,* July-August 1972.

Grimm, C. M., and Smith, K. G. *Strategy as Action: Industry Rivalry and Coordination.* Cincinnati, Oh.: South-Western College Publishing, 1997.

Groves, R.E.V., Pendlebury, M. W., and Stiles, D. R. "A Critical Appreciation of the Uses for Strategic Management Thinking, Systems and Techniques in British Universities." *Financial Accountability and Management,* November 1997, *13*(4), 293–312.

Hackman, J. R., Lawler, E. E. III, and Porter, L. W. *Perspectives on Behavior in Organizations* (2nd ed.). New York: McGraw-Hill, 1983.

Harrigan, K. R. *Strategic Flexibility: A Management Guide for Changing Times.* Lexington, Mass.: Lexington Books, 1985.

Harvey, D. F., and Brown, D. R. *An Experiential Approach to Organization Development* (4th ed.). Englewood Cliffs, N.J.: Prentice-Hall, 1992.

Hightower, L. "Fact or Fiction: The Relevance of the Strategic Planning Literature to Planning Practices at Small Colleges and Universities."

Paper presented at the 35th annual forum of the Association of Institutional Research, Boston, Mass., May 1995.

Hirschman, A. O. *Exit, Voice, and Loyalty: Responses to Decline in Firms, Organizations, and States.* Cambridge, Mass.: Harvard University Press, 1970.

Huse, E. F., and Cummings, T. G. *Organization Development and Change* (3rd ed.). New York: West Publishing Company, 1985.

IBM. "Information." [http://www.pc.ibm.com/training/na/na_info_about_pci.html], 2000.

Integrated Postsecondary Education Data System. U.S. Department of Education. [http://nces.ed.gov/ipeds/index.html], 2000.

Janis, I. L. *Victims of Groupthink.* Boston: Houghton-Mifflin, 1972.

Jewell, L. N., and Reitz, H. J. *Group Effectiveness in Organizations.* Glensview, Ill.: Scott, Foresman, 1981.

Johnson, C. A., and Orr, C. L. "Promoting the Work Ethic Among Generation X and N-Gen Students." In P. A. Gallo Villee and M. G. Curran (eds.), *The 21st Century: Meeting the Challenges to Business Education.* Reston, Va.: National Business Education Association, 1999, 16–26.

Johnson, M. D. *Customer Orientation and Market Action.* Upper Saddle River, N.J.: Prentice Hall, 1998.

Katz, D., and Kahn, R. L. *The Social Psychology of Organizations.* New York: Wiley, 1966.

Katz, R. L. "Skills of an Effective Administrator." *Harvard Business Review,* September/October 1974.

Katz, R. N. "Competitive Strategies for Higher Education in the Information Age." In R. N. Katz and Associates (eds.), *Dancing with the Devil: Information Technology and the New Competition in Higher Education.* San Francisco: Jossey-Bass, 1999.

Katzenbach, J. R., and Smith, D. K. *The Wisdom of Teams: Creating the High Performance Organization.* Boston: Harvard Business Press, 1993.

Keller, G. *Academic Strategy.* Baltimore: Johns Hopkins University Press, 1983.

Keller, G. "The Changing Milieu of Education Planning." *Planning in Higher Education,* Winter 1994–1995, *23*(2), 23–26.

Kember, D., and Gow, L. "Orientations to Teaching and Their Effect on the Quality of Student Learning." *Journal of Higher Education.* January/February 1994, *65*(1), 58–74.

Kerin, R. A., Varadarajan, P. R., and Peterson, R. A. "First-Mover Advantage: A Synthesis, Conceptual Framework, and Research Propositions." *Journal of Marketing,* October 1992, 33–52.

Kerr, S. "On the Folly of Rewarding A While Hoping for B." *Academy of Management Journal,* 1975, *18,* 769–83.

Kiker, B. F. *Investment in Human Capital.* Columbia: University of South Carolina Press, 1971.

Kochan, T. A., and Useem, M. (eds.) *Transforming Organizations.* New York: Oxford University Press, 1992.

Kotter, J. P. *Organizational Dynamics.* Reading, Mass.: Addison-Wesley, 1978.

Larkley, P. D., and Sproull, L. W. *Advances in Information Processing in Organizations* (Vol. 1). Greenwich, Conn.: JAI Press, 1984.

Lawrence, P. R., and Lorsch, J. W. *Organizations and Environment: Managing Differentiation and Integration.* Boston: Division of Research, Graduate School of Business Administration, Harvard University, 1967.

Lawrence, P. R., and Lorsch, J. W. *Developing Organizations: Diagnosis and Action.* Reading, Mass.: Addison-Wesley, 1969.

Leslie, D. W., and Fretwell, E. K. Jr. *Wise Moves in Hard Times: Creating and Managing Resilient Colleges and Universities.* San Francisco: Jossey-Bass, 1996.

Levine, A. "Higher Education's New Status as a Mature Industry." *Chronicle of Higher Education,* 1997, *43*(21), A48.

Levy, F. S., Meltsner, A. J., and Wildavsky, A. *Urban Outcomes: Schools, Streets, and Libraries.* Berkeley: University of California Press, 1974.

Lewin, K. "Field Theory in Social Science." In D. Cartwright (ed.), *Selected Papers.* New York: Harper, 1951a.

Lewin, K. *Field Theory in Social Science.* New York: Harper, 1951b.

Lewis, R. G., and Smith, D. H. *Total Quality in Higher Education.* Delray Beach, Fla.: St. Lucie Press, 1994.

Likert, R. *The Human Organization: Its Management and Values.* New York: McGraw-Hill, 1967.

London, H. L. "The Death of the University." *The Futurist,* May/June 1987, *21,* 17–22.

Maghroori, R., and Rolland, E. "Strategic Leadership: The Art of Balancing Organizational Mission with Policy, Procedures, and External Environment." *The Journal of Leadership Studies,* 1997, *2,* 62–81.

Marcus, L. R. "The Micropolitics of Planning." *The Review of Higher Education,* Fall 1999, *23*(1), 45–64.

Marguiles, N., and Raia, A. P. *Conceptual Foundations of Organizational Development.* New York: McGraw-Hill, 1978.

Marguiles, N., and Wallace, J. *Organizational Change: Techniques and Applications.* Glenview, Ill.: Scott, Foresman, 1973.

McClelland, D. C. *The Achieving Society.* New York: Van Nostrand Reinhold, 1961.

McGill, M. E. *Organization Development for Operating Managers.* New York: Amacom, 1977.

McGregor, D. *The Human Side of Enterprise.* New York: McGraw-Hill, 1960.

McKeachie, W. J. *Teaching Tips: A Guidebook for the Beginning College Teacher* (8th ed.). Lexington, Mass.: Heath, 1986.

McLean, A. J., Sims, D.B.P., Mangham, I. L., and Tuffield, D. *Organization Development in Transition: Evidence of an Evolving Profession.* New York: Wiley, 1982.

Melan, E. H. *Process Management: Methods for Improving Products and Services.* New York: McGraw-Hill, 1993.

MEMEX Press. "Critical Comparisons of American Colleges and Universities." http://www.memex-press.com//cc/reports/nutshells/188429a.html, 1997.

Miles, R. E., and Snow, C. C. *Organizational Strategy, Structure, and Process.* New York: McGraw-Hill, 1978.

Miles, R. E., and Snow, C. C. "Fit, Failure, and the Hall of Fame." *California Management Review,* Spring, 1984, *26*(3), 10–28.

Mintzberg, H. *The Nature of Managerial Work.* Englewood Cliffs, N.J.: Prentice-Hall, 1973.

Mintzberg, H. "Concept I: Five P's for Strategy." *California Management Review,* Fall 1987, *30*(1), 11–24.

Mintzberg, H. *The Rise and Fall of Strategic Planning.* New York: The Free Press, 1994a.

Mintzberg, H. "The Fall and Rise of Strategic Planning." *Harvard Business Review,* January/February 1994b, *72*(1), 107–114.

Modern Language Association. "Foreign Language Enrollments in United States Institutions of Higher Learning." [http://www.infoplease.com/ipa/ A0193892.html]. Fall, 1995.

Morrill, R. L. "Centre College of Kentucky." In D. W. Steeples (ed.), *Successful Strategic Planning: Case Studies.* New Directions for Higher Education, no. 64. San Francisco: Jossey-Bass, 1988.

Morrison, J. L., Renfro, W. L., and Boucher, W. I. *Futures Research and the Strategic Planning Process: Implications for Higher Education.* Washington, D. C.: ASHE-ERIC, 1984.

Mosher, F. C. *Democracy and the Public Service* (2nd ed.). Oxford: Oxford University Press, 1982.

Motorola. "Frequently Asked Questions." [http://mu.motorola.com/]. 2000.

Nadler, D. A. *Feedback and Organizational Development: Using Data-Based Methods.* Reading, Mass.: Addison-Wesley, 1977.

National Research Council. *Research Doctorate Programs in the United States:*

Continuity and Change. Washington, D.C.: National Academy of Sciences, 1995.

Nutt, P. C., and Backoff, R. W. *Strategic Management of Public and Third Sector Organizations.* San Francisco: Jossey-Bass, 1992, 56–72.

Nutt, P. C. *Managing Planned Change.* New York: Macmillan, 1992.

Ouchi, W. G. *Theory Z: How American Business Can Meet the Japanese Challenge.* Reading, Mass.: Addison-Wesley, 1981.

Pascarella, E. T., and Terenzini, P. T. *How College Affects Students.* San Francisco: Jossey-Bass, 1991.

Pearce, J. A. III, and Robinson, R. B. Jr. *Formulation, Implementation and Control of Competitive Strategy* (7th ed.). New York: Irwin McGraw-Hill, 2000.

Penn State University at Hazleton. *Strategic Plan Update: 1999–2000.* [http://www.hn.psu.edu/planning/st_plan_update.htm], 2000.

Peters, T. *Thriving on Chaos: Handbook for a Management Revolution.* New York: Knopf, 1987.

Peters, T., and Waterman, R. H. *In Search of Excellence.* New York: Random House, 1982.

Pfeffer, J. *Organizations and Organization Theory.* Boston: Pitman, 1982.

Pfeffer, J. *Managing with Power.* Boston: Harvard Business School Press, 1992.

Pfeffer, J., and Salancik, G. R. *The External Control of Organizations: A Resource Dependence Perspective.* New York: Harper and Row, 1978.

Porter, M. E. "How Competitive Forces Shape Strategy." *Harvard Business Review,* March/April 1979, 137–145.

Porter, M. E. *Competitive Strategy: Techniques for Analyzing Industries and Competitors.* New York: Free Press, 1980.

Porter, M. E. *Competitive Advantage: Creating and Sustaining Superior Performance.* New York: Free Press, 1985.

Pressman, J. L., and Wildavsky, A. *Implementation: The Oakland Project.* Berkeley: University of California Press, 1973.

Rivlin, A. M. *Systematic Thinking for Social Action.* Washington, D.C.: The Brookings Institution, 1971.

Roach, E. D. "West Texas State University." In D. W. Steeples (ed.), *Successful Strategic Planning: Case Studies.* New Directions for Higher Education, no. 64. San Francisco: Jossey-Bass, 1988.

Robbins, S. P., and De Cenzo, D. A. *Fundamentals of Management: Essential Concepts and Applications* (2nd ed.). Upper Saddle River, N.J.: Prentice-Hall, 1998.

Roethlisberger, F. J. *Management and Morale.* Cambridge, Mass.: Harvard University Press, 1941.

Roskilde University. "A Brief Introduction to Roskilde University." [http://ruk.dk/eng/general/inf-kontor/into.html]. 2000.

Rowley, D. J. "Using KPIs to Start Planning." *Planning for Higher Education,* Winter, 1997, *25*(2), 29–32.

Rowley, D. J., Lujan, H. D., and Dolence, M. G. *Strategic Change in Colleges and Universities: Planning to Survive and Prosper.* San Francisco: Jossey-Bass, 1997.

Rowley, D. J., Lujan, H. D., and Dolence, M. G. *Strategic Choices for the Academy: How Demand for Lifelong Learning Will Re-Create Higher Education.* San Francisco: Jossey-Bass, 1998.

Russell, R. D. "Developing a Process Model of Intrapreneurial Systems: A Cognitive Mapping Approach." *Entrepreneurship Theory and Practice,* Spring 1999.

Schein, E. H. *Process Consultation: Lessons for Managers and Consultants,* vol. 2. Reading, Mass.: Addison-Wesley, 1987.

Schein, E. H. *Process Consultation: Its Role in Organization Development.* Reading, Mass.: Addison-Wesley, 1969.

Scott, W. R. *Organizations: Rational, Natural and Open Systems.* Englewood Cliffs, N.J.: Prentice-Hall, 1981.

Segev, E. "Analysis of Two Business-Level Strategic Typologies." *Strategic Management Journal,* Sept./Oct. 1989, *10*(5), 487–501.

Senge, P. M. *The Fifth Discipline.* New York: Doubleday, 1990.

Sherman, H. *The Strategic Management Process: Readings, Cases and Exercises.* Needham Heights, Mass.: Ginn Press, 1989.

Sherman, H. "A Typology of Strategic Management: Rational, Natural, and Ecological Approaches." *Journal of Management Science and Policy Analysis,* Spring/Summer 1991, *8*(3/4), 332–345.

Sherman, H. "Merging Mini-Paradigms: Organizational Development and Strategic Management." *Proceedings of the Northeast Business and Economics Association.* New Haven, Conn.: Northeast Business and Economics Association, 1999, 34–37.

Shirley, R. C. "Strategic Planning: An Overview." In D. W. Steeples (ed.), *Successful Strategic Planning: Case Studies.* New Directions for Higher Education, no. 64. San Francisco: Jossey-Bass, 1988.

Simon, H. A. *Administrative Behavior: A Study of Decision-Making Process in Administrative Organizations* (3rd ed.). New York: Free Press, 1976.

Southampton College of Long Island University. *Undergraduate and Graduate Bulletin: 1999–01.* Southampton, N.Y.: Southampton College, 1999.

Steeples, D. W. "Concluding Observations." In D. W. Steeples (ed.), *Suc-*

cessful Strategic Planning: Case Studies. New Directions for Higher Education, no. 64. San Francisco: Jossey-Bass, 1988.

Steiner, G. A., Miner, J. B., and Gray, E. R. *Management Policy and Strategy* (2nd ed.). New York: Macmillan, 1982.

Stitt-Gohdes, W. L. "Teaching and Learning Styles: Implications for Business Teacher Education." In P. A. Gallo Villee and M. G. Curran (eds.), *The 21st Century: Meeting the Challenges to Business Education.* Reston, Va.: National Business Education Association, 1999, 7–15.

Stonich, P. J. (ed.) *Implementing Strategy: Making Strategy Happen.* Cambridge, Mass.: Ballinger, 1982.

Swain, D. C. "The University of Louisville." In D. W. Steeples (ed.), *Successful Strategic Planning: Case Studies.* New Directions for Higher Education, no. 64. San Francisco: Jossey-Bass, 1988.

Swan, J. A., and Clark, P. A. "Organisational Decision-Making in the Diffusion and Appropriation of Technological Innovation: Cognitive and Political Dimensions." *European Work and Organizational Psychologist,* 1992, *2,* 103–127.

Swenk, J. "Planning Failures: Decision Cultural Clashes." *The Review of Higher Education,* Fall 1999, *23*(1), 1–21.

Taylor, F. W. *The Principles of Scientific Management.* New York: Harper and Brothers, 1911.

Thompson, J. D. *Organizations in Action.* New York: McGraw-Hill, 1967.

Thurow, L. C. "The New Economics of High Technology." *Management,* Spring/Summer 1992, 1–7.

Toffler, A. *Future Shock.* New York: Bantam Books, 1970.

Toffler, A. *Powershift: Knowledge, Wealth, and Violence at the Edge of the 21st Century.* New York: Bantam Books, 1990.

Trachtenberg, S. J. "Preparing for 'Baby Boomers.'" *Chronicle of Higher Education,* March 21, 1997, *43*(28), B7.

Treacy, M., and Wiersema, F. *The Discipline of Market Leaders.* Reading, Mass.: Addison-Wesley, 1995.

Tubbs, S. L. *A Systems Approach to Small Group Interaction* (2nd ed.). Reading, Mass.: Addison-Wesley, 1984.

Ulschak, F. L. *Human Resource Development: The Theory and Practice of Needs Assessment.* Reston, Va.: Reston Publishing, 1983.

University of Maastricht, Maastricht, the Netherlands. "Education." [http://www.unimaas.nl/pbl/fdcw/fdcweduc.htm]. 2000.

Van Dusen, G. C. "The Virtual Campus: Technology and Reform in Higher Education." *ERIC Digest.* [http://www.ed.gov/databases/ERIC-Digests/ed412815.html]. 2000.

Vietor, R. H. K. *Strategic Management in the Regulatory Environment: Cases and Industry Notes.* Englewood Cliffs, N.J.: Prentice, 1989.

Walker, O. C. Jr., and Ruekert, R. W. "Marketing's Role in the Implementation of Business Strategies: A Critical Review and Conceptual Framework." *Journal of Marketing,* July 1987, 15–33.

Weick, K. E. *The Social Psychology of Organizing* (2nd ed.). Reading, Mass.: Addison-Wesley, 1979.

Weick, K. E. "Technology as an Equivoque: Sensemaking in New Technologies." In P. Goodman and L. Sproull (eds.), *Technology and Organizations.* San Francisco: Jossey-Bass, 1990.

Western Governors' University. "Vision, History, and Mission." [http://www.wgu.edu/wgu/about/vision_history.html]. 2000.

Western Interstate Commission for Higher Education (WICHE). *Exploring the Relationship: A Survey of the Literature on Higher Education and the Economy.* Boulder, Colo.: Western Interstate Commission for Higher Education, 1992.

Whetten, D. A., and Cameron, K. S. *Developing Management Skills: Gaining Influence and Power.* New York: Harper-Collins, 1993.

Wick, C. W., and Leon, L. S. *The Learning Edge: How Smart Managers and Smart Companies Stay Ahead.* New York: McGraw-Hill, 1993.

Wilkerson, L., and Gijselaers, W. H. "Editors' Notes." In L. Wilkerson and W. H. Gijselaers (eds.), *Bringing Problem-Based Learning to Higher Education: Theory and Practice.* New Directions for Teaching and Learning, no. 68. San Francisco: Jossey-Bass, 1996.

Woodside, A. G., Sullivan, D. P., and Trappey, R. J. III. "Assessing Relationships Among Strategic Types, Distinctive Marketing Competencies, and Organizational Performance." *Journal of Business Research,* 1999, *45*(2), 135–146.

Wren, D. A. *The Evolution of Management Thought.* New York: Wiley, 1979.

Yin, R. K., Heald, K. A., and Vogel, M. E. *Tinkering with the System.* Lexington, Mass.: Lexington Books, 1977.

Young, D. W. *Introduction to Financial and Management Accounting: A User Perspective.* Cincinnati, Ohio: South-Western Publishing, 1994.

Yukl, G. *Skills for Managers and Leaders: Text, Cases and Exercises.* Englewood Cliffs, N.J.: Prentice-Hall, 1990.

Zand, D. E. *Information, Organization, and Power: Effective Management in the Knowledge Society.* New York: McGraw-Hill, 1981.

Name Index

Subject Index